100 THINGS
PADRES FANS
SHOULD KNOW & DO
BEFORE THEY DIE

100 THINGS PADRES FANS SHOULD KNOW & DO BEFORE THEY DIE

Kirk Kenney

TRIUMPH
BOOKS

This book is available in quantity at special discounts for your group or organization. For further information, contact:

Triumph Books LLC
814 North Franklin Street
Chicago, Illinois 60610
(312) 337-0747
www.triumphbooks.com

Printed in U.S.A.
ISBN: 978-1-62937-200-6
Design by Patricia Frey

To Leanne, for going all nine innings

Contents

Foreword *by Randy Jones* xi

Acknowledgments. xv

1 Tony Gwynn 1

2 Ray Kroc 10

3 Jerry Coleman 14

4 1984 World Series Team. 17

5 Garvey's Homer. 23

6 Garvey's Number. 27

7 1998 World Series Team. 29

8 C. Arnholdt Smith. 33

9 Hoffman in the 9th 35

10 The Chicken 37

11 Tim Flannery. 40

12 The Wizard of Oz 43

13 Tempy. 45

14 .394. 47

15 Bruce Bochy 50

16 John Moores and Larry Lucchino 52

17 Back-to-Back-to-Back 55

18 Tony Talks with Ted. 56

19 Tony's Number 60

20 Mr. Indispensable—Whitey Wietelmann 62

21 Ken Caminiti. 65

22 Randy Jones Wins the 1976 Cy Young Award 68

23 Yo, Adrian. 71

24 1978 All-Star Game 75

25 1992 All-Star Game 77

26 Ollie Brown—the Original Padre 79

27 Petco Park. 81

28 Get a Foul Ball at Petco 83

29 San Diego Stadium 88

30 Buzzie Bavasi. 90

31 Dave Winfield. 93

32 Trader Jack McKeon. 98

33 Dick Williams. 101

34 Rollie Fingers 105

35 Randy Jones 107

36 Gaylord Perry 112

37 Yuma. 114

38 Visit Peoria for Spring Training 117

39 Visit Cooperstown. 118

40 The Crowd in Cooperstown 122

41 Jones vs. Kaat 124

42 Preston Gomez 127

43 Gwynn's World Series Homer off David Wells. 129

44 Jake Peavy. 131

45 Catfish Gets off the Hook. 133

46 Draft Flops 137

47 Chris Gwynn's Big Hit 140

48 Mark Davis. 142

49 A.J. Preller's 36-Hour Makeover 144

50 The Fire Sale. 146

51 Trevor Hoffman 149

52 Sounding "Hells Bells" 154

53 Trevor's 500th Save 156

54 Atta Baby! 157

55 The 5.5 Hole. 159

56 Prop C Gets an Aye. 160

57 Benito's 34-Game Hitting Streak 162

58 Tony's 3,000th Hit. 163

59 Rickey's 3,000th Hit. 168

60 12 Hours in Philly. 170

61 Rocky Mountain Low 172

62 Wear Camo to a Game 174

63 Before It Was the Q 176

64 Matt Kemp's Cycle. 177

65 See a Padres Player Pitch a No-No 180

66 Why the Padres? 183

67 The Swinging Friar 185

68 The 1968 Expansion Draft 186

69 The First Game. 190

70 Dock's No-No 194

71 The Curse of Clay Kirby 198

72 Nate Colbert's Big Day. 200

73 Collect Washington Padres Cards 204

74 "I've Never Seen Such Stupid Ballplaying" 207

75 Short-Order Cook at Third. 208

76 Big Mac Sundays. 210

77 History from the Other Dugout 212

78 Alvin Dark's Spring Cleaning 216

79 Jerry—Not Gary—Coleman Hired 217

80 Hang a Star on That, Baby! 219

81 Finishing Last Twice in '81 220

82 Gwynn's Debut 222

83 Skunks in the Tarp 226

84 Beanballs with the Braves 227

85 Eric Show Sits Down on Mound 230

86 LaMarr Hoyt Trade Goes South 233

87 Jimmy Jones' One-Hitter 235

88 The Feeney Finger 237

89 Clark vs. Gwynn—'89 Batting Title 239

90 Barr-Strangled Banner 243

91 Name All the Managers—in Order 249

92 Take a Tour of Petco Park 252

93 Western Metal Supply Co. Building 254

94 Going 82–80 255

95 Going Ape on the Padres' Plane 257

96 Cammy's Snickers Bar 258

97 Enzo Hernandez 260

98 Buy a Painting from Gene Locklear 261

99 Garth Brooks Makes a Hit 263

100 In Closing… 264

Sources 267

Foreword

I was seven years old when I first took the mound in a Pee Wee League game. I knew that day what I wanted to do—be a major league pitcher.

As many of us did in our younger years, I chased that dream until I was 23 years old, when my dream became a reality in a San Diego Padres uniform.

It didn't take me long until I was welcomed to the big leagues by giving up my first major league hit, a home run to none other than Willie Mays.

Yep; like my dad always said, "Do it right or don't do it at all."

As I came off the mound that night, even my manager, Don Zimmer, had a smile on his face and a glimmer in his eye. We both knew it wouldn't be the last one I would give up. That started a run of 42 years being involved in the game I've always loved and I'm still trying to add to that number.

Except for two years with the New York Mets, my life has been Padres baseball in San Diego. With the first eight years pitching in a Padres uniform, I had a front-row seat to many of the stories you'll be introduced to in this book.

I broke in with Dave Winfield in 1973 and played with Clay Kirby, Ollie Brown, Nate Colbert, Cito Gaston, and Steve Arlin in those early years. We just couldn't quite get the winning formula with Ray Kroc and Buzzie Bavasi at the helm. They certainly tried, with players like Willie McCovey, Dave Kingman, Rollie Fingers, Oscar Gamble, Gene Tenace, Ozzie Smith, and Gaylord Perry, to name a few. Even Tim Flannery couldn't work his magic until a few more years passed. But through all these players, the history and stories of the San Diego Padres was born.

After my playing days ended, I've had the privilege of being around Padres baseball as a radio voice, community relations speaker, TV personality, and owner of the Randy Jones BBQ at the ballpark. I've always embraced the Padres fans on and off the mound. Whether we were at Jack Murphy Stadium or Petco Park today, it's a joy to talk baseball with them.

I recall when Roger Craig managed us to our first winning season in 1978. It gave us hope until the magical 1984 World Series team that Trader Jack McKeon put together. That taste of success would elude us until the 1998 season with another visit to the World Series. The 2000s have seen some successful years, but the World Series has eluded us.

All these years have continued to breed new Padres baseball stories—none better than the incredible career of Mr. Padre, Tony Gwynn. For 20 years, we had the honor of watching one of the greatest players play the game. When we couldn't watch him, Hall of Fame broadcaster Jerry Coleman would be on the radio describing the action for us.

As more chapters are added to the Padres story, it's important we don't forget how we got here.

Like when Jim Kaat and I pitched a game that took an hour and 29 minutes at the Murph or when I became the first Padres pitcher to win the Cy Young Award in 1976 and started and won the All-Star game that year. Or Gaylord Perry winning the Cy Young in 1978 for the Padres; Tony Gwynn's 3000th hit; and watching Trevor Hoffman notch his 500th save at Petco Park.

When you're reading *100 Things Padres Fans Should Know & Do Before They Die*, you're getting a great glimpse of past Padres lore as well as getting to know a few characters who have worn the Padres uniform. You'll also enjoy many stories of the people wearing suits who continued to try to make this franchise better.

This book reminds me why I have been so passionate about this game for nearly 60 years. I hope it's a reminder to you all that sometimes dreams do come true.

Enjoy the book.

—Randy Jones
January 2016
RandyJonesbbq.com

Acknowledgments

I first crossed paths with a Padre in the cafeteria of Maryland Avenue Elementary School in La Mesa, California.

Catcher Mike Ivie was the special guest at our Cub Scouts meeting. I have to thank Ivie for drawing my ticket during a raffle that night. The autographed Padres baseball I won still sits on the mantle in our den.

Writing *100 Things Padres Fans Should Know & Do Before They Die* revived memories that had faded with time and reminded me how much my life has been intertwined with the Padres for the better part of half a century.

I spent most of my high school and college years working in the vending department at the stadium, with one eye on work and the other eye on the game. I proposed to my wife, Leanne, standing in the outfield at the stadium—"I know this is coming out of left field, but will you marry me?"—a few hours before a game during the 1990 season.

I have been fortunate enough to attend or cover a majority of the franchise's most memorable moments.

I watched Steve Garvey's Game 4 home run against the Cubs in the 1984 NLCS from down the right-field line. From my perspective, I could not see the right-field wall. So I just looked out at the stands at the crowd's reaction. I still get chills remembering the roar from that moment.

Other memories are of things most people would never have noticed.

I remember closer Rollie Fingers hitting fungoes to the outfielders before games. Fingers would hit the last ball over the left-field wall. I tried to give him a big target with my first baseman's glove. He frequently hit the mark.

I have to congratulate pitcher Randy Jones for making the mid-1970s special for San Diego baseball fans. His home starts created a buzz we had never seen before. Also, a tip of the cap to Jones for making it acceptable to be a curly left-hander (his hair permed, mine natural).

And I have to thank Tony Gwynn for two decades of excellence on the field and a lifetime of decency off it. The past decade was especially meaningful. I will forever miss our postgame chats in his office at the stadium that bears his name.

It is at San Diego State that I got my first glimpse of Gwynn—and nearly two dozen others who would play pro ball from the 1981 Aztecs team—as a reporter for the school newspaper.

I always will be indebted to Frank Mickadeit for hiring me at a time when "paper route" was the only journalism-related experience listed on my resume.

SDSU coach Jim Dietz and the Aztecs sparked an interest in baseball that made me want to chronicle it as a career.

Those I want to acknowledge for their help along the way include three longtime editors I have always appreciated—Bill Pinella, Jess Kearney, and Doug Williams. They make writers better and make them want to be better.

I want to recognize three former colleagues—John Shea, Buster Olney, and Bill Center—whose passion for the game has been an inspiration.

I can't fail to mention friend and colleague Tod Leonard for having (and hitting) my back.

Andy Strasberg was particularly helpful with this project, offering ideas, insight, and photos that made the book better.

Finally, I want to thank San Diego County high school baseball coaches, who have fueled my interest in the game for more than three decades. Their dedication and commitment are two reasons San Diego ranks among the nation's hotbeds for baseball talent.

1 Tony Gwynn

On the first day of the 1981 Major League Baseball draft, Tony Gwynn was sitting by the telephone waiting for it to ring.

And it did.

"A secretary called," Gwynn said, "and didn't tell me who she was calling from, just that she needed my middle name."

"Keith," he told her.

When the phone rang a second time, five minutes later, that same secretary revealed a little more. He had been drafted by San Diego.

"I remember the first words out of my mouth were, 'Aw, (bleep),'" Gwynn said. "The Padres. That damn brown and gold.

"But I sat there with my brother and started thinking about it and I said, 'You know, they're letting a lot of young players play there.' I thought I might move up real quickly."

Thirteen months later—on July 19, 1982—Gwynn was in San Diego making his major league debut.

So began the career of the greatest player in Padres history—and the most beloved citizen of San Diego.

Gwynn got the first two hits of his career that night against the Philadelphia Phillies. Who knew there were 3,139 more hits where those came from?

"I was like most young guys," Gwynn said. "I came up and wanted to establish myself in the big leagues....I think I developed because I was a workaholic as far as this game is concerned. I've tried to do everything I can to get better."

Gwynn's .338 career batting average—which ranks 22nd all-time—is the highest in the majors since Ted Williams hit .344.

Gwynn's eight National League batting titles equaled the mark set by Honus Wagner. Only Ty Cobb won more.

Gwynn's 3,141 career hits ranked 17th on the all-time list when he retired.

Gwynn had the distinction of playing all of his 20 seasons in a Padres uniform. When he retired he was only the 17th player in history to have played 20 or more seasons all with the same team.

It easily could never have happened.

When Gwynn went off to college, he was not yet on a path that would lead to the major leagues and, eventually, the National Baseball Hall of Fame.

Gwynn, who was born in Los Angeles and grew up in Long Beach, originally came to San Diego on a scholarship to play basketball.

Gwynn was SDSU's point guard. He would hold game (18), season (221), and career (590) assist records by the time his career was over. Those records still stand.

Gwynn didn't want to limit himself to basketball, but that's what he was asked to do his freshman year at State.

"The basketball coach [Tim Vezie] asked me to focus on basketball," Gwynn said. "What could I really do? So that first year I just sat on Raggers' Rail (just beyond the right-field fence at the baseball field) and watched them play."

Along comes Bobby Meacham on his recruiting visit to San Diego State. Meacham, a shortstop from Santa Ana's Mater Dei and one of the nation's prize recruits, was sitting in SDSU baseball coach Jim Dietz's office when Gwynn poked his head in the door, said hello, and continued on his way.

"Coach, I didn't know he was playing here," said Meacham.

"No, he's on the basketball team," Dietz said. "Does he play baseball, too?"

Basketball? Meacham knew Gwynn only as a baseball player from Long Beach Poly High.

"In high school, he was a great hitter, a guy who could fly around the bases, could steal a base, a great center fielder," said Meacham, who got to know Gwynn when they played summer league baseball in Long Beach. "I thought he was the best player I ever played against."

And someone Meacham desperately wanted to play with.

"I thought, *This is crazy. He's got to play baseball*," said Meacham.

Gwynn had met Dietz briefly when Gwynn visited the campus before making his commitment. But, again, he was there on a basketball scholarship. He was a walk-on in baseball. And that was a year after their brief encounter.

"They had 80 or 90 walk-ons a year in baseball and here comes this guy out of basketball trying to play baseball," Gwynn said.

But Gwynn had someone on the inside putting in a good word for him.

"If Bobby doesn't say anything, I probably don't even play baseball," said Gwynn. "Bobby told Coach Dietz, 'You've got a hell of a baseball player on the basketball team.'

"Bobby was Dietz's prize recruit. Meach could have gone anywhere in the country and decided to go to San Diego State. Lucky for me. I eventually proved my worth."

It may not have been evident initially. Gwynn batted .301 his first season. He had one home run and 11 RBIs in 34 games as he removed the cobwebs from his swing. He came around the second year, leading the team in batting at .423 with six homers and 29 RBIs in 41 games.

Then there was his third year. What a season. Gwynn batted .416 with 11 homers and 62 RBIs in 52 games.

The statistics weren't what garnered Gwynn attention, however. Once again, he thanked Meacham for that.

"All the scouts came to our games to see him, not me," Gwynn said.

Meacham was selected in the first round, the eighth pick overall, by the St. Louis Cardinals. After a trade, he would play six years in the majors with the New York Yankees.

"I still chuckle when I think that we went in the same draft and I went so much higher than him," Meacham said. "The Cardinals picked the wrong guy from San Diego State."

The Padres selected Gwynn in the third round with the draft's 58th overall pick. Before the day was over, he had been drafted again—in the 10th round of the NBA draft by the San Diego Clippers.

There was a time when Gwynn considered basketball his sport.

"Baseball was just something to do in the spring and summer," Gwynn once said. "I told my mom I didn't think I would try baseball in college. She and my dad told me it was something I might want to fall back on."

Baseball turned out to be a good Plan B, and Gwynn set off on a whirlwind tour of the minor leagues.

In the summer of 1981, Gwynn won a Class-A batting title in the Northwest League by hitting .331 at Walla Walla, Washington. He was promoted to Double-A Amarillo (Texas) for the last three weeks of the season and hit .462 in 23 games. Gwynn opened the 1982 season at Triple-A Honolulu and batted .328 in 93 games before being called up by the Padres.

Gwynn batted .289 during his rookie season in San Diego. He was two hits shy of batting .300. Gwynn hit better than .300 each of the following 19 seasons.

He stumbled onto something early that would be an asset throughout his career. Sometimes inspiration comes from desperation.

Gwynn was concerned about his swing during a slump midway through the 1983 season that dropped his average as low as .229. That led to his pioneering use of videotape to review at-bats and search for flaws in his swing.

Tony Gwynn peppered plenty of hits around the ballpark—3,141 of them, to be exact—during his 20-year career as the Padres' right fielder. (San Diego Padres)

"We were on the road and I saw the game was going to be tele-cast back to San Diego," Gwynn recalled. "My wife and I had just gotten some video-recording equipment for our television.

"So I called Alicia and asked her to tape that night's game for me. We were headed home, and I wanted to see if I could spot something wrong with my swing."

Gwynn did identify an issue, corrected it, and was on his way again.

"(Video) was so basic when I started," Gwynn said. "I was at the mercy of what they showed on the television. If the TV cameras caught a shot of me swinging, I had a piece of tape to work with. If they didn't, I didn't, and it was back to the drawing board."

Gwynn gives much of the credit to his wife.

"She was taking care of the baby (son Tony Jr.) and running to the tape machine when I hit. I'm sure she wasn't happy with the program at times. But she helped turn my career around. We were a team."

Gwynn batted .333 over the final two months of the season. It included a 25-game hitting streak, which would be the best of his career.

Gwynn's five Gold Gloves didn't set any records, but in some ways were an even greater accomplishment than his hitting.

The knock on Gwynn when he reached the majors was that he was not a good defensive outfielder. John Boggs, Gwynn's longtime agent and friend, had the pleasure of giving Gwynn the good news when the right fielder won his first Gold Glove in 1986.

"He was on a trip," Boggs said. "When I finally reached him, he sounded terrible."

'Tony, what's wrong?' Boggs said.

"I'm sick," Gwynn replied.

"Hopefully, I have something that will make you feel better," Boggs said. "I just got the news that you won your first Gold Glove.

"And he went nuts. He started yelling and screaming, from his death bed, it sounded like, to the most euphoric I've ever heard him."

"Tony, what's going on?" Boggs asked.

"I'm jumping up and down on the bed and pumping my fist," Gwynn said. "That's great news."

Said Boggs: "I've never heard him that excited about something, which told you how hard he worked at it and accomplished it. Tony knew he needed to improve defensively, and he worked on that just like he worked on everything in life. He really paid special attention to the defensive component of his game."

Even when the Gold Gloves started coming, Gwynn would forever be known by the way he swung the bat.

"Tony Gwynn is the Picasso of modern-day hitters," Ted Williams once said. "Nobody studies the game harder, pays more attention to detail and goes to the plate with a better idea of what he wants to do."

But it was much more than Gwynn's prowess at the plate that endeared him to San Diego.

It was showing loyalty to stay with the Padres when he could have made more money elsewhere. It was his good works in the community. It was a friendly, outgoing personality when dealing with the fans. It was returning to his alma mater when his career ended and becoming head coach of the baseball team.

"As far as San Diego, he was a consistent sign of stability," Tony Gwynn Jr. said of his father. "When it comes to sports or when you think of the city of San Diego, a lot of people think of my father. Because he was here for so long and everything he did professionally involved the city of San Diego. Everything he did in his life involved the city of San Diego."

Every person who watched Gwynn play right field for the Padres for 20 years felt like they knew him. Seemingly everyone met him at one time or another, at an autograph signing, at the store or the gas station.

And Gwynn could meet someone for 20 minutes and you would think they had been friends for 20 years.

Informed once that his autograph on a baseball was selling for more than $100, Gwynn was dumbfounded.

"How could it be worth anything?" he asked. "I've signed for everyone."

Then he laughed that incredible laugh of his.

When you read about those who played the game, some nearly a century ago now, guys like Babe Ruth and Lou Gehrig and Jackie Robinson and Williams, their accomplishments seem almost mythical. Generations to come will view Gwynn in the same regard.

His most amazing season, when he batted .394 in 1994 before the strike wiped out the last six weeks of the season, he had the highest average since Williams batted .406 in 1941.

It goes far beyond what Gwynn did with a bat and glove. That much was evident when about 25,000 people showed up to pay their respects at Petco Park for a memorial service after Gwynn died of cancer in 2014 at the age of 54.

"He will in some sense be a mythical icon in a lot of kids' minds because they will have never seen him up close and in person," Gwynn Jr. said, "but they will have many, many stories to tell about him....

"Ultimately, his legacy will be who he was as a man and how he treated people. I try to live my life the same way he did as far as his interaction with people that weren't family. I think he genuinely felt that anybody he came across he wanted to treat them as such, as family."

Cooperstown had a family atmosphere in 2007 when Gwynn (97.6 percent of votes) and Baltimore's Cal Ripken (98.5) were enshrined at the National Baseball Hall of Fame. A crowd estimated at 82,000—the largest ever for Hall of Fame Induction Weekend—showed up to honor the players.

At one point during his induction speech, Gwynn said: "I worked hard in the game because I had to. I wasn't talented enough to just get by on a billing. I really had to work at it. I had to do the video stuff. I had the extra hit(ting). I had to go about my business and do things the way I did. I think people, we make a big deal about work ethic.

"We make a big deal about trying to make good decisions and doing things right, and you know what, we are supposed to. That is what they pay us for....I'm a big believer when you sign your name on a dotted line, there's more than just playing the game of baseball. I think if you look out here today, you see all these people out here today, they love the game, too. And there's a responsibility when you put that uniform on that those people, the people who pay to go watch you play, you're responsible, you've got to make good decisions and show people how things are supposed to be done."

A quarter century had passed since that day Gwynn had been drafted by the Padres. The "brown and gold" had changed to blue and orange by the time he was done playing. Either way, that franchise and that city had come to mean the world to Gwynn.

"I'm proud as heck to be a San Diego Padre," he said. "I played for one team. I played in one town. I told the people of San Diego when I left to come to Cooperstown, they were going to be standing up here with me, so I hope they are just as nervous as I am, because this is a tremendous honor to be here today."

A 9½-foot statue of Gwynn in Petco's Park at the Park was unveiled a week before Gwynn's induction at Cooperstown.

Gwynn walked completely around the statue, admiring the work of the sculptor. He had captured the hitter in midswing.

The inscription on the front reads: Tony Gwynn, Mr. Padre.

On the back is a quote from Gwynn's father Charles: "If you work hard, good things will happen."

Isn't that the truth.

Ray Kroc

Ray Kroc was reading the sports pages one day when he came across a story about the Padres being for sale.

My God, Kroc thought. *San Diego is a gorgeous place. Why don't I go over there and look at that ballpark?*

Kroc's interest was sufficiently sparked that he told wife Joan, "I'm thinking of buying the Padres."

"Why would you want to buy a monastery?" she replied.

Joan didn't know much about baseball.

Of course, baseball didn't know much about the Krocs, either.

The McDonald's magnate had already sold more than a billion burgers by the time he turned to baseball.

That was news to Padres president Buzzie Bavasi, who had never eaten at the restaurant.

When Kroc's lawyer, Don Lubin, first contacted the Padres to inform them of Kroc's interest, Bavasi seemed unimpressed.

"That's fine," Bavasi said. "Who else is in the group?"

"He *is* the group," came the reply.

Bavasi was told that Kroc owned 7½ million shares of McDonald's stock, but he was still puzzled. That's because Bavasi had mistakenly confused McDonald's with McDonnell-Douglas, the aerospace manufacturing corporation.

Stock in McDonnell-Douglas was selling for $2.50 a share at the time, which would have put their value at $18.75 million. That wouldn't have left much for operating expenses after purchasing the team.

It all sunk in for Bavasi when son Peter explained that it was McDonald's the fast-food chain that Kroc owned.

"Seven-and-a-half million shares of McDonald's stock at $45 a share was $337.5 million," Buzzie said. "Ray Kroc could afford to buy the Padres, or anything else, for that matter."

Kroc was a self-made millionaire. His big break came in the mid-1950s when he was selling milkshake mixers and happened across the McDonald's brothers and their hamburger stand in San Bernardino, California.

Kroc recognized a business opportunity, bought out the brothers, franchised the fast-food concept, and the rest is history.

Kroc was born in 1902 in Oak Park, Illinois, and grew up a baseball fan cheering for the Chicago Cubs. In 1972, Kroc wanted to buy the Cubs from owner Philip Wrigley, but his calls weren't returned.

With original Padres owner C. Arnholdt Smith in financial turmoil, the opportunity to purchase the Padres followed a year later.

Kroc went to lunch with Smith and asked what the purchase price was for the team. Smith told him it was $12 million.

"Deal," Kroc said.

Smith would say later that he thought he could have doubled the price and Kroc would have said the same thing.

The sale was finalized on January 25, 1974, less than a month before spring training was to begin.

After Smith's penny-pinching ownership for five years, the Padres were in for a refreshing change.

At his introductory press conference, Kroc emphasized the financial commitment he was willing to make to field a winning team.

"After all, what do I need with more money?" he said.

Padres owner Ray Kroc, pictured with the Swinging Friar logo used when San Diego hosted the 1978 All-Star Game, gained folk hero status among fans when he saved the franchise from moving to Washington, D.C. (Fantography.com/Andy Strasberg)

Kroc saved baseball for the city, then promised to give it a winner.

Three months later, he forever endeared himself to fans when he commandeered the PA microphone in the eighth inning of the team's home opener, a 9–5 loss to the Houston Astros.

"Fans, I suffer with you," Kroc said. "I've never seen such stupid ballplaying in my life."

The crowd, at least those left from the 39,083, cheered its approval.

The Padres were no more successful on the field during Kroc's first year of ownership than they had been the year before he purchased the team. They finished 60–102 both seasons.

The Padres were much more popular, however. The club drew more than one million fans for the first time in franchise history. That, after barely attracting 600,000 (last in the NL) the year before.

And Kroc would live up to his commitment. He actively pursued the game's top players when free agency arrived. Although the Padres missed out on players like pitchers Catfish Hunter and Andy Messersmith and slugger Reggie Jackson, Kroc did make a splash with signings such as Oakland A's pitcher Rollie Fingers and catcher Gene Tenace.

Kroc died on January 14, 1984, just as his dream of success was on the verge of being realized.

The players wore his initials—RAK—on their uniform sleeves that season.

More than a few people believed Kroc was looking down from above, enjoying every minute of the Padres' championship season—even if it meant the greatest moments did come at the expense of his beloved Cubs.

Kroc became a San Diegan as soon as he purchased the Padres. And to baseball fans here, he always will be.

Jerry Coleman

One of the most beloved figures in Padres history spent only one season in the dugout and never played an inning for the team.

Yet Jerry Coleman easily is the most heroic figure the franchise has ever known.

Coleman became the lead announcer for the Padres in 1972, serving behind the microphone for all but one of the next 42 years.

He endeared himself to Padres fans with signature phrases such as "Oh, Doctor!" and "Hang a star on that one" as well as malaprops that became known as Colemanisms.

But what set him apart was service to his country, not the ballclub. Coleman's baseball career was interrupted twice by military service—in World War II and the Korean War.

Coleman spent 70 years in baseball, but it still finished second when prioritizing his life.

"The most important thing in my life was not what I did in baseball," Coleman said, "but what I did in the service of the Marines during two wars—five years on active duty."

Coleman played on six World Series teams—winning four times—during a nine-year career with the New York Yankees. He was American League Rookie of the Year in 1949 and World Series MVP in 1950.

Coleman, who was born in San Jose in 1924, joined the Marines when he was 18 years old. He would fly 120 combat missions over two wars. Among the honors he received were two Distinguished Flying Crosses.

"To him, the Marine Corps was No. 1 after family," longtime broadcast partner Ted Leitner said. "This is a guy who wore the pinstripes at Yankee Stadium, who roomed with Mickey Mantle, who had his picture taken with Joe DiMaggio, who played in World Series and was MVP of one of them. Yet he'd tell you that his time with the Marines was more important to him. Nobody shot at him at Yankee Stadium."

Coleman's broadcast career began not long after his playing career ended in 1957. He shared the Yankees broadcast booth with Red Barber, Mel Allen, and Phil Rizzuto.

A decade later, Coleman was eager to get back to the West Coast. He inquired about doing Padres broadcasts in 1970, but there wasn't an opening, so he went to work for the California Angels.

Jerry Coleman endeared himself to Padres fans during more than four decades as a broadcaster with the franchise. (Kirk Kenney)

Two years later, he joined the Padres broadcast team. This is where fans came to be aware of some of his Colemanisms.

One of their favorites was a description of pitcher Randy Jones—"On the mound is Randy Jones, the left-hander with the Karl Marx hairdo" (he meant Harpo Marx).

Another fan favorite was describing Dave Winfield making a play in the outfield—"Winfield goes back to the wall, he hits his head on the wall and it rolls off! It's rolling all the way back to second base. This is a terrible thing for the Padres."

Coleman shrugs it off: "All this has been well-recorded for years. I don't pay attention to that stuff."

Coleman came down from the press box one season to manage the 1980 Padres. The team finished 73–89, which was then the second-best record in team history. He returned to the broadcast booth the following season.

"There were some Padres who never really accepted me as their manager," said Coleman, who had been out of uniform for more than two decades when he took the job. "Three or four didn't like me—who I was or what I represented—right from the start. I wasn't surprised. Not that it changed where we finished, but when you have that, you don't get the full energy you need....

"Maybe the players who turned away from me were right. I don't blame them. In fact, had I to do it all over again, I wouldn't have taken the managing job. There was too much of a problem from the standpoint of 'Who is this guy?'"

Former Dodgers manager Tommy Lasorda believes Coleman could have done well had he been given a chance.

"I don't think he really wanted to do that," Lasorda said. "He could've been a good manager, though, if he'd had a real opportunity to do it. Jerry was a great ballplayer, an intelligent player, and he was a bomber pilot. With those qualifications, you think he couldn't have been a good manager, too?"

Back in the broadcast booth, Coleman was there to call virtually every one of the team's biggest moments, from the 1984 and 1998 World Series appearances to Tony Gwynn's 3,000th hit—"You can hang a star on that, baby! A star for the ages for Tony Gwynn!"—to the last game at Qualcomm Stadium and the first game at Petco Park.

Coleman's presence can still be felt at Petco.

In 2004, a star was painted on the wall beneath the press box. In 2012, the Padres honored Coleman with a statue. Fittingly, The Colonel is depicted in his Marine Corps uniform.

Coleman was inducted into the Padres Hall of Fame in 2001. He received the Ford C. Frick Award in the National Baseball Hall of Fame in 2005.

"Bottom line: People loved Jerry and respected him, because you could tell from listening to him what a wonderful person he was," legendary Dodgers broadcaster Vin Scully said. "I considered it a great privilege for me to be one of those who voted for Jerry's induction into Cooperstown. What an amazing life."

4 1984 World Series Team

The movie *Ghostbusters* debuted on June 8, 1984.

The following day, the Padres moved into first place in the National League West, where they would stay for the remainder of the season.

Fifteen years of futility finally came to an end when the Padres chased the ghosts away, reaching the postseason for the first time.

It was magical. There is no other word for it.

"There is only one first time, and that is something they can't take away from you," former Padres infielder Tim Flannery said years later. "And I think the people who experienced it as fans feel the same way."

Indeed. The Padres' first NL West championship, first NL pennant, and first World Series appearance still resonate with fans more than three decades later.

Those familiar with the team could see everything coming together as the season approached. GM Jack McKeon had assembled just the right mixture of young players and veterans.

The Padres had one of the least productive farm systems in the major leagues through the years, but it produced plenty of talent in the years immediately leading up to that magical season.

Flannery and pitchers Eric Show and Andy Hawkins were selected in the 1978 draft, pitcher Mark Thurmond came in the 1979 draft, and outfielders Kevin McReynolds and Tony Gwynn and pitcher Greg Booker were selected in the 1981 draft.

In 1984, McReynolds and Gwynn would start alongside each other in the outfield. Flannery was a reserve who provided a spark off the bench. Show, Hawkins, and Thurmond would comprise three-fifths of the starting rotation and Booker would work out of the bullpen.

The rest of the roster was constructed through a couple of key free-agent acquisitions and some shrewd trading by Padres GM Jack McKeon.

The Padres made perhaps the best free-agent signing in club history, certainly to that point, when they signed first baseman Steve Garvey before the 1983 season. Then they signed free-agent closer Goose Gossage before the 1984 season.

Two other starting pitchers, Tim Lollar and Ed Whitson, had come over in earlier trades, as did reliever Dave Dravecky.

The glue to the infield was shortstop Garry Templeton, who had been acquired after the 1981 season in the trade with St. Louis that sent Ozzie Smith to the Cardinals. St. Louis proved a good trade partner. A year earlier, McKeon had acquired catcher Terry Kennedy from the Cardinals.

Left fielder Carmelo Martinez and reliever Craig Lefferts were acquired in a trade with the Chicago Cubs at the 1983 Winter Meetings.

The addition of Martinez enabled the team to move Alan Wiggins from the outfield to second base, an experiment that would pay huge dividends. Wiggins had been acquired in 1980 in the Rule 5 draft for unprotected minor league players. He would be a catalyst for the offense hitting at the top of the order.

The final piece came from the Yankees. Third baseman Graig Nettles, a local product who played at San Diego High and San Diego State, was acquired in a trade just four days before the season began.

"I really thought the Nettles deal put us over the hump," McKeon said. "Before we had him, there was no doubt in my mind we had a good chance to win the pennant. But when we got him, it psychologically lifted the ballclub. The players were thinking, *Hey, management's behind us. They're interested in winning.*

"It was the icing on the cake. In my opinion, the day we acquired Nettles was the day we won the pennant."

Guiding this group was Dick Williams, the gruff manager who had taken two other teams—the 1967 Red Sox and 1972–73 A's—to the World Series in a career that would take him to Cooperstown.

Everything was taking shape when news came on January 14, 1984, that owner Ray Kroc had died.

"The guys who had been around the longest knew best what Ray was about and what he thought of the Padres," Templeton said. "We took it hard."

The Padres received approval from Major League Baseball to put Kroc's initials—RAK—on the sleeves of the players' uniforms.

The 1984 Padres Roster

Starting Lineup
Alan Wiggins, 2B
Tony Gwynn, RF
Steve Garvey, 1B
Graig Nettles, 3B
Terry Kennedy, C
Kevin McReynolds, CF
Carmelo Martinez, LF
Garry Templeton, SS

Reserves
Bruce Bochy, C
Tim Flannery, INF
Bobby Brown, OF
Champ Summers, OF
Kurt Bevacqua, UTL
Luis Salazar, 3B

Starting Rotation
Eric Show, RHP
Tim Lollar, LHP
Ed Whitson, RHP
Mark Thurmond, LHP
Andy Hawkins, RHP

Bullpen
Greg Harris, RHP
Luis DeLeon, RHP
Greg Booker, RHP
Dave Dravecky, LHP
Craig Lefferts, LHP
Goose Gossage, RHP

"I remember getting chills looking down at those initials anytime we won a close game," Gwynn said. "It affected all of us."

The Padres got off to a solid start, winning 14 of their first 20 games, before a tough stretch that included a seven-game losing streak dropped them to .500.

Then they flipped a switch with another hot stretch that began in late May and carried into most of June.

The Padres were never really challenged thereafter. They finished 92–70 to win the NL West by 12 games over the second-place Atlanta Braves.

The most noteworthy event of the summer was a beanball war in Atlanta with the Braves that remains one of the most notorious brawls—three or four of them, actually—in baseball history.

But that didn't overshadow what the team accomplished over the 162-game grind.

"Every day it turned out to be someone else, which I thought turned out to be one of the best parts of 1984," Garvey said. "We didn't have one or two guys. We had about 20."

It truly was a team effort.

Gwynn won the first of his eight NL batting championships with a .351 average, but there were no real statistical standouts on the team.

Garvey was the team's top run producer with 86 RBIs. Nettles and McReynolds shared the team lead in home runs with 20 apiece. Wiggins did open some eyes with 70 stolen bases.

On the mound, the wins were spread pretty evenly among starters Show (15), Whitson (14), Thurmond (14), and Lollar (11). Gossage had 10 wins to go along with 25 saves.

The euphoria coming into the playoffs against the Chicago Cubs was quickly doused with a dose of reality.

The Cubs won the first two games of the best-of-five series at Wrigley Field by 13–0 and 4–2 scores.

The Padres were a somber group on the flight home.

Their spirits soared around midnight, though, when their bus pulled into the parking lot at San Diego Jack Murphy Stadium. Thousands of fans were there clapping and cheering.

They still believed.

"Suddenly, we believed, too," Williams said.

Gossage, who had been critical of San Diego fans during the season for being too laid-back, was among those moved by the outpouring.

"I said to the guys, 'Are we really down two to nothing?'" Gossage said. "These people weren't frontrunners. They were behind us after we lost. I walked around the parking lot, shaking hands with people, and I saw love in their eyes. I suddenly realized how much this all means to them. You know, us winning for the first time."

The Padres were re-energized when they took the field at home.

The atmosphere was electric.

Kroc's widow, Joan, went to the mound wearing a Padres uniform to throw out the first pitch. A crowd of 58,346—the first of three straight sellouts—produced more noise than anyone could remember.

Stadium speakers blared "Cub Busters," a variation on the "Ghostbusters" theme song, with a reworked refrain—"I ain't afraid of no Cubs."

The Padres won 7–1 in Game 3, with Whitson and Gossage combining on a five-hitter.

Game 4 featured the biggest home run in Padres history, the two-run blast in the bottom of the ninth by Garvey that delivered a 7–5 win to tie the series.

In Game 5, the Padres trailed by three runs through five innings before rallying for six unanswered runs in a 6–3 win to capture the series.

The word *bedlam* is defined as "a scene of uproar and confusion." That summed up the scene after Gossage got the final out.

The 10th Man made a big difference, according to Williams.

"I firmly believe [the fans at the stadium when the team returned from Chicago] set the tone for what happened the next three days," Williams said. "Coming from a hardened baseball man like me, this sounds blasphemous, I know.

"But all you baseball fans who think you never directly affect a team or a game, you're wrong. That weekend you may just have won us a playoff."

The World Series wasn't nearly as dramatic. The Detroit Tigers, who had opened the season with 35 wins in their first 40 games, won in five games.

The Padres won Game 2 by a 5–3 score. Kurt Bevacqua provided the most memorable moment, doing a pirouette at first base when he hit a three-run homer in the fifth inning.

The Padres returned home—after a harrowing experience on the team bus leaving Tiger Stadium amid rioting fans—to another lovefest with their fans.

A crowd of more than 35,000 saluted the team at the stadium upon its return.

"Hitting the home run to win the second game of the World Series was the thrill of my life," said Bevacqua as he looked into the crowd. "But tonight means more to me than that home run."

The three-hour celebration included fireworks, marching bands, and dancers, among other things. Players and coaches came onto the field in convertibles that delivered them to an infield stage.

"I can't believe what's happening here tonight," catcher Bruce Bochy said. "I will remember it the rest of my life."

The scene included souvenir vendors in the stands, hawking commemorative items.

The most popular item was a pennant that read: "Padres World Series 1984: I Was There."

Garvey's Homer

All that was missing was the lightning—although there was electricity in the air when Steve Garvey provided the thunder.

The movie *The Natural* was among the 1984 summer blockbusters. Robert Redford's Roy Hobbs had nothing on Garvey.

Reality was more exciting, more dramatic, more unbelievable than fiction when The Garv hit the biggest home run in Padres history and provided the most memorable moment in San Diego sports history.

"Time stopped. Sound stopped," said Garvey, describing the moment he hit a two-run homer in the bottom of the ninth inning of Game 4 of the NLCS for a 7–5 win over the Chicago Cubs.

Tony Gwynn was on first base with a one-out single when Garvey stepped to the plate against Cubs closer Lee Smith. Garvey took a ball, then smashed a 95-mph fastball over the 370 sign on the wall in right-center field. A sellout crowd of 58,354 fans roared at San Diego Jack Murphy Stadium.

"It's gone!" Padres broadcaster Jerry Coleman exclaimed. "The Padres win!...Oh, doctor!"

Garvey raised a clenched fist into the air as he rounded first and circled the bases.

Padres teammates couldn't wait for Garvey to reach the plate, meeting him halfway up the third-base line to escort him home. They lifted him on their shoulders and carried him away from the plate amid bedlam.

"I think our future senator picked up a few votes tonight," the Padres' Champ Summers said.

"The last person I saw do something like this was Roy Hobbs," quipped Padres infielder Tim Flannery.

"Wonderboy, it wasn't," Garvey said. "Just good, solid ash."

Added Garvey: "I love the situation. I love the challenge. And it's my pleasure to come through."

The first baseman, who had signed as a free agent with the Padres the previous season, didn't even know if he would be able to play coming into the game.

Garvey said he began to feel the effects of a virus the day before, an off-day when the Padres had a light workout.

"I had some soup for dinner and was in bed by 7 o'clock," Garvey remembered in his 1986 autobiography. "All night I was cramped up, pulled into a fetal position. Every couple of hours I would wake up, soaked with sweat."

He felt a little better when he got to the ballpark the following day and worked out "gingerly," taking a few ground balls and swings in the batting cage. Then he lay down in the trainers' room with a towel on his face.

Garvey said he was still a little queasy during his first at-bat, a fly-out to right field.

"After that I got more into the game and forgot about my stomach," Garvey said.

Could one swing of the bat compel a franchise to retire a player's jersey number? It did in the case of first baseman Steve Garvey. (Fantography.com/Madres)

In the third inning, Garvey doubled to left field, driving in teammate Alan Wiggins to give the Padres a 1–0 lead.

The Cubs pulled ahead 3–2 by the fifth inning, when Garvey came to the plate again and delivered an RBI single to score Flannery and make it 3–3.

In the seventh, Garvey singled to left field to drive in Gwynn and Bobby Brown for a 5–3 lead.

The Cubs tied the game again with two runs in the eighth inning off Padres closer Goose Gossage.

That set the stage for Garvey's ninth-inning heroics.

"Smith lives or dies by power," Garvey said. "I didn't think he was going to fool around with breaking pitches."

Smith didn't.

"He threw another fastball," Garvey said. "I was striding into the pitch and got my arms fully extended. Crack! I knew it was gone. I can still see the white ball rising into the semi-dark background, a halo of light around it."

Naturally.

"I remember hitting first base and raising my arm in this euphoric feeling," Garvey said. "Everything around me was frozen. The noise was muffled. The movement stopped.

"Touching second base, I was coming down to earth. I could see the crowd and distinguish voices, though they were a loud echo.

"By the time I got to third base, I could see the stands, see the Cubs walking off the field.

"At home plate, our whole team was waiting. Somebody stepped on my heel and my shoe came off. I grabbed it, just as they were picking me up and putting me on their shoulders."

Said Smith: "I threw up my best pitch and Garvey hit it out. If it came up in the same situation, I would do the same thing. I'm not second-guessing myself."

"Mr. Garvey got us all night," said Cubs manager Jim Frey. "He got a two-out base hit to tie the game. He got another two-out base hit to put them ahead. He accounted for five runs. He's been doing it a long time. I guess that's why they paid him all that money to come down here and play."

The Cubs were finished off the following day. The Padres reached the World Series for the first time in the franchise's 16-year history while preventing the Cubs from getting back to the series for the first time since 1945.

Garvey still hears from Cubs fans more than anyone else—more than 30 years after he broke their hearts with the biggest home run in Padres history.

"October 6, 1984," said Garvey, reciting the date of the homer 30 years later. "Every day Cubs fans come up to me and say, 'How could you do that to us?' They were so frustrated. They beat us twice (in the best-of-five series) and thought they were all set....It was voted the greatest sports moment in San Diego history, which I take a lot of pride in.

"But that was when the Padres fans realized this is what you do when you're a winner. Guys do that kind of stuff."

6 Garvey's Number

Steve Garvey left the Dodgers following the 1982 season.

Garvey visited with five teams he considered signing with as a free agent—the Giants, Cubs, Yankees, Astros, and Padres.

"I mostly discussed personality and philosophy," Garvey said.

The first baseman left details to his agent, Jerry Kapstein, who negotiated a five-year, $6.6 million contract with the Padres. The deal included all kinds of incentives, from a $150,000 bonus for being named playoffs MVP to $25,000 for being named to the National League All-Star team.

One thing that wasn't in the contract was any assurance that Garvey could continue to wear the No. 6 jersey that he had worn for 14 seasons with the Dodgers.

That was the number utilityman Tim Flannery wore during his first five seasons with the Padres. Not to worry. Flannery had no problem giving No. 6 to The Garv.

"Even before Steve signed with San Diego, I knew he was coming. I just knew," Flannery said. "And one day when we were playing the Dodgers and I got on first base, I told him he could have my number.

"When he signed, he accepted—No. 6 belonged to him, not me."

Most players are pretty particular about their number. Those who are traded or sign with a new team as a free agent usually want to keep the same number, and they frequently have to pay for the privilege.

Sometimes it's cold, hard cash that gets the deal done. Rickey Henderson paid $25,000 to Turner Ward in 1993 so he could wear No. 24.

But more often than not it's a gift of some kind that completes the transaction.

When he joined Toronto in 1997, Roger Clemens gave Carlos Delgado a $15,000 Rolex watch in order to get No. 21. Then again, in 1991 the Phillies' John Kruk turned over No. 28 to Mitch Williams in exchange for two cases of beer.

Garvey was very gracious following Flannery's kind gesture.

"He said 'I'll give you any suit you want in the world,'" said Flannery. "I said, 'OK, I want a wet suit.'"

An avid surfer, that would suit Flannery just fine.

"But he didn't let it happen," said Flannery. "He made me go to Ralph Lauren and buy a $600 three-piece suit.

"The first time I wore it all these guys, I think (Bruce) Bochy was one of them, him and Goose (Gossage), they hit me in the back with buttered rolls on the airplane."

The suit has been hung up in Flannery's closet ever since.

7 1998 World Series Team

Here's a tip to those franchises trying to get approval for a new stadium: put a championship product on the field right before constituents head to the ballot box.

With a vote for a new downtown ballpark looming in November of 1998, the Padres picked the perfect time to assemble their best team in franchise history.

How important was it to do well? Padres owner John Moores said "Major League Baseball cannot survive in San Diego without the new ballpark."

Most of the key pieces for success already were in place coming into the season.

Padres third baseman Ken Caminiti and center fielder Steve Finley had come over in a 1994 trade with Houston. First baseman Wally Joyner and left fielder Greg Vaughn both arrived in 1996 in trades with Kansas City and Milwaukee, respectively. Catcher Carlos Hernandez signed as a free agent following the 1996 season.

And, of course, Tony Gwynn had been a fixture in right field since 1982.

Those six players—along with the steady double-play combination of second baseman Quilvio Veras and shortstop Chris Gomez—provided a solid everyday lineup.

The pitching staff was slightly above average, but it needed an ace.

Enter Florida right-hander Kevin Brown, who was available when the Marlins held a fire sale after winning the 1997 World Series. The Padres traded two of their top prospects, first baseman Derek Lee and pitcher Rafael Medina, to get Brown, whose price wasn't higher because he would be a free agent after the season. They also included minor leaguer Steve Hoff.

Medina played just two seasons in the big leagues, winning three games. Lee would play 15 years in the majors and collect more than 300 career home runs. But you do what you have to do when the opportunity to win presents itself.

Brown went 18–7 with the Padres with a 2.38 ERA and a career-high 257 strikeouts. He was everything the team hoped he would be—and more.

The 1998 Padres Roster

Starting Lineup
Quilvio Veras, 2B
Tony Gwynn, RF
Greg Vaughn, LF
Ken Caminiti, 3B
Wally Joyner, 1B
Steve Finley, CF
Carlos Hernandez, C
Chris Gomez, SS

Reserves
Mark Sweeney, UTL
Andy Sheets, MI
Ruben Rivera, OF
Greg Myers, C
John Vander Wal, OF
Jim Leyritz, UTL

Starting Rotation
Kevin Brown, RHP
Andy Ashby, RHP
Joey Hamilton, RHP
Sterling Hitchcock, LHP
Mark Langston, LHP

Bullpen
Brian Boehringer, RHP
Scott Sanders, RHP
Randy Myers, LHP
Donne Wall, RHP
Dan Miceli, RHP
Trevor Hoffman, RHP

Brown's presence took pressure off others in the rotation. Andy Ashby (17–9, 3.34 ERA) set a career-high in wins and Joey Hamilton (13–13, 4.27) also reached double figures in wins. Sterling Hitchcock (9–7, 3.93) had his brightest moment in the playoffs when he earned National League Championship Series MVP.

Closing out most of the team's victories was Trevor Hoffman, who saved a club-record 53 games. It's not quite clear if Hoffman was buoyed more by strong starting pitching, a potent offense, or entering the game to AC/DC's "Hells Bells."

Injuries were catching up with Caminiti, who was the 1996 NL MVP, but he still contributed 29 homers and 82 RBIs during the season.

Vaughn was the big bopper, collecting a team-high 119 RBIs and team-record 50 home runs—No. 50 coming in his final at-bat of the regular season.

The contributions of Gwynn (16 HR, 69 RBIs), Finley (14 HR, 67 RBIs), Joyner (12 HR, 80 RBIs), and Hernandez (9 HR, 52 RBIs) made for a formidable offense.

The Padres were in first place in the NL West for all but six days of the season. Four of those days were in May, a month in which the team went just 16–14. An 11-game winning streak in mid-June fueled a 56–22 stretch that pretty much put away the division.

"I don't think we've ever played better for an extended period of time," Padres manager Bruce Bochy said. "We had a lot of guys who contributed...not just in one game but night after night. We were dangerous any time a number of guys came up."

A cold streak down the stretch in which they went 3–8 cost the Padres a 100-win season. Their 98–64 mark was still a franchise record. They finished 9.5 games ahead of San Francisco for the team's third NL West title.

The Padres defeated Houston in four games in the best-of-five NL Division Series. Two of the victories came over future Hall of Famer Randy Johnson. The Astros came into the series with the

NL's highest-scoring offense, but were limited to eight runs in four games.

The Padres advanced to the NLCS against Atlanta, which had won a franchise-record 106 games behind a powerful offense and the Big Three—future Hall of Fame pitchers Greg Maddux, Tom Glavine, and John Smoltz.

The Padres threatened to sweep the best-of-seven series, winning the first three games. The Braves came back with two wins before the Padres closed them out with a 5–0 win in Game 6. Hitchcock was named series MVP after throwing five scoreless innings with eight strikeouts in the decisive game.

The Padres finally met their match in the World Series when they were swept by a Yankees team that had won 114 games in the regular season and ranked among baseball's all-time best clubs.

The most memorable moment for the Padres was a fifth-inning home run Gwynn hit off David Wells in Game 1. The ball hit the upper-deck facade of Yankee Stadium and provided the Padres with a 5–2 lead. The Yankees rallied to win and were on their way to the franchise's 24th World Series title.

The 1998 postseason provided the city with the most exciting baseball it had seen since the 1984 World Series season.

And it made it possible for the franchise to push for a new baseball-only facility.

Qualcomm had been expanded to accommodate the Chargers—and attract another Super Bowl. Construction entailed filling in the bowl, which completed a circle of seating.

One of the by-products of this is that the enclosed stadium captured the crowd noise, making it reverberate throughout the place.

No one remembers crowds being any louder. Nor were they any bigger. Qualcomm Stadium attendance records for baseball were set throughout the postseason, culminating with a record 65,427 for Game 4 of the World Series.

So thankful was the crowd—even in losing—that thousands remained in the stands long after the game was over. They remained to cheer Padres players for an outstanding season.

The Padres were honored with a downtown parade after the World Series.

"Don't forget: November 3 [Election Day] is coming quickly. You know what we need to do. Yes on C," Gwynn said to the crowd when he took the podium.

They listened.

Two weeks after the season ended, city voters went to the polls. Proposition C for a new downtown ballpark was overwhelmingly approved by nearly 60 percent.

C. Arnholdt Smith

The excitement of Major League Baseball coming to San Diego in 1969 was short-lived in the office of the San Diego Padres.

"We were doomed from the beginning," Buzzie Bavasi said.

Not exactly encouraging words coming from the franchise's original president.

That was Bavasi's assessment within weeks of being around owner C. Arnholdt Smith.

Smith was known as Mr. San Diego, with real estate, business, and banking holdings that made him one of the city's most influential civic leaders.

Smith purchased the minor league Padres for $300,000 in 1955. A decade later, he was interested in acquiring a major league team.

Smith's efforts were rebuffed again and again, until he lured Bavasi, the longtime Dodgers GM, down from Los Angeles. Bavasi's extensive baseball contacts were instrumental in helping Smith receive approval from National League owners for an expansion franchise in 1969.

"When he got the franchise, his financial empire had already begun to crumble," Bavasi said. "I had anticipated we'd get into the league for $7 million. When I learned the price would be $10 million, I advised Smith to back out. At that price, we would not have enough money left to properly operate the ballclub. He went ahead and got the franchise, anyway.

"He never understood baseball or anything necessary to run a club. He would not allow us to spend money, failing to understand that you had to sign players for the four minor league clubs.

"By the time he was forced to sell, money was so scarce we could not afford to sign anyone."

One such player Bavasi mentioned was third baseman Doug DeCinces.

The Padres drafted DeCinces out of high school, selecting him in the 18th round of the 1969 June major league draft. The Padres offered a $4,000 signing bonus, but DeCinces wanted $6,000.

"The Padres did not sign DeCinces," Bavasi said, "because they could not afford the extra $2,000."

DeCinces enrolled in junior college. Six months later he was drafted in what was then the January phase of the draft and signed by Baltimore. DeCinces split a productive 15-year career between the Orioles and Angels and one four-game stint with St. Louis in 1987.

"Every time we got a decent player, we would have to sell him," Bavasi said. "It had come to the point where we'd pay the players on a Friday and ask them not to cash their checks until Monday."

Smith's U.S. National Bank collapsed, becoming the nation's biggest bank failure at the time, and he had the SEC breathing down his neck.

Smith would be charged with embezzlement and commingling of funds from other businesses and eventually served seven months at a county honor camp.

Of bigger concern to local baseball fans was the fact that Smith had to sell the Padres. The prospective new owner, grocery magnate Joseph Danzansky, planned to move the team to Washington, D.C., in 1974.

A historical footnote—while Ray Kroc is credited with saving baseball for the city, San Diego city attorney John Witt deserves a tip of the cap for his role.

It was Witt who filed a lawsuit for breaking the San Diego Stadium lease, which still had 15 years remaining. The added cost of having to pay off the lease made purchase of the team unfeasible.

Danzansky backed out and Kroc eventually stepped in to save the day.

As for Smith? It's safe to say he was no fan favorite thereafter.

9 Hoffman in the 9th

Entering the game to get the last three outs sounds like good work if you can get it.

And it is.

But a tremendous amount of pregame and ingame preparation is required if one is to be ready to pitch the ninth inning.

Trevor Hoffman, a creature of habit growing up, perfected a routine that helped him collect a franchise-record 552 saves for the Padres (and 601 saves for his career).

Here was a typical day from the time Hoffman arrived at the ballpark until the moment he was summoned to the mound in the ninth:

- Hoffman, who arrived as many as six hours before the game, goes to his locker and throws on his green hospital scrub shirt.
- Because strong legs and trunk are essential to a pitcher's success, he runs lap after lap around the field.
- Run pregame sprints in the outfield with other relievers to work the "fast twitch" muscles.
- Do some pregame throwing—not too much, not too little—to assess the shoulder and arm and make sure everything is good to go for that evening's contest.
- Do abdominal crunches to maintain a strong core.
- Do hydrotherapy, alternating between cold and hot water to constrict and dilate, respectively, blood vessels. This would promote recovery, speeding up the process of removing waste from tissues.
- Spend the first five innings of the game in the bullpen with the other relievers. Conversations could be about anything and everything while passing the time out there. At some point, the focus would be on the opposing lineup and what insight could be gained on how to pitch to particular hitters.
- At about the sixth inning, Hoffman would return to the clubhouse to get his mind right and have a hot shower and ultrasound treatment to his shoulder and/or arm. That stimulation, along with other stretching, would get him ready to pitch.
- Return to the bullpen in time to throw some warmup pitches before the call comes in the ninth.

- Jog to the mound, get three outs for the save, get the game ball to add to the collection, high-five teammates, head back to the clubhouse.

The Chicken

The most famous graduate of San Diego's Hoover High is definitely named Ted.

Hall of Famer Ted Williams?

Maybe. Maybe not.

Ted Giannoulas just may be better known around the globe.

After all, Williams mostly limited himself to eight American League cities during his 19-year career with Boston. Giannoulas has performed in all 50 states and eight countries across more than four decades.

Can't place the face?

How about the name—The San Diego Chicken?

In his bio, Giannoulas is described as reaching "icon status as a sports and entertainment personality throughout the nation and the world. In his element as an outrageous comic actor, he's as unique and gifted a humorist as any stage has ever seen."

It's no exaggeration.

Former *San Diego Union* sports editor Jack Murphy once said: "The Chicken has the soul of a poet. He is an embryonic Charles Chaplin in chicken feathers." *The Sporting News* placed him among The Top 100 Most Powerful People in Sports of the 20ᵗʰ Century.

The first time Giannoulas had such an opportunity, he thought it was for the birds.

The San Diego Chicken debuted in 1974 and had more success on the field than almost anyone else until the Padres made the playoffs for the first time a decade later. (Fantography.com/Andy Strasberg)

"When I was a kid at Hoover, they had an open tryout for the Cardinal mascot," Giannoulas said. "Nobody wanted to do it. My friends said, 'Ted, you should do that.' I turned and said, 'I'm way too hip to be doing anything like that. You guys really think I'm that stupid? To be a goof like that?'"

Giannoulas didn't squawk the next time such an opportunity presented itself, even if his salary was chicken feed.

As a student at San Diego State in 1974, Giannoulas was offered $2 an hour to put on a chicken suit promoting radio station KGB for a one-week gig handing out Easter eggs at the San Diego Zoo.

When the promotion ended, Giannoulas pitched the idea of going to Padres games to promote the station (and get into baseball games for free).

"I had to watch through a bothersome beak, but hey, it was better than a knothole," Giannoulas said.

Five hundred straight Padres games later, Giannoulas had developed and honed an act that made him the biggest hit at the ballpark.

Giannoulas' own comedic tendencies borrowed on "slapstick, parody, and visual antics, all woven throughout interludes of ballgames, much to the surprised delight of sports fans."

In one moment he was bringing out an eye chart for the home plate umpire and in another instance he led a conga line of chicklets (children dressed as little chickens) who each lifted a leg as they passed by one of the men in blue.

He performed routines to music long before players approached the plate to walk-up songs. And he spent more time in the crowd than the vendors.

He is recognized as the father of professional mascots, spawning the proliferation of costumed characters throughout the sports world.

A sellout crowd of 47,000 filled San Diego Stadium in 1979 when The Chicken "rehatched," going off on his own in a new red, white and blue costume after having a falling out with the radio station.

The Chicken was well on his way to becoming a national figure by that time. He performed at 250–275 events a year in his heyday. Giannoulas does approximately 75 events a year these days. By his count, Giannoulas has performed more than 8,500 times—and has never missed a show—in more than 900 venues. His appearances total more than 17,000 when parades, trade shows, banquets, conventions, and TV and radio dates are included.

While he is getting a little long in the beak, Giannoulas still gets as much enjoyment out of being the chicken as he ever did.

"I get very passionate about performing for thousands of people," Giannoulas said. "It's intoxicating....It's been (almost) 42 years. It was a radio station promotion that wasn't supposed to last 42 days."

Tim Flannery

Tim Flannery never made an All-Star team. He never won a batting title. Heck, he was a backup infielder for virtually his entire major league career.

And yet Flannery is among the most beloved Padres players of all time. His hustle and enthusiasm—not to mention surfing and guitar playing—touched fans from virtually the moment Flannery received a September call-up in 1979.

"I told all the people that I just wanted to play for the pure joy of baseball," said Flannery, whose 11 seasons with the Padres were more than any player but Tony Gwynn (20 seasons). "That's the reason I got into this game in the first place."

The 5'11" Flannery was drafted in the sixth round of the 1978 major league draft out of Chapman University. He reached the major leagues a little more than a year later, and, though he always seemed to be battling to keep his spot on the roster, Flannery became a fixture with the Padres for the next decade.

"He's a great guy to have on the team," former Padres first baseman Steve Garvey said. "He's always ready. He understands his role but he doesn't necessarily like not playing. He does the next best thing by staying ready. He's what I call a true professional."

Flannery figured prominently in the Padres' first playoffs appearance in the dramatic comeback against the Chicago Cubs in the 1984 NLCS.

He had a pinch-hit single and scored a run midway through Game 4, before Garvey's two-run homer won the game in the bottom of the ninth.

A day later in the decisive Game 5, Flannery came to the plate as a pinch-hitter in the seventh inning. He hit a sharp ground ball through the legs of Cubs first baseman Leon Durham to drive in the tying run, then came around to score the go-ahead run in the victory that sent the Padres to the World Series for the first time.

Flannery's best year came in 1985, when he was the Padres' regular second baseman. He set career highs, batting .281 with 40 RBIs and 50 runs scored.

Future Hall of Famer Roberto Alomar took over at second base toward the end of Flannery's career, but it didn't faze Flannery.

"I would like to have been an All-Star second baseman for 15 years," said Flannery, who had a .255 career batting average. "I thought I was gonna be. I wasn't, but it doesn't mean I wasn't a success."

Flannery's legion of fans would agree.

"You prepare yourself and give 100 percent and do your very best," Flannery said. "Do that and you are a success. You don't have to be pressured by expectations, trying to reach expectations to be successful. When you're done, when you walk out the door, you don't want to say you regret that there were a couple of years you might have played harder. You want to be able to say, 'Thank you, I gave it all I had. I have no regrets.'"

Midway through the 1989 season, Flannery announced that it would be his last as a player.

"I am very happy," Flannery said as his final game approached, "and when I tear up and I get emotional, it's not because I'm disappointed in my decision. It's because I'm overwhelmed by the way my teammates and this city have embraced me the last couple of months—well, for the last 10 years, but I never stopped to think about it until the last two months."

Jack McKeon, who was Padres manager for Flannery's final two seasons, said, "I hate to see him go. He's a fine young man and a great asset to any ballclub. He was an important guy in things that didn't show up in the box scores—the intangibles. He was a positive influence in the clubhouse."

Flannery picked September 29, 1989—his 32nd birthday—to play his last game.

The next night was declared Flan Appreciation Night, with commemorative pins given out to those in attendance—and 47,787 people showed up.

"I never thought I'd play long enough to enjoy a last night," Flannery said. "I'd always thought the end was going to be me getting released, or them telling me, 'You can't play anymore.' That's why I feel so fortunate.

"Ninety-nine percent of the guys leave the game bitter, because they've either been released or they continue to play too long, and their physical capability doesn't match up to what they always thought it was. I didn't want that."

Said Padres shortstop Garry Templeton: "He will be missed around here. I've enjoyed playing with him. Since I've been here, they have always tried to give his job away to someone else. A lot of guys would have given up, but he stuck through it."

Flannery would have a second career coaching in the Padres organization, first as a minor league manager, then on Padres manager Bruce Bochy's staff.

When Bochy left to manage the San Francisco Giants in 2007, Flannery went with him. They won three World Series championships together, in 2010, 2012, and 2014.

The Wizard of Oz

In 1978, the Padres took the virtually unprecedented step of firing their manager during spring training.

Alvin Dark was axed for his inability, one executive said, "to communicate effectively with his players, coaching staff, and those of us in the front office."

There was at least one effective move Dark made that no one will ever forget. On the first day of spring training, Dark named Ozzie Smith the Padres' starting shortstop.

The Padres drafted Smith in the fourth round of the 1977 major league draft. Ten months later he was playing in the major leagues, making the jump from Class-A Walla Walla.

Smith never forgot the support he received from Dark, making mention of him 24 years later during his induction speech at the National Baseball Hall of Fame.

Smith taking over at shortstop was seriously questioned at the time, however, because it entailed moving incumbent Padres shortstop Bill Almon, a former No. 1 overall draft pick, to second base.

It wasn't long before Padres fans realized they had someone special in Ozzie.

Smith made the greatest play of his career just days into his rookie season, scrambling to his feet to throw out Atlanta's Jeff Burroughs at first base after making a diving, barehanded stop on a ball hit up the middle.

The play is still shown among highlights four decades later and, in fact, was selected as the greatest defensive play in major league history.

"The one word to best describe Ozzie is *spectacular*," Dodgers broadcaster Vin Scully once said. "In the old days you had steady guys like [Pee Wee] Reese and [Marty] Marion. You never thought of them making the great play. They were always just there in the right spot. But Ozzie is an acrobat, and that makes him stand out."

Smith was overmatched at the plate in his first few years. He batted .258 as a rookie, then slipped to .211, .230, and .222. He was a threat on the base paths when he did reach base, however, averaging more than 36 stolen bases a year during his first four seasons.

Any offense Smith provided was a bonus, of course. That's because his play in the field at a premium position was off the charts.

Roger Craig, who replaced Dark as Padres manager, would say: "He's the best defensive shortstop who ever played the game. Ever."

The Gold Gloves started coming by Smith's third season, in 1980. He won 13 in a row. Baltimore's Brooks Robinson, who won 16 straight, is the only position player to win more consecutively and overall.

The downside for Padres fans is that Smith did most of his glove work for the St. Louis Cardinals.

Smith, or more specifically his agent, Ed Gottlieb, had trouble reaching contract terms with the Padres almost from the get-go.

Unable to reach a contract agreement with Smith before the 1980 season, the Padres renewed him at $72,500, the same amount he made in 1979.

Gottlieb was angered and tried to embarrass the club by taking out a help-wanted ad in the *San Diego Union*. It read, in part: *Padre baseball player wants part-time employment to supplement income.*

So Joan Kroc, the wife of Padres owner Ray Kroc, offered Smith a job as an assistant gardener at their Rancho Santa Fe estate.

Of course, Smith, always known for his defense, never claimed he could rake.

That incident was pretty much the last straw between the two sides. Smith was traded after the 1981 season to the Cardinals in a six-player deal in which the teams basically exchanged disgruntled shortstops.

As it worked out, life was happier for everyone with their new surroundings.

 **Tempy**

St. Louis was for the birds in more ways than one on an August afternoon in 1981, when Cardinals shortstop Garry Templeton let it be known that he had had enough with the city and its fans.

The seeds of resentment began to grow two years earlier when Templeton declined an invitation to the 1979 All-Star Game because he had not been voted in as a starter.

It all came to a head two years later, when Templeton struck out in the first inning of a game against the San Francisco Giants.

The ball got away from the catcher, but Templeton, perhaps not realizing, didn't run down to first base.

Fans at Busch Stadium booed as he returned to the dugout and Templeton responded with his middle finger to the Ladies Day crowd.

Boos continued when Templeton came off the field in the second inning and in the third inning, when Templeton again flipped off the fans.

This time, he was ejected by home plate umpire Bruce Froemming. Templeton made one more gesture, grabbing his crotch, before he left the field. St. Louis manager Whitey Herzog got Templeton into the dugout, where they scuffled briefly.

After the incident, Templeton was fined $5,000 and suspended for three weeks.

Templeton was as talented as they come when he reached the major leagues in the mid-1970s. He took over as St. Louis' starting shortstop when he was only 20 years old. By his sixth season, Templeton had worn out his welcome after speaking up about his desire to bat leadoff, wanting to be traded to a team in California, and grumbling about his salary.

Trading Templeton was a top priority following that 1981 season. When Herzog, who was also the Cardinals' GM, bumped into Padres GM Jack McKeon during the Winter Meetings, they quickly struck a deal to exchange shortstops.

Padres shortstop Ozzie Smith had fallen out of favor with Padres management. He and Templeton were the key pieces in a six-player trade.

The change did wonders for Tempy, who played a steady shortstop, provided more offense for the Padres, and also was an important influence in the clubhouse.

"They wanted me to take a leadership role because of the younger players they had on the team," Templeton said. "It made me focus on what I had to do.

"I just tried to keep the team together. I had the opportunity to talk to the young kids—and back then the kids listened. I also had the veterans' ears."

Templeton was an important member of the Padres' 1984 National League championship team. In fact, the switch-hitter picked up the Silver Slugger Award and led the National League in fielding that season.

In 1987, Templeton was named team captain by manager Larry Bowa, who recognized the influence his shortstop had on the Padres.

"I knew my role on the team was to be a leader," Templeton said.

Templeton spent nine-plus seasons with the Padres. By the time he was done, he ranked among the Top 10 all-time in several offensive categories for the franchise, including second in hits (1,135), doubles (195), and games played (1,286) and sixth in runs scored (430) and RBIs (427).

In 2015, Templeton was named to the Padres Hall of Fame. He was the first shortstop so honored.

14 .394

One of the biggest disappointments from the 1994 major league strike—and there were many—was it cheated Tony Gwynn out of the chance to hit .400.

Gwynn was batting .394 when baseball came to an abrupt halt on August 12 that season.

Six weeks remained for Gwynn to make history. Would he have done it? That's a question that will never be answered.

But, boy, would it have been fun watching him try to become the first .400 hitter since Ted Williams, another San Diegan, accomplished the feat 53 years earlier.

The subject of batting .400 came up several times in conversations between Tony Gwynn and Williams, who hit .406 for the Boston Red Sox in 1941.

"Ted looked at me and said, 'If I knew that hitting .400 would have been so damn important, I would have done it more often,'" Gwynn said. "I just laughed. But the more I thought about that, he probably could have hit .400 again if he had wanted."

Gwynn actually did hit .400 during the 162-game stretch from August 1, 1993, to May 9, 1995, batting .406 by going 242-for-596.

Doing it in 1994 is what would have made it so special, though.

"I'd be lying if I didn't say I want to make a crack at .400," Gwynn said in the midst of that '94 campaign. "But it's not going to be easy. It's going to be a lot more difficult than I think people think, but I just go out and play. I don't worry about the numbers. I just go out there and just play because that's where I'm having the most fun."

Gwynn opened the season by batting .395 in April. He was still at .393 at the end of May, which included nine days at or above .400. He was at .391 through June and .385 by the time July was in the books.

When August arrived, Gwynn really got going on one of his patented hot streaks.

With the strike looming, the Padres headed to Houston for what would be the final series of the season.

Gwynn was batting .392 going into the series. He needed to go 9-for-14 to get to .400. He went 6-for-13. That included collecting three singles in five at-bats in an 8–6 win over Houston in the Padres' final game of the season.

Gwynn's .394 average was the highest in the majors—and remains so—since Williams hit .406. Gwynn was later asked if he felt deprived of an opportunity to hit .400.

"Deprived? I don't feel that way," Gwynn said. "We (players) all were in the same boat. But in my mind, I thought I could. I sure wanted the chance. I was squaring the ball up nicely, hitting lefties, righties. I would have given it a run. I'm not sure how I would have handled it in September. But I think I had the type of personality to handle it. We'll never know, but I have no regrets."

But would he have done it?

"I really believe I'd have hit .400," Gwynn said.

Gwynn was 19-for-40 (.475) during the Padres' 10 games in August, which began with a series in Los Angeles against the Dodgers.

Gwynn's brother, Chris, then an outfielder for Los Angeles, remembers his Dodgers teammates talking about Tony.

"He was on a tear, making it look easy," Chris Gwynn said. "The guys couldn't get him out. He was either walking or hitting a rocket somewhere. And all of them were falling.

"It was steadily climbing and everybody was like, 'Oh, my God, he's going to do it.'"

Chris Gwynn said his brother wasn't concerned so much with the on-the-field task but potential off-the-field distractions.

"What he was worried about was how he was going to handle the media," Chris Gwynn said. "As he got closer, the media attention was going to go through the roof. He was starting to let his mind figure out how he was going to do it.

"I don't know if he said that out loud, but you could just tell. He was trying to stay in the moment.

"He normally had five to 10 writers around him every BP. Then it became 20, 25, 30. He's thinking how's he going to handle this. Because after a while there's going to be a press conference every day."

Gwynn certainly would have had a plan in place.

"I'm kind of upset I'm not going to get those extra six points," Gwynn said after the strike came. "But I've done everything I wanted to do offensively this year."

Gwynn was on pace for career highs in several offensive categories. He had 165 hits, 35 doubles, 12 home runs, 79 runs scored, and 64 RBIs when the strike came.

"Deep down in my heart, I think he would have done it," Chris Gwynn said.

We'll never know.

It will remain one of those "what if?" subjects for decades to come.

Bruce Bochy

Bruce Bochy had his moments on the field during a nine-year major league career, but where he really made his mark was in the dugout.

Bochy was a career backup—including five seasons playing for the Padres—but he did get the opportunity to catch a 1984 World Series game against the Detroit Tigers.

He can probably recall the circumstances of each of his home runs—all 26 of them. There was one in particular worth remembering. In 1985, Bochy hit a walk-off home run against Houston's Nolan Ryan—the only walk-off homer Ryan allowed in his career.

Bochy was part of baseball history again later that season. He is pictured behind the plate catching for the Padres as Cincinnati's Pete Rose strokes his record-breaking 4,192nd hit.

But much of Bochy's time was spent on the bench. He made the most of it.

"He's one of those guys that has incredible instincts," said Kevin Towers, a former teammate and later his general manager with the Padres. "As a backup catcher he spent all those years watching the game, studying the game."

Bochy spent 24 years in the Padres organization, beginning as a player from 1983 to 1987.

"He was the perfect guy to have on your ballclub," then Padres GM Jack McKeon said. "Great personality, a clubhouse leader even though he wasn't playing," McKeon said. "He wasn't in position to be the No. 1 catcher, and he never bitched or complained. He accepted the role and remained dedicated."

McKeon had that in mind when Bochy retired, offering him a chance to manage in the Padres' minor league system.

By 1993, Bochy was back in the big leagues as the Padres' third-base coach. Two years later, he was named Padres manager.

Bochy, who went 951–975 over 12 seasons, brought managerial stability previously unknown by the Padres.

Fourteen managers preceded him over the first 25 years of Padres history. None lasted longer than four years, that being Dick Williams, who managed Bochy for three of the five years the catcher played for the Padres.

Bochy guided the team to four National League West Division championships, beginning with a 1996 title that earned him NL Manager of the Year. Two years later, Bochy took the Padres to the 1998 World Series.

Despite back-to-back NL West titles in 2005–06, Padres CEO Sandy Alderson preferred going in another direction and allowed Bochy to become manager of the San Francisco Giants.

"We've had a great run together here," Towers said at the time. "It's been a tremendous run. Bochy is a great friend and was a great working partner. We made a lot of great memories that I'll cherish."

Bochy certainly landed on his feet in San Francisco, guiding the Giants to three World Series championships in five years (2010, 2012, 2014).

Bochy entered the 2016 season with a career record of 1,702–1,682, ranking 16th in career victories among managers.

If he sticks around four more years, Bochy should reach 2,000 career wins. Only 10 managers have ever reached that plateau. All 10 men are in the National Baseball Hall of Fame.

"He's very quietly putting together a Hall of Fame career," Angels manager Mike Scioscia said. "When you talk about Joe Torre, about Tony La Russa, about Bobby Cox, about guys that have made it, Bochy is going to be right there when it's all said and done.

"And it will be very deserving if he gets in."

16 John Moores and Larry Lucchino

John Moores and Larry Lucchino arrived in San Diego during one of Major League Baseball's darkest hours and guided the Padres to some of the franchise's brightest moments.

The lasting legacy for Moores and Lucchino is Petco Park.

The downtown ballpark was promised as a springboard to success for the Padres, putting them on equal footing with the big boys in baseball.

It didn't turn out that way on the field, but Petco did serve as a catalyst for downtown redevelopment.

And it is a beautiful ballpark.

Moores, who made his millions in computer software, was approved in December of 1994 as the new owner of the Padres. The purchase came in the middle of the baseball strike that wiped out the playoffs and World Series.

Moores purchased the Padres for $80 million from the ownership group led by Tom Werner. Moores became chairman of the board in a group that included Lucchino as the team's president and CEO.

Within two weeks of acquiring the team—and with settlement of the strike still four months away—the Padres made one of the biggest trades in their history.

They acquired center fielder Steve Finley and third baseman Ken Caminiti, among others, from the Houston Astros in a 12-player deal that was the largest in baseball in 37 years.

It was the first move among many that would point the Padres toward a 1996 West Division championship and a 1998 World Series berth.

"The Padres were a challenge because the stone was at the bottom of the hill," Lucchino said. "When we got to San Diego, there was a major reclamation project. Then the ballpark."

Lucchino, who had been the driving force behind marketing and community involvement for the Padres, spearheaded the effort to get a new ballpark.

Lucchino was the man for the job after also serving as president and CEO for the Baltimore Orioles when the team built Camden Yards.

The Padres' World Series appearance coincided with a ballot measure to approve funding of the new park. It was overwhelmingly approved.

The city benefitted greatly from Moores' philanthropy—especially contributions to San Diego State University and local hospitals—around town. Moores benefitted greatly from downtown real estate he acquired during redevelopment.

The new ballpark was scheduled to open in time for the 2002 season, although several legal challenges caused a two-year delay in funding and construction.

Lucchino and Moores had a falling out during that time and Lucchino left. In 2002, he became part of a new ownership group for the Boston Red Sox.

Lucchino returned to town when Petco Park debuted in 2004, throwing out the first pitch when San Diego State met Houston in the first game played at the ballpark.

"It's such a tremendous civic success," Lucchino said of Petco during a visit in 2007 when the Padres played the Red Sox. "The ballpark wasn't one of those false promises. It's hit a home run. When we started, they were talking about $500 million in construction around the ballpark. I'm now told it's at $4.3 billion."

The product the Padres put on the field was not their best in the five years between reaching the World Series and the opening of Petco. They finished fourth or fifth in the NL West each season.

The Padres' Opening Day payroll was slashed in 1999 and ranked among baseball's bottom six teams from 2001 to 2003.

The payroll was boosted when the ballpark opened, ranging from $66 to $74 million from 2004 to 2006. That placed it in the middle of the pack among baseball's 30 teams.

The 2005 and 2006 seasons brought NL West titles, but a playoff drought would follow over the next decade.

Payroll was slashed again—ranking it in the bottom three teams from 2009 to 2012 and last at $44 million in 2010—when Moores went through a divorce that forced him to sell the team.

He originally sold the ballclub for $540 million to a group led by former agent Jeff Moorad. The sale did not gain the approval of major league owners, however. An ownership group headed by members of the O'Malley family, the longtime owners of the Los Angeles Dodgers, and San Diego businessman Ron Fowler did win approval to purchase the team for $800 million in 2012.

Moores was at the owners meetings when the sale was approved.

"It was an out-of-body experience," said Moores, who was reflective after nearly two decades of owning the Padres. "It was more emotional than I thought it would be. I was on the phone afterward and I couldn't keep my voice from cracking. It's been 18 years. All I keep thinking about at this point is baseball. It's just weird. But it's time to move forward."

17 Back-to-Back-to-Back

The National Baseball Hall of Fame hasn't asked for a lot of Padres memorabilia through the years.

But Cooperstown came calling for three bats following the team's home opener on April 13, 1987.

And the Padres didn't even win the game. They lost 13–6 to the San Francisco Giants.

The game was memorable—and historical—for the way it started for the Padres.

After San Francisco scored two runs in the first inning, Giants pitcher Roger Mason took the mound in the bottom half of the inning.

Padres center fielder Marvell Wynne led off. Wynne worked the count to 3–2 when Mason tried to get him with a slider. Wynne wasn't fooled, lining the ball for a home run to right field.

Right fielder Tony Gwynn was the second hitter. He hit a 1–1 fastball for a home run to right-center.

Left fielder John Kruk was the third hitter. He had a 1–1 count when Mason threw him a split finger fastball that Kruk sent over the fence in left-center.

It marked the first time in major league history that a team started a game with back-to-back-to-back home runs.

First baseman Steve Garvey was the fourth hitter. He hit a fly ball to deep center field that captured the crowd for a few moments before the fans realized the ball was staying in the ballpark. Giants center fielder Chili Davis gloved it for the out.

How unlikely was it for Wynne, Gwynn, and Kruk to go back-to-back-to-back?

Consider this: Wynne would hit just one other home run in 213 plate appearances. And Wynne was only put into the starting lineup an hour before the game when regular center fielder Stan Jefferson begged off with a sore left ankle.

Gwynn finished with seven homers in 680 plate appearances. Kruk showed some pop, collecting 20 homers in 527 times at the plate.

18 Tony Talks with Ted

Bob Costas reviewed Tony Gwynn's accomplishments in an interview conducted during the winter of 1994–95, when Major League Baseball was in the middle of the strike that wiped out the World Series for the first time in 90 years.

Gwynn has been hailed as the greatest hitter of his generation, a genius with the bat who was in the middle of a career in which he would average .338 and collect eight batting titles.

Gwynn seemed less than sure of himself, however, because of the man seated next to him during the interview—Ted Williams—who was firing question after question at Gwynn about hitting.

Tony Gwynn loved to talk baseball with everyone, but there was no one he enjoyed talking hitting with more than Hall of Famer Ted Williams. (Fantography.com/Andy Strasberg)

"When Ted Williams said, 'Now, do you swing all the way through in this situation or do you push at the ball?'" said Costas, "you had the look of a schoolboy hoping he would have the right answer or the teacher would slap his hand with a ruler."

"No question about it," Gwynn replied. "Lots of people look toward Ted Williams as their teacher, whether they were fortunate enough to work under him or do like I did reading books and stuff.

"If anybody else asked me that question, there's no doubt I would say I try to stay behind the ball and block the ball off. But with Ted sitting there I had to think about it a minute, and I was a bit nervous."

John Boggs, Gwynn's longtime agent and friend, was off to one side of the room listening during the interview.

"Ted is a very forceful guy," Boggs said. "It was like John Wayne interviewing you. Ted would ask a question like, 'Tony, what are you looking for on a 2–2 pitch?' and he'd go through this scenario. I'm sitting there going, 'Oh, my gosh, hopefully, you say the right thing T.'"

Gwynn did come up with the right answers. And each time, Williams would respond with a booming: "Correct!"

The interview took place in Florida after a luncheon at Williams' Hitters Hall of Fame. Costas sat down for a chat with two of the game's greats. It turned into one of the most fascinating hitting conversations ever filmed and made a great impression on Gwynn.

"After that interview Tony was so pumped and so excited," Boggs said, "that we talked about it from the time we left to go to the airport, flying all the way back to San Diego, and the next day. It was an impactful time for him."

Said Gwynn years later: "First of all, I was scared to death. Second of all, it was like being a kid in the candy store. Imagine sitting next to the man who knew more about hitting a baseball than anyone who ever played the game. If you had any questions about hitting, here was the man who had all the answers....The thing I remember most, we talked about the ball inside because that's where he really got testy."

Williams, who retired with a .344 lifetime average and 521 home runs, had a saying: "History is made on the inner third of the plate."

"By the time I walked out of there," Gwynn said, "I started to realize that this guy was the supreme authority, so why shouldn't I go ahead and try out some of the stuff that we had talked about?

"It took me a year and a half to figure it out, but he had been absolutely right. It made a huge difference for me in the last five full seasons of my career."

At one point during that initial conversation, Williams asked Gwynn: "How many homers you hit last year?"

"I hit 12, which is a lot for me," Gwynn said.

Williams predicted Gwynn would hit more.

"Certainly, don't change what you're doing," Williams said. "But take more advantage of the count, more advantage of the type pitcher you're hitting against, crowd the plate once in a while, because you know you can pull the ball better in, you can hit the ball hard when it's over the plate up the middle...."

Three of Gwynn's five seasons with double-figure home runs came in his last three full seasons.

In 1997—Gwynn's 16th year in the big leagues—he had statistically his best year. He batted .372 (his highest average for a full season) with a career-high 220 hits, 17 home runs, and 119 RBIs.

"He said that whatever type of hitter I wanted to be, I would be better at it if I learned to handle the ball inside," Gwynn remembered. "My argument was, 'I can already handle the ball in.' And he laughed. He thought I was hilarious.

"He didn't just lay it out for you, saying, 'Look, you need to do this, this, this, and this,'" Gwynn said. "Good hitters have a sense of just trying to figure stuff out."

Gwynn and Williams would cross paths several times over the next few years—most notably before the 1999 All-Star Game at Boston's Fenway Park—and develop quite a friendship.

"He truly enjoyed talking about the art of hitting a baseball, and he truly enjoyed the banter going back and forth on how to best get it done," Gwynn said. "Believe me, there were times when he was pissed at me and I was pissed at him and we went back and forth.

"I was similar to a lot of guys who've had success and who think their way is the right way. That's the stubbornness that good hitters have and I'm thinking, *Mr. Williams, he doesn't know*, but it turns out he was right. I had to kind of eat crow."

Said Boggs: "They genuinely had a great friendship from that (first meeting). Ted loved the way Tony played the game, and vice versa.

"Ted became very, very fond of Tony and Tony fond of Ted."

Tony's Number

Tony Gwynn never liked his 1983 Topps rookie card.

The photo was taken during a spring training game in 1982. Gwynn is pictured coming out of the batter's box, his eyes locked on the batted ball heading to the outfield as he runs down the first-base line.

What Gwynn didn't appreciate was the photographer's perspective. The hitter was shot from behind. All Gwynn could see was his behind.

"I hate that card," Gwynn said. "All you see is my big booty."

Gwynn is wearing jersey No. 53. It's one of those high numbers they give to players who aren't expected to make the team.

And Gwynn didn't make the big club out of spring training. He was farmed out to Triple-A Hawaii. He wasn't away long, getting called to the big leagues July 19, 1982.

In the Padres clubhouse, equipment manager Ray Peralta directed Gwynn to his locker. Longtime clubhouse man Whitey Wietelmann brought Gwynn his jersey.

"When he handed it to me it was No. 19," said Gwynn. "When I looked at it, I was just happy it was lower than 53."

Gwynn said Wietelmann told him that only a few players had worn No. 19 for the Padres. In fact, outfielder Gene Richards, who wore No. 19 during the 1978 season, is the only other player to wear it in the majors for the organization.

Ted Williams was the first player to wear No. 19 in San Diego. He put it on for the minor league Padres in their inaugural season in the city after signing out of San Diego's Hoover High.

The number also was worn in the minors by Wietelmann when he played shortstop for the club from 1949 to1952.

Wietelmann made sure Gwynn knew a little about the history of the number when he gave it to the young outfielder, concluding his comments by saying, "So don't disgrace it."

"I'll try to do the best that I can, Mr. Wietelmann," Gwynn said.

Eight batting titles and 3,141 hits later, Gwynn's best wasn't bad.

When Gwynn retired following the 2001 season, the No. 19 was retired along with him. It was three years before the franchise made it official, however.

The Padres retired the Hall of Fame right fielder's number in 2004 during a ceremony at Petco Park. The No. 19 was placed above the batter's eye at the ballpark, alongside Steve Garvey's No. 6, Dave Winfield's No. 31, and Randy Jones' No. 35 (Trevor Hoffman's No. 51 would join them in 2011).

"I wasn't as talented as some of these guys here," Gwynn told the sellout crowd for his jersey retirement before that night's game against the Colorado Rockies. "I knew I had to work. So I rolled up my sleeves and got to work. You saw me play for 20 years, and now here's my number."

The number also was outside on a street sign. Petco Park is located at 19 Tony Gwynn Drive.

Gwynn, who wore No. 24 on the basketball court and No. 28 on the baseball field at San Diego State, donned No. 19 when he served as head coach for 12 years for the Aztecs.

SDSU retired the No. 19 during a ceremony before its 2015 season opener against Valparaiso, honoring Gwynn in the first baseball game played since his death the previous June.

In March 2015, actor Will Ferrell made a spring training appearance in Arizona as part of a cancer awareness promotion.

Ferrell played 10 different positions for 10 teams in one day. He wore No. 19 for nine of the teams.

Ferrell's 10th and final team of the day was the Padres. He played right field. And wore No. 20.

No one—no one—will ever wear No. 19 again on the field for the Padres.

There are still plenty of people wearing No. 19 in the Petco Park stands.

20 Mr. Indispensable— Whitey Wietelmann

The last pitch of Game 4 of the 1984 NLCS was hit over the right-field wall by Steve Garvey.

Everybody knows that.

What many people don't know is that the first pitch of the game was thrown out by Whitey Wietelmann.

"I didn't want to do it," Wietelmann said. "I did it as a favor to Mrs. (Joan) Kroc because she wanted me to. After I did it, it was all right. But it just wasn't like me to do it."

Wietelmann was given the honor of throwing out the first pitch because of his four-decade association with the Padres, dating back to when he joined the team as an infielder in 1949.

He played for the minor league Padres from 1949 to 1952, then coached for the club from 1960 to 1965 and again in 1968. He was among the coaches for the original Padres in 1969, serving on the staff through 1979. Whitey served a variety of roles thereafter over the next decade.

He was born William Frederick Wietelmann in Zanesville, Ohio, in 1919. It was there that he served as a batboy for the semipro team owned by his father. In the team photo for the 1925 Zanesville Greys baseball team, Wietelmann is seated in front of an outfielder named Jim Thorpe.

Wietelmann played nine seasons in the major leagues from 1939 to 1947. He hit a modest .232 with seven home runs over 580 games. He came away with a nickname, however. His first manager with the Boston Braves, a fellow by the name of Casey Stengel, dubbed him "Whitey."

Wietelmann wore No. 19 for the minor league Padres, and memorably presented it in 1982 to a young outfielder named Tony Gwynn. He cooked many a meal in the clubhouse for the players. His chili was described as "world renowned" in the team's media guide.

He was likely to be found mending an old glove one moment and any of a thousand things the next.

"If it breaks, I fix it," he said.

He even invented a baseball-cleaning machine to brighten up batting practice balls.

Irascible, feisty, and *crusty* all were words used to describe Wietelmann, but around the Padres clubhouse he was known as "Mr. Indispensable." In fact, that was his title in the 1985 Padres media guide.

Wietelmann frequently could be seen driving a golf cart running errands around San Diego Stadium.

On one occasion in 1986, Wietelmann was going down the hallway in the bowels of the stadium when he came upon another cart coming from the other direction.

In the other cart was Peter Tork, a keyboardist and guitarist for the rock group the Monkees, being driven to his dressing room. The Monkees were to play a postgame concert that afternoon.

There was room for only one cart at a time in the narrow hallway. The 67-year-old Wietelmann had no idea who Tork was and commanded the driver of the other cart to "back up."

Tork, then 42 years old, said, "No, you back up, old man."

"That's all Whitey needed to hear," said Andy Strasberg, then the Padres' vice president of public relations. "He quickly got out of his cart, walked over to Peter and cold-cocked him—hitting him in the face with a right hook."

That there was a "situation" was relayed to Strasberg in the fourth inning of the Padres' game against the Phillies. So Strasberg hustled down to the Monkees' dressing room.

"In disbelief, I slowly entered the dressing room," Strasberg said. "I saw Peter sitting on a table with a towel on the side of his face, but didn't see any blood or bruises. I introduced myself, apologized for what happened, and asked if he was okay. Peter said, 'Yes,' and then he apologized for calling Whitey an old man."

A music review in the *San Diego Union* two days after the concert mentioned that Tork "looked sickly and gaunt."

Guess he could have used a bowl of Whitey's chili.

Ken Caminiti

Ken Caminiti was one of the Padres' biggest stars.

And one of the franchise's most tragic figures.

Caminiti came to the Padres from Houston, along with center fielder Steve Finley, in a 12-player trade that was the largest in baseball in 37 years.

Caminiti became hugely popular among Padres fans. He was a striking figure with a chiseled build, piercing blue eyes, and goatee that would inspire a promotional giveaway.

His fierce competitiveness manifested itself in many ways, most memorably when he broke a bat over his knee after a strikeout.

Caminiti earned three straight Gold Gloves at third base from 1995 to 1997, routinely making highlight-reel plays at the hot corner.

In 1996, Caminiti put together one of the finest seasons in Padres history. He batted .326 with 40 home runs and 130 RBIs, the latter two statistics single-season club records at the time. After the All-Star break, Caminiti led the National League in batting (.360), home runs (28), and RBIs (81).

"He's the best I've ever been around," Padres right fielder Tony Gwynn said. "I always thought that (San Francisco's) Matt Williams was the best third baseman I've seen since Mike Schmidt. But this guy, wow, he's right there. Let me put it this way, we wouldn't be here without him."

Caminiti was a unanimous choice as NL MVP for his efforts.

"I'm excited, but I don't play for the awards," Caminiti said after the announcement. "I play to do the best I can. I consider myself a player who can help his team win, but I never felt I could put up the type of numbers that an MVP does. I remember when

Padres third baseman Ken Caminiti put together the greatest season in franchise history in 1996 when he won the NL MVP. (Fantography.com/Madres)

(former Houston teammate) Jeff Bagwell won the MVP (in 1994) and he'd tell me he couldn't believe what was happening and I'd look at him and say, 'Hey, man, you're doing it, that's all.'

"That's the same way it was with me this year. I got on my knees every night and said a prayer that I could play (despite a shoulder injury), but my attitude is that if I can get to the park, I'm going to play."

Caminiti played much of the '96 season with a torn rotator cuff in his left shoulder that would require surgery over the winter.

"What Cammy did for this club was more than just numbers," said Kevin Towers, then the Padres' general manager. "He was a real presence, leading by example and playing through more than just aches and pains. There were points in the season when he literally carried the club."

Caminiti remains the only Padres player to win the MVP award. Outfielders Dave Winfield (1978) and Tony Gwynn (1984) and third baseman Gary Sheffield (1992) all finished as high as third.

Caminiti's four years with the Padres concluded following a 1998 season in which his 29 homers and 82 RBIs helped the Padres to the World Series.

He played two more seasons with Houston, then split the 2001 season between Texas and Atlanta before retiring.

Caminiti later would admit to using steroids during his 15-year career, including his years with the Padres.

He battled alcoholism and drug abuse throughout his life, which came to a tragic end in 2004 from an accidental drug overdose. He was 41 years old.

"I don't think this puts an asterisk by my name," said Caminiti, commenting on steroid use in a *Sports Illustrated* article published two years before his death. "I worked for everything I've got. I played the game hard, gave it everything I had. Nothing came easy. I could sit here and lie and try to make myself look like a better person, but I'm not going to do that.

"I take responsibility for what I've done. I'm guilty of some bad behavior. It's embarrassing, some of the things I've done. But like I said, I don't consider steroids to be one of them."

22 Randy Jones Wins the 1976 Cy Young Award

If anyone ever asks when the Padres finally made the big time, tell them it was July 12, 1976.

That was the date *Sports Illustrated* featured a Padres player on its cover for the first time.

Under the headline "Threat to Win 30" was the pitcher described as "San Diego's Confounding Randy Jones."

Seven years into the franchise's existence and two years after the team nearly relocated to Washington, D.C., Padres fans finally had reason to cheer.

"My proudest thing," Jones said, "was in the '70s, putting the franchise on the map."

The United States celebrated the bicentennial while San Diego celebrated a curly left-hander who had captured the baseball world's attention.

Jones would win the 1976 National League Cy Young Award after leading the league in wins (22), games started (40), complete games (25), innings pitched (315⅓), and WHIP (1.027).

Jones received 15 of 24 first-place votes for the Cy Young Award, finishing ahead of the Mets' Jerry Koosman and the Dodgers' Don Sutton.

"It's like a boyhood dream come true," Jones said. "It shows I am for real. When you achieve your boyhood dream, it's an incredible thrill. It really hasn't sunk in yet."

The award was made possible by a monster first half of the season.

Jones came into the All-Star break with a 16–3 record, something no pitcher has accomplished in the four decades since. He was a threat to win 30 games in a season for the first time since Denny McClain went 31–6 with the 1968 Tigers.

"Randy has three outstanding pitches—a sinker, a slider, and a curve—and he usually needs only two," Padres pitching coach Roger Craig said at the time. "He never throws the ball straight, but he has the best control of any pitcher in the game.

"The sinker is unusual in that it breaks late; it looks like a fastball down the middle before it drops four to eight inches. And Randy turns it over so that it breaks a little like a screwball. To a right-handed hitter, the sinker breaks down and away and the slider down and in. If you're looking for the sinker, no way you're gonna hit the slider."

Jones' starts captivated the crowd like no one before or since. Perhaps it was because he looked like an everyman on the mound. He stood barely 6'0" and threw a fastball that barely touched 73 mph.

In his first 12 starts at San Diego Stadium in 1976, attendance averaged 32,775 when Jones pitched. When another starting pitcher was on the mound, the Padres averaged about 21,000.

"I was cruising along fine at the start of this season," Jones said, "then after I'd won a few I started looking ahead, thinking about how many I could win. That's not my style. I must stay relaxed. If I'm too anxious, pressing too hard, I defeat my purpose. For one thing, my sinker works best when I throw it at slower speeds. I don't get the movement on the ball when I overthrow."

During a six-week period—from May 17 through June 26—Jones pitched 68 innings without allowing a walk, tying a 63-year-old record by the New York Giants' Christy Mathewson.

Jones was the starting pitcher of the 1976 All-Star Game in Philadelphia, pitching three shutout innings in which he allowed two hits to pick up the win for the NL in a 7–1 victory over the American League.

Jones' success was not altogether unexpected. He had finished second to the Mets' Tom Seaver for the 1975 NL Cy Young Award after going 20–12 with an NL-best 2.24 ERA. That, after Jones led the league in losses in 1974 when he went 8–22.

"It's not hard to stay humble," Jones said in the middle of his Cy Young season. "Twenty-two losses will do that for you. Besides, I don't particularly care to change my personality. I can see how some people would change, though. You can be leading a simple life with not too much exposure, then it all explodes in your face. All of a sudden you have no private life."

Jones won two of his next three starts after the All-Star Game, putting him within two victories of another 20-win season with two full months left in the season.

Jones lost his first two starts in August, however. A 1–0 defeat in Atlanta on August 4 concluded a road trip. The Padres returned to San Diego late that night, and Jones was involved in a car accident on the way home.

"Randy lost control of his car on a curve and the next thing he knew the telephone pole was sitting in the front seat," Marie Jones, the pitcher's wife, told a reporter after the accident. "He has some minor glass cuts on his face and had stitches for a cut chin and two cuts on his neck."

Jones was treated and released at a local hospital.

An investigating officer said Jones "probably was bushed from pitching twice this week," according to a newspaper account.

Jones didn't miss a start, although any thoughts of winning 30 games were dashed. He went 4–8 over his last 12 starts. He didn't pitch poorly, but the Padres offense didn't give him much support.

He allowed three runs or fewer in five of those eight losses down the stretch.

On September 28, Jones faced Cincinnati in his 40th and final start of the season. It was one he would just as soon forget.

With one out in the second inning, Jones felt something in his arm and was replaced by reliever Rick Sawyer with the Reds' Cesar Geronimo at the plate.

"I felt something pop in my left arm," Jones said. "It was like a rubber band unraveling. I called manager John McNamara to the mound, told him I was done for the year, and left the game."

Jones visited Dodgers orthopedic surgeon Dr. Frank Jobe during the team's season-ending road trip to Los Angeles. At one point during his examination, Jobe asked Jones to make a muscle, but the pitcher was unable to do it.

"That's not good," Jobe said.

"I figured that," Jones responded.

Exploratory surgery was done after the season. It was discovered that Jones had a nerve injury. It healed on its own, but was reinjured several more times over the remainder of his career.

"I still had the sinker," Jones said, "but I could never again throw that good slider."

Jones never approached the same success, but the pinnacle of his career is something Padres fans have never forgotten.

Yo, Adrian

Everything might have been different if the Texas Rangers had only given Adrian Gonzalez 300 plate appearances before giving up on the 23-year-old first baseman.

"At every level I've ever played, it's taken me about 300 plate appearances to get comfortable and do what I can do," Gonzalez said. "I have a plan....

"I told the Rangers that and they didn't seem to believe me."

He was traded after he had but 206 plate appearances over parts of two seasons with the Rangers.

"I don't know why," Gonzalez said, "but it's taken me about the same number of at-bats at every level before I get my swing down."

Padres fans might not have enjoyed Gonzalez's hitting prowess—not to mention his Gold Glove fielding at first base—had the San Diego native been given more of an opportunity in Texas.

Of course, the Rangers weren't the first team that failed to realize what it had in Gonzalez.

The Florida Marlins used the first pick in the 2000 major league draft to select Gonzalez out of Chula Vista's Eastlake High. He was traded to Texas on July 11, 2003, but didn't get much of a chance playing behind first baseman Mark Teixeira.

The Rangers traded Gonzalez, along with pitcher Chris Young and outfielder Terrmel Sledge, before the 2006 season for pitchers Adam Eaton and Akinori Otsuka and minor league catcher Billy Killian.

It turned out to be one of the best trades in Padres history, primarily because Gonzalez blossomed into one of the game's best players.

In his first full major league season, Gonzalez helped the Padres to the 2006 NL West championship. He led the club with a .304 batting average and 24 home runs and was second with 82 RBIs.

Gonzalez benefitted when Ryan Klesko was disabled with a shoulder injury in spring training that opened the door for an everyday job at first base.

Gonzalez had impressed Padres manager Bruce Bochy by mid-season, who said, "He's smart and he works hard. You can see he's getting more and more comfortable at the plate."

Added Padres hitting coach Merv Rettenmund: "Adrian has a beautiful swing. He's got the stroke, along with the idea of what he wants to do with the ball."

Gonzalez's left-handed swing delivered even more power in 2007, when he had 30 homers and 100 RBIs, and 2008, when he had 36 homers and 119 RBIs. In 2009, he belted 40 homers. His RBIs slipped to 99, perhaps because he was walked an NL-high 119 times.

Even when he had established himself, Gonzalez sounded as if he was one bad swing, one poor throw, or one booted ball from being banished to the bench. Or worse, kicked to the curb.

"I still feel like I've got to get better every day in order to stay up here," Gonzalez said. "Although I know I am (secure), I still don't feel that. Because the minute anybody takes a step back or takes their foot off the gas pedal, that's when everything is going to start going downhill. You've always got to try to get better."

Gonzalez's drive is almost an obsession, which can be traced to his earliest days on sandlots in both San Diego and across the Mexican border in Tijuana. Perhaps it provides the explanation for how he used to shrug off comparisons to some of the game's greats and why he will never be satisfied with his success.

For Gonzalez, it isn't a fear of failure. It's a concern for complacency.

"You see it happen a lot," said Gonzalez. "Guys that have great years and then two years later they're out of the game. And you say, 'What happened?' Well, what happened is they got comfortable. They thought they had it all made, stopped working, and the next thing they knew they were out of the game."

The landscape is littered with can't-miss prospects and once-in-a-lifetime phenoms—even at the top of the draft. Ken Griffey Jr.

(1987), Chipper Jones (1990), and Alex Rodriguez (1993) all were first overall picks. So were Steve Chilcott (1966) and Brien Taylor (1991), who never reached the major leagues.

Dave Finley was a scout for the Florida Marlins when Gonzalez was a senior at Eastlake High, which is just 18 miles southeast of Petco Park.

Finley remembers seeing Gonzalez's sweet left-handed swing, defensive prowess, and off-the-charts makeup and strongly encouraging the Marlins to select him.

"When you're a scout and seeing a 180-pound kid in high school, you're projecting all the positives and envisioning what he's going to look like in five or 10 years," Finley said. "It's not always the case, but with him it's exactly what I thought he was going to be....

"We thought he was going to hit for average and develop power. I'd be lying if I said he was going to hit 40 homers (like in 2009). But I thought he had a chance to hit 25 or 30 and bat .300.

"We were thinking bottom line you get Mark Grace and top of the line you get Rafael Palmeiro. And if you get Mark Grace in this draft, not a bad pick. Mark Grace was a helluva player.

"Adrian just needed a chance to play."

Gonzalez amassed 161 home runs and 501 RBIs from 2006 to 2010, the most in either category by any Padres player over a five-year period. In fact, he finished within two home runs of Padres record holder Nate Colbert.

After he was traded to the Boston Red Sox following the 2010 season, Gonzalez took out a full-page ad in the *San Diego Union-Tribune* to say thank you to the fans.

The feeling was mutual.

24 1978 All-Star Game

On July 11, 1978, a crowd of 51,549 watched the National League beat the American League 7–3 in the 49th All-Star Game, which was at San Diego Stadium.

This was the first big moment for a Padres franchise in just its ninth year of existence.

Steve Garvey is best remembered by Padres fans for the game-winning home run he hit at Jack Murphy Stadium against the Chicago Cubs in the 1984 National League Championship Series. It wasn't the first big hit for Garvey in Mission Valley, however. An eighth-inning triple six years earlier helped Garvey earn MVP honors at the 1978 All-Star Game.

Three days before the game, Garvey had been struck in the chin by an errant throw to first base. The wound required 22 stitches to close. The thought of missing the game because of the injury never entered his mind.

"The fans voted me into the starting lineup," Garvey said. "I had to play and had to give them my best shot."

Besides, Garvey said, "You don't hit with your chin."

Yankees closer Goose Gossage gave up Garvey's triple, then threw a wild pitch to let the Dodgers first baseman score. Gossage, who allowed three more hits and three runs before the inning was over, took the loss in the game.

"My only disappointment was in that triple," Garvey said. "When I hit the ball, I thought it was out of the park. That would have been perfect, hitting a homer to win the game."

Garvey's heroics should have come as no surprise. He had a flair for the dramatic almost from the moment his career began.

In 1974, after all, The Garv was voted to his first All-Star Game as a write-in candidate. He was MVP of that game, too.

Garvey joined Willie Mays as the only two-time All-Star Game MVPs. Gary Carter, Cal Ripken Jr., and Mike Trout have since joined them.

Chicago Cubs closer Bruce Sutter was the winner of the '78 game. Sutter came on in the eighth inning and struck out Jim Rice and Dwight Evans during a 1–2–3 inning. Sutter did not allow a hit over 1⅔ innings before giving way to Phil Niekro for the final out.

Former president Gerald Ford was on hand and expected to throw out the first pitch. But it was Padres owner Ray Kroc, perhaps in honor of saving the franchise in 1974, who picked up the ball and fired it to the plate. It seemed appropriate enough. After all, the game wouldn't even have been taking place in San Diego had Kroc not stepped in at the 11th hour four years earlier to purchase the Padres.

Keith Jackson, Howard Cosell, and Don Drysdale called the action on television for ABC. Vin Scully and Brent Musberger handled the CBS radio broadcast.

The Padres were represented by closer Rollie Fingers and right fielder Dave Winfield, who received the loudest, longest ovation during pregame introductions.

The National League was managed by the Dodgers' Tommy Lasorda and the American League by the Yankees' Billy Martin.

San Francisco left-hander Vida Blue was the starting pitcher for the NL. Baltimore right-hander Jim Palmer got the nod for the AL.

Cincinnati's Big Red Machine was well represented with catcher Johnny Bench, second baseman Joe Morgan, third baseman Pete Rose, and outfielder George Foster voted into the game as starters. Shortstop Dave Concepcion was a reserve and right-hander Tom Seaver was among the pitchers. Bench, Morgan, and Seaver were among eight future Hall of Fame players playing for the NL.

Winfield, Fingers, first baseman Willie Stargell, and pitchers Bruce Sutter and Phil Niekro were the others.

The roster for the American League included nine players who would be enshrined in Cooperstown: pitchers Palmer and Gossage, outfielders Reggie Jackson, Jim Rice, and Carl Yastrzemski; infielders George Brett, Rod Carew, and Eddie Murray; and catcher Carlton Fisk.

25 1992 All-Star Game

On July 14, 1992, a crowd of 59,372 watched the American League beat the National League 13–6 in the 63rd All-Star Game, which was played at San Diego Jack Murphy Stadium.

The first pitch, thrown by San Diego native Ted Williams with President George H.W. Bush by his side, had barely crossed the plate before American League hitters began bashing balls all over the place.

Atlanta left-hander Tom Glavine, the starting pitcher for the National League, gave up four runs in the first inning. He allowed five runs on nine hits over the 1⅔ innings he was on the mound.

The AL built a 10–0 lead before Padres first baseman Fred McGriff singled home Pittsburgh's Barry Bonds from second base for the NL's first run.

There was still plenty for Sean McDonough and Tim McCarver to talk about on the CBS television broadcast. Padres broadcaster Jerry Coleman joined John Rooney and Johnny Bench for the radio broadcast.

Seattle outfielder Ken Griffey Jr. was selected as the game's MVP, lacking only a triple for the cycle. Griffey singled in the first inning off Glavine, homered in the third off the Cubs' Greg Maddux, and doubled in the sixth off St. Louis' Bob Tewksbury.

As excited as the 22-year-old Griffey was to be named the game's MVP, he said it wasn't his biggest thrill in baseball.

"Playing with my father (was)," said Griffey, who shared the Seattle outfield with Ken Griffey Sr. during the 1990–91 seasons. "No matter if I win a World Series or a league MVP, playing with him will be the biggest thing that I have ever done."

Texas Rangers right-hander Kevin Brown, who would help lead the Padres to the World Series six years later, started for the AL. Brown was credited with the win after he retired the NL in order in the first inning, getting Ozzie Smith on a strikeout and Tony Gwynn and Bonds on fly balls to left field.

Gwynn, catcher Benito Santiago, and McGriff gave the Padres three starters in the NL lineup. Third baseman Gary Sheffield and shortstop Tony Fernandez came off the bench in Padres uniforms. McGriff had the best day at the plate among the five players, going 2-for-3 with an RBI.

Gwynn was hitless, but he did throw out two runners at second base from right field, short-circuiting AL rallies in the first and sixth innings.

"If there is anything to feel good about, it is that defensively I was into the game," Gwynn said.

A pair of former Padres outfielders, John Kruk and Bip Roberts, also had two hits for the NL. Roberts added two RBIs. San Francisco first baseman Will Clark led the NL with a game-high three RBIs, all the runs supplied by Clark's three-run homer.

The AL had 19 hits spread among 15 players. Griffey, with three hits, along with Chicago White Sox third baseman Robin Ventura and Toronto outfielder Joe Carter, with two hits apiece, were the only players with multihit games for the squad.

The National League roster included seven future Hall of Famers—Craig Biggio, Glavine, Gwynn, Maddux, Ryne Sandberg,

Smith, and John Smoltz. The American League roster countered with seven players who would wind up in Cooperstown—Roberto Alomar, Wade Boggs, Dennis Eckersley, Griffey, Paul Molitor, Kirby Puckett, and Cal Ripken Jr.

This was the second time in 14 years the Midsummer Classic was hosted in San Diego, although the city would have to wait another 24 years before having the opportunity to host the 2016 All-Star Game at Petco Park.

Ollie Brown—the Original Padre

You have to start somewhere.

The Padres began with Ollie Brown.

Brown would forever be known as the "Original Padre" after the Padres used the first pick in the 1968 National League expansion draft to select the outfielder off the San Francisco Giants roster.

"I figured that once the Giants put me on the expansion list, I thought I might have a good chance of getting picked," Brown said. "But I had no idea I would be the first one picked. It came at a good time in my career because I got the chance to play on an everyday basis."

Brown provided a big bat for the Padres in their formative years. His 20 home runs and 61 RBIs in 1969 were second on the team to Nate Colbert.

In 1970, Brown had a career-high 23 homers and 89 RBIs, joining Colbert and Cito Gaston as the team's biggest run producers.

The Padres traded Brown to Oakland one month into the 1972 season. He played for six teams during his 13-year career, finishing with a .265 average, 102 homers, and 454 RBIs.

The Original Padre also may have been the franchise's first player with a memorable nickname. He was called "Downtown" even before his 1965 debut in the major leagues.

"I got it when I was playing in the minor leagues in Fresno," said Brown, who was the Pacific Coast League's MVP in 1964 when he hit 40 home runs. "That year, I had a pretty good year. I hit a lot of balls to center field. And the way the ballpark was situated, when you did hit it over the fence, the ball was going the direction of downtown.

"One day, after I hit a home run, the radio announcer said the ball was going downtown. That's how I got my nickname."

Brown was noted for his strong throwing arm. Fans marveled during warmups as Brown fielded balls deep in the right field corner and made throws to third base—on the fly.

The strong arm was a trait shared by Hall of Famer Dave Winfield, who became a fixture in right field for the Padres a year after Brown was traded. Brown also had a connection to another Padres Hall of Fame right fielder, Tony Gwynn. Both graduated high school from Long Beach Poly.

Those early Padres teams didn't have an overabundance of fan support, but those who did come to games had their favorites. Brown was definitely a fan favorite.

When Brown died in April of 2015 from mesothelioma, online news reports drew warm remembrances from fans. Don Frazier, who lives in Missouri now, recalled childhood memories of watching Brown.

"I was just a little kid, but I remember his laser beam throws from the outfield," Frazier said. "I would try to throw his line drive throws, but as a little second baseman I couldn't pull them off. I could pretend though."

It's too bad the Padres couldn't pretend they had better pitching in those early years.

"They wanted more wins out of us," Brown said in an interview with mlb.com in 2012. "It's kind of tough to put an expansion club together with new players....It helps to have good pitching.

"At the time, we had pretty good hitting. Just didn't have enough overall good pitching."

27 Petco Park

"Nothing in the world is worth having or worth doing unless it means effort, pain, and difficulty."

President Theodore Roosevelt said that. He may have been the first Teddy Ballgame. He was definitely a heavy hitter. And everyone knows he carried a big stick.

When it comes to effort, pain, and difficulty, nothing fits that description better than Petco Park.

Proposition C received nearly 60 percent voter approval in 1998, paving the way for Petco. Groundbreaking for the ballpark was in May of 2000. Construction was halted five months later because of financial and political problems.

The project had to survive 16 lawsuits and six appeals that were responsible for delaying funding and causing a two-year delay in opening. But the $474 million ballpark opened to rave reviews in 2004. A $60 million, 22-year naming rights deal with Petco, the San Diego–based pet supplies retailer, supplied the place's alliterative name.

"I sense I've spent 14 years on it the last seven years," said Larry Lucchino, the former Padres president who was one of the driving forces behind the ballpark. "It feels good. There's a positive buzz about the place and it's certainly a beautiful ballpark. If I had to give it a marketing theme, it would be 'A Ballpark Like No Other.'"

Lucchino's comments came on the occasion of the first baseball game played at Petco.

It was March 11, 2004. San Diego State beat Houston 4–0 before a crowd of 40,106, the largest gathering ever to watch a college baseball game. The contest matched the Aztecs team coached by Tony Gwynn against the alma mater of then-owner John Moores.

SDSU's Lance Zawadzki hit a double for the first hit and teammate Rielly Embrey launched a ball over the right-field wall for the first home run. Right-hander Scott Shoemaker pitched a three-hit shutout with 14 strikeouts to get the first win.

Four weeks later, on April 8, the Padres would play the first major league game at Petco, beating San Francisco 4–3 in 11 innings before 44,400. The Padres' Brian Giles singled for the first hit. The Giants' Marquis Grissom hit the first homer with a 10th-inning blast. Left-hander David Wells pitched seven shutout innings for the Padres, but it was little-known reliever Eddie Oropesa who got the first win.

The Pacific Coast League Padres came to San Diego in 1936, moving into Lane Field at the foot of West Broadway. Things came full circle 68 years later when Petco Park opened downtown at 19 Tony Gwynn Dr.

Petco originally measured 334 feet down the left-field line, 396 feet to center, and 322 feet down the right-field line.

The impact of the ballpark extended well beyond those boundaries, however. It served as the catalyst for revitalizing the East Village area of downtown San Diego.

28 Get a Foul Ball at Petco

There are few sports souvenirs as coveted and memorable as getting a foul ball at a baseball game.

Here are a few foul-ball stories from Padres fans interviewed in 2004 during the opening season at Petco Park.

* * *

Marvin Hamilton remembers being a member of the Padres' "Little Swingers" club back in 1969 during the franchise's inaugural season.

Kids paid a couple of dollars to join, and they received tickets to 11 games (each National League opponent) a season. As much as Hamilton enjoyed the experience, there was one he missed out on: getting a foul ball.

"Never got one as a kid," said Hamilton. "Came close a few times."

Hamilton camped out in left field at Qualcomm Stadium during the 2002 season, determined to get his glove on a ball in batting practice. And he did.

"It was such a thrill," he said.

He became hooked. At Petco Park, Hamilton found a good spot in the second level in left field. He caught four batting practice balls in six games, including one when the Cubs were in town. Hamilton remembers that one in particular. After he caught the ball, there was a tug at his shirt. Or was it his heartstrings?

"I had a kid come up and ask for the ball," Hamilton said. "I asked him if he had ever gotten one and he said, 'No.' Couldn't resist. I just had to give it to him."

* * *

The proximity of the seats to the field at Petco Park provides more opportunities than ever for kids—big and small—to get a ball.

An average of nearly four dozen baseballs—fouled off or homered into the stands, tossed or handed to the fans—find their way into the stands each game.

One thing has remained constant: many fans still scramble after balls with complete disregard for themselves and those around them.

For instance, there was the fan who made an acrobatic catch of a home-run ball hit during a game against the Giants.

The man tightroped across the netting between the left-field wall and front-row seats as he tracked the ball's trajectory. Then he made the catch. Hold your applause.

After he snagged the ball, the guy landed in the laps of two fans seated in the stands.

* * *

Longtime Padres fan David Krohn is old-school. His approach to foul balls is reminiscent of running backs who simply tossed the football to the referee after scoring a touchdown: act as if you've been there before.

It's old hat for Krohn, who estimates he's gotten 250 baseballs during games or batting practice. His season seats, like the ones he had at Qualcomm, are in a perfect location in the front row in the left-field corner of the field level.

Krohn doesn't jump at every crack of the bat.

"I'll go for it if I have a better chance than someone else," he said. "So I can get it for someone and the chance isn't lost for the souvenir. I give them to the kids, for the most part."

Krohn even gave a ball to one youngster after the child's father accidentally knocked Krohn onto the field while going for the foul grounder.

"He was pretty good about it," Krohn said. "He apologized. He also gave me a ticket to the Founders Club behind home plate. I went up there and sat at the beginning of the game, but I decided I liked my seats better and came back down."

* * *

There's been an appreciable increase in fouls in the upper sections of Petco compared with the Q, although not just any player has the ability to reach the seats.

"Phil Nevin constantly hits foul balls in this area," said Tom Skrobut, an usher who worked the upper level at both Qualcomm Stadium and Petco Park.

Skrobut specifically recalls back-to-back games in 2004 when Nevin hit two balls within a foot of each other off a wall in Section 313.

"The reason I remember," Skrobut said, "is that everybody was in such a rush (to get to one of the balls) that a lady got knocked over backward and I had to call the paramedics."

Although the seats at Petco are closer to the action, this hasn't resulted in more frequent or more serious injuries than in previous years. In fact, most of the bumps and bruises are created by the fans, not the balls.

"We have people come in with scratches all over their arms," nurse coordinator Janie Kramer said.

Surveying the crowd, Kramer shakes her head in wonder that more people aren't injured.

"A lot of people talk on their cell phones," she said. "They really should be keeping their eye on the ball."

* * *

Scott Smith falls somewhere between the cell phone users and the ballgame watchers.

Smith was sitting in the area known as the ring during a game against the Pirates. The ring is a row of seats located just below the press box. It's prime foul ball territory.

Smith's brush with foul ball fame came in the ninth inning when Padres catcher Ramon Hernandez lined one back.

"The minute it came off the bat I knew it was my ball," Smith said. "And then I lost it. It had too much spin on it...I heard a lot of boos."

That wasn't the worst of it.

As Smith leaned over to reach for the ball, his cell phone slipped from the left breast pocket of his shirt, slid down an awninglike covering, and landed on a table in the Garden Suite owner's box.

The phone found its way into the hands of then-Padres owner John Moores.

"It was in three pieces," said Moores, who marveled that the thing still worked after he reassembled it.

A Padres representative returned the phone to its owner, although it would have been only fair for Moores to keep the souvenir after it fell out of Smith's pocket.

After all, the baseballs everyone else gets to keep are coming out of the owner's pocket.

* * *

Foul ball tips:
- Bring a glove. Those who try to barehand a ball usually end up with sore hands—but not the ball. It bounces off the hands and lands in the lap of someone in the next row.
- Opportunities are much greater during batting practice, when there are fewer fans in the ballpark competing for the souvenirs. The Padres allow fans to go down to the field level seats—regardless of where their actual seats are—until the end of batting practice.

- Players frequently toss balls into the stands—to kids—as they come off the field in BP, so stand along the rail.
- The words "please" and "thank you" are preferred over "Hey, you" when trying to persuade a player to toss you a ball.

Foul ball hot spots:
- During batting practice, most fouls go into the field level seats adjacent to left field and most home run balls go into the left- and right-field bleachers within two to three sections of the foul poles.
- Remember, right-handed hitters foul off balls to the right side and left-handed hitters foul off balls to the left side. Curving fouls land in the field level seats adjacent to either first or third base and extending toward the foul poles. Sharper fouls are lined back primarily in the two levels above field level, fanning out behind the plate in about a 60-degree arc. Pop fouls land directly behind the plate.
- Players toss balls into the seats behind the dugouts at the end of innings.
- Young fans have balls handed to them when a ball girl fields a foul grounder.
- One note: MLB has plans in 2016 to extend the protective netting down the lines, which will likely change some of the interaction with fans.

29 San Diego Stadium

There was a time when building a stadium in San Diego met with overwhelming support.

It was 1965 and both the Chargers and the Padres were looking for a new place to play.

The Chargers wanted 50-year-old Balboa Stadium replaced. The Padres, playing at 8,000-seat Westgate Park, needed a larger venue if they were to step up from the Triple-A Pacific Coast League to the major leagues.

The San Diego City Council approved a 50,000-seat multipurpose stadium in May of 1965. Cost for the stadium was $27.5 million. *San Diego Union* sports editor Jack Murphy rallied community support, writing columns promoting a new stadium. When the proposal was placed on the ballot, voters approved it with an overwhelming 72 percent majority.

The stadium was completed in time for the Chargers to move in for the 1967 season.

The minor league Padres played there during the 1968 season. A National League franchise was approved for the city that year, and the major league Padres made their debut in 1969. The stadium was their home for 35 seasons.

Original stadium dimensions were 330 feet to left and right fields, 420 to center, and 375 to the gaps, surrounded by a 17½-foot outfield wall.

The Padres defeated Houston by a 2–1 score in the franchise's inaugural game. It was not the first game at San Diego Stadium between two major league teams. That distinction belonged to the San Francisco Giants and Cleveland Indians, who played an exhibition game there in April of 1968.

When the Padres were nearly sold and moved to Washington D.C. following the 1973 season, it was the 30-year lease on the stadium that ultimately saved baseball for the city. Buying out the lease would have proven too costly for the new owners, and the sale fell through, opening the door for McDonald's owner Ray Kroc to step in and purchase the team.

When Murphy died in 1980, the stadium was renamed in his honor. The named was changed again in 1997 when Qualcomm stepped forward to bridge a financing gap for stadium expansion. The local company paid $18 million and was given naming rights for 20 years.

The stadium was completely enclosed during the second expansion project, which was done specifically to appease the NFL for the 1998 Super Bowl.

One benefit was that it took crowd noise to new levels during the Padres' 1998 playoff run. The extra seating also enabled a crowd of 65,427 to attend Game 4 of the 1998 World Series between the Padres and Yankees. It was the largest gathering ever to witness a major league game at Qualcomm Stadium.

But the cavernous stadium was no longer a suitable site for baseball, which was being played in more intimate venues. Another proposal was put to voters following the '98 season, this one to approve construction of a new downtown ballpark.

Six years later, the Padres moved into Petco Park.

30 Buzzie Bavasi

Major League Baseball may never have come to San Diego had it not been for Buzzie Bavasi.

C. Arnholdt Smith, the longtime owner of the minor league Padres, wanted to bring Major League Baseball to town. Smith didn't have the support of owners, however. He needed help.

That's where Bavasi came in.

Baseball nicknames were commonplace when Bavasi broke into baseball in the 1930s. But Bavasi had been called Buzzie long before then.

Emil Joseph Bavasi was given his alliterative nickname early in life by his sister, who said he was "always buzzing around."

Bavasi buzzed around the Dodgers organization for 30 years, learning early on at the foot of Branch Rickey. Bavasi would rise to Dodgers general manager, where over 18 seasons the franchise won eight National League pennants and four World Series championships for owner Walter O'Malley.

"By 1968, I could see the son rising, and in the process, the sun setting on my Dodger career," Bavasi said in his book *Off the Record* about his life in baseball. "The son was Peter O'Malley, whose father, Walter, had been grooming him for the job, and rightfully so. I was aware that blood was thicker than water, but it did not make leaving my life behind any easier."

The opportunity in San Diego came at the perfect time.

"At least I wasn't going far, and it was in every regard an upward move," Bavasi said. "I was to become a part owner of a National League expansion franchise....If I had gone to an established club, I'd have felt bad, as if I had betrayed the O'Malleys.

In my mind, I justified it by the fact I would be building a new club."

Smith enticed Bavasi with a 32 percent ownership stake in the team if Bavasi could secure the franchise for him. After three decades with the Dodgers, Bavasi had the contacts and reputation in the game to make it happen.

Among the cities being considered for NL expansion at the time were Montreal, Denver, Dallas, Buffalo, and San Diego. Montreal and San Diego were chosen.

And Buzzie was soon busy building a ballclub as Padres president. He oversaw the 1968 NL expansion draft and everything thereafter leading up to the team's 1969 debut.

Padres president Buzzie Bavasi and manager John McNamara put their heads together in spring training in the mid-1970s—as reliever Butch Metzger posed for a photographer—but couldn't come up with any winning seasons.
(Fantography.com/Andy Strasberg)

The franchise's formative years were not easy, much of it because Smith ran the Padres on a shoestring. A frayed shoestring.

"He never understood baseball or anything necessary to run a club," Bavasi said. "He would not allow us to spend money, failing to understand that you had to sign players for the four minor league clubs."

The easygoing Bavasi has said that he got along with everyone. In the front office, he was responsible for acquiring players. He left most everything else to the manager and coaches.

"All I demanded of players was that they stand for the national anthem before games," Bavasi said. "Respect the flag of the United States or it was a $100 fine if you didn't.

"One day one kid comes to me and says, 'Geez, Buzzie, every time I stand for 'The Star-Spangled Banner,' I have a bad night.' I said, 'No problem.' He said, 'You mean I don't have to stand?' I said, 'No, just give me a check for $16,200.' Turns out he wasn't that superstitious."

The Padres finished last in the NL West in each of their first six years of existence. That included 1974, the year McDonald's magnate Ray Kroc had stepped in at the 11th hour to purchase the franchise from the financially floundering Smith.

Kroc's ownership was decidedly different than that of Smith. Kroc had the deep pockets and desire to get good players.

It was the dawn of free agency and the Padres jumped in with both feet, going after big prizes like pitcher Catfish Hunter and slugger Reggie Jackson. The Yankees swooped in to sign them instead.

The Padres did come away with their share of free agents, Bavasi getting pitcher Rollie Fingers and catcher Gene Tenace, among others, to come to San Diego. They joined a couple drafted players who became stars—pitcher Randy Jones and outfielder Dave Winfield—to put the Padres in position to compete.

The franchise finally enjoyed its first winning season in 1978.

Bavasi left a year earlier, retiring to his hilltop home in La Jolla. He was quickly lured out of retirement by Angels owner Gene Autry, who needed help with his struggling franchise.

"Long as I've been around it, baseball's remained a fascinating game to me," Bavasi said, "no matter what they keep trying to do with it. It touches so many people."

Buzzie was a big part of baseball touching people in San Diego.

In 2001, he was inducted into the Padres Hall of Fame. Six years later, Bavasi was inducted into the Breitbard Hall of Fame at the San Diego Hall of Champions.

31 Dave Winfield

Dave Winfield played for six major league teams during his 22-year Hall of Fame career.

There was some controversy in 2001 when he was enshrined in Cooperstown wearing a Padres hat. He was the first player in the Hall of Fame who had an SD insignia on his cap.

Winfield's nine seasons with the Yankees was more time than he spent with any other team. But his eight years with the Padres was nothing to sneeze at. After all, that's where he started. And became a star.

"I didn't anticipate there'd be this much discussion or thought about the hat," Winfield said after his Hall hat was revealed. "It caused me to be very introspective. It caused me to reach out and talk to a lot of people. The essence of this is I feel that I belong to all of baseball, more than just one city or one team."

Winfield had plenty of reasons to go with the Padres cap.

"When I look at everything," he said, "it's kind of like, who gave me the first opportunity, where do I come from, where did I emerge? All this started a long time ago. They saw me, drafted me first, gave me a chance to play in the big leagues right away. I was an All-Star there; I was their first captain."

He debuted on June 19, 1973, in left field at San Diego Stadium, although you have to wonder if Cooperstown still would have been Winfield's destination had he started on the mound.

After all, the 6'6" Winfield was more accomplished as a right-handed pitcher than a hitter when the Padres used the fourth pick in the first round of the 1973 draft to select him out of the University of Minnesota.

"I really think I could do either," Winfield said at the time. "But they think of me as an outfielder, so that's what I'll be."

Winfield was the eighth player in the draft era to go straight to the majors, playing for the Padres one week after pitching for the Gophers in the College World Series.

Winfield batted seventh—between third baseman Dave Roberts and second baseman Rich Morales—on that June night in Mission Valley. He collected the first of his 3,110 hits in a 7–3 loss to the Houston Astros. There were 5,338 witnesses to his debut. The fan base was turned off more, no doubt, by the prospect of seeing a 20–46 team than it was turned on by the chance to get a glimpse of someone who would become one of the game's all-time greats.

"We want him as an everyday player," said Bob Fontaine, the Padres' player personnel director, after Winfield signed for a $100,000 bonus. "With his ability to run and hit and throw, we think he would be more of an asset in the lineup every day."

Fontaine and the Padres were right.

Winfield would become a fixture in right field for the Padres over the next eight seasons, developing into one of the National League's most complete all-around players.

Dave Winfield was drafted by four teams in three sports, but chose to sign with the Padres after being selected in the first round of the 1973 amateur draft. It was a wise choice, leading to a 22-year Hall of Fame career. (San Diego Padres)

He thrilled fans with a big swing that produced long home runs, a strong arm that made runners think twice about going from first to third, and long legs that made it seem like he could steal second base in three strides.

Winfield provided a power bat for the Padres, highlighted in 1979 when he hit 34 homers with an NL-leading 118 RBIs.

Such statistics drew interest outside of San Diego, and the Yankees signed Winfield to a record $23 million, 10-year free-agent contract following the 1980 season.

Winfield recorded a .283 batting average over his 22-year career, accumulating 465 home runs, 1,833 RBIs, and 223 stolen

Straight to the Majors

Players who went straight to the major leagues during the draft era, which began in 1965:

Mike Adamson, RHP, USC—Orioles, 1967
Steve Dunning, RHP, Stanford—Indians, 1970
Burt Hooton, RHP, Texas—Cubs, 1971
Rob Ellis, OF, Michigan State—Brewers, 1971
Pete Broberg, RHP, Dartmouth—Senators, 1971
Dave Roberts, 3B, Oregon—Padres, 1972
Dick Ruthven, RHP, Fresno State—Phillies, 1973
Dave Winfield, OF, Minnesota—Padres, 1973
David Clyde, RHP, Westchester (Houston) High—Rangers, 1973
Eddie Bane, LHP, Arizona State—Twins, 1973
Mike Morgan, RHP, Valley (Las Vegas) High—A's, 1978
Bob Horner, 3B, Arizona State—Braves, 1978
Tim Conroy, LHP, Gateway (Penn.) High—A's, 1978
Brian Milner, C, TCU—Blue Jays, 1978
Pete Incaviglia, OF, Oklahoma State—Rangers, 1986
Jim Abbott, LHP, Michigan—Angels, 1989
John Olerud, OF, Washington State—Blue Jays, 1989
Darren Dreifort, RHP, Wichita State—Dodgers, 1994
Ariel Prieto, RHP, Fajardo (Cuba) College—A's, 1995
Xavier Nady, OF, Cal—Padres 2000
Mike Leake, RHP, Arizona State—Reds, 2010

bases. He was a 12-time All-Star who won seven Gold Gloves and sic Silver Sluggers.

He was the 19th player in major league history to reach the 3,000-hit milestone—collecting the big hit in 1993 with his hometown Minnesota Twins.

Winfield was a first-ballot Hall of Famer in 2001. He was inducted into the Padres Hall of Fame a year earlier, and his No. 31 is among six numbers retired by the franchise.

During his induction speech in Cooperstown, Winfield said, "I chose baseball because, to me, baseball is the best game of all."

He had plenty of other options after being drafted by four teams in three sports.

A starting forward on the Gophers' basketball team, Winfield was drafted by the NBA's Atlanta Hawks and the ABA's Utah Stars. Winfield never played a down of college football, but the NFL came calling, too. The Minnesota Vikings drafted him as a potential tight end.

Before Winfield could sign with the Padres after being drafted, there was the matter of leading Minnesota into the College World Series.

Winfield beat Oklahoma in one game, striking out 14 batters in a 1–0 win over the Sooners.

In the semifinals against USC, Winfield limited a Trojans lineup that included four future major leaguers—Fred Lynn, Roy Smalley, Steve Kemp, and Rich Dauer—to one hit with 15 strikeouts through eight shutout innings. He tired in the ninth inning, and coach Dick Siebert brought in a reliever with the Gophers leading 7–0. The Trojans rallied for an 8–7 win and went on to win their fourth straight national championship.

In 2010, the Minnesota–USC game was voted the No. 3 most memorable moment at the CWS. Not for the right reasons, in Winfield's mind.

In addition to his pitching performance, Winfield batted .467 (7-for-15). He was selected Most Outstanding Player of the series, despite his team not making the final.

Winfield finished the college season with a 9–1 record and 109 strikeouts in 82 innings—and never took the mound in a game again.

Imagine what could have been.

32 Trader Jack McKeon

Jack McKeon was a lot of things over the first 50 years of his life.

Taxi driver. Bus driver. Gas station attendant. School teacher. Mailman. Mechanic. Appliance salesman. Ballplayer. Scout. Manager. And, finally, importer-exporter.

It was the last job that finally earned him his nickname.

Trader Jack.

What he imported and exported was ballplayers.

McKeon spent a decade as Padres general manager. He assembled the team that went to the 1984 World Series, then spent the next five years trying to get them back there. The last three years of his tenure, from 1988 to 1990, he also sat in the dugout as Padres manager.

That managerial stint came after he had managed in Kansas City and Oakland but before he had moved on to Cincinnati and Florida (where he won a 2003 World Series title).

In San Diego, McKeon always will be known for his wheeling and dealing. With his ever-present cigar, of course.

"I make trades that help the team, not just to make trades," McKeon has said. "But then, I'd be lying if I said I didn't like trades. If another GM asks me if I want a certain guy, I rarely say no. Maybe I don't have a need for a guy, but maybe I can acquire the guy anyway, and trade him for someone I do need."

McKeon was originally hired by the Padres as an assistant to general manager Bob Fontaine in 1979, then became GM when Fontaine was fired during the 1980 All-Star break.

His first big trade came two months after the season ended. It involved 11 players.

"Why do I trade?" McKeon asks. "I'm aggressive. I'm confident. I'm a gambler. I'm willing to make a trade and not be afraid I'll get nailed."

Asked about one of his most memorable trades McKeon recalls a deal at the Winter Meetings that brought some integral pieces to the Padres team that would reach the 1984 World Series. Walking through the lobby in Nashville in 1983, McKeon bumped into a Montreal executive, who was interested in Padres left-hander Gary Lucas. The Expos offered right-hander Scott Sanderson.

"I said I had no interest in Scott Sanderson," said McKeon. "Later on that evening, Dallas Green and Hughie Alexander from the Cubs were walking by. We were pretty good friends and I had made a few deals with them. I said, 'How you guys doing?'"

McKeon quickly learned the Cubs were trying to get Sanderson.

"Scott Sanderson?" asked McKeon. "I can get him for you."

McKeon wanted first baseman/outfielder Carmelo Martinez and left-handed reliever Craig Lefferts in exchange for Sanderson.

McKeon was told, "OK, go get Sanderson and you got 'em."

"I didn't need to go upstairs and look at scouting reports," McKeon said. "I knew who I wanted and we got them. They helped us win the pennant the next year."

Martinez batted .250 with 13 home runs and 66 RBIs for the 1984 Padres, starting in left field in an outfield that included Kevin McReynolds in center and Tony Gwynn in right. Lefferts was a key pitcher for the Padres, throwing 105.2 innings in 62 games out of the bullpen. He went 3-4 with 10 saves and a 2.13 ERA.

McKeon could strike up a trade just about anywhere.

"I made one checking out of the hotel in Dallas," said McKeon. "Bill Lajoie from Detroit was in line two guys in front of me. I said, 'Let's make a deal.' He said, 'OK, what do you want?'"

Jack McKeon's Biggest Trades for the Padres

December 1980: Pitchers Rollie Fingers and Bob Shirley and catchers Gene Tenace and Bob Geren to St. Louis for catchers Terry Kennedy and Steve Swisher; infielder Mike Phillips; and pitchers John Urrea, John Littlefield, Kim Seaman, and Al Olmstead

February 1982: Shortstop Ozzie Smith to St. Louis for shortstop Garry Templeton and others

December 1983: Pitcher Gary Lucas to Montreal and pitcher Pitcher Scott Sanderson from Montreal to the Cubs; first baseman/outfielder Carmelo Martinez and pitcher Craig Lefferts from the Cubs to the Padres

December 1984: Shortstop Ozzie Guillen to the White Sox for pitcher LaMarr Hoyt and others

December 1986: Outfielder Kevin McReynolds and pitcher Gene Walter to the Mets for outfielders Shawn Abner and Stan Jefferson and third baseman/outfielder Kevin Mitchell

July 1987: Third baseman/outfielder Kevin Mitchell and pitchers Dave Dravecky and Craig Lefferts to San Francisco for infielder Chris Brown and pitchers Mark Davis, Mark Grant, and Keith Comstock

February 1988: Pitchers Goose Gossage and Ray Hayward to the Chicago Cubs for infielder/outfielder Keith Moreland and infielder Mike Brumley

October 1988: Outfielder Stanley Jefferson and pitchers Jimmy Jones and Lance McCullers to the Yankees for first baseman Jack Clark and pitcher Pat Clements

November 1988: Infielders Chris Brown and Keith Moreland to Detroit for pitcher Walt Terrell

They settled on a couple of players to swap, whose names escape McKeon now, and announced the deal after each of them flew home.

"Just like that," said McKeon. "You couldn't do that today. You'd have to go upstairs, get a printout, watch some video....The contracts make it tough today. There's a lot of money and the clubs are conscious about being budget wise now. Before it was simple. I had no problem writing contracts because there wasn't that much money involved."

One of McKeon's biggest trades late in his Padres tenure sent pitchers Dave Dravecky and Craig Lefferts and outfielder Kevin Mitchell to San Francisco. The Giants got the best of that deal, Lefferts and Mitchell helping lead the team to the 1989 World Series.

"That's how this business works," McKeon said. "Like I said, I'm not in this business to rip people off. I'm here to smoke cigars and make a trade or two."

Dick Williams

Dick Williams was just the man the Padres needed when he was hired as the team's manager before the 1982 season.

The Padres had gone through a stretch in which they were managed by six men in five years.

Enter Williams, a tough, no nonsense, old-school manager who was the most experienced and successful skipper in the franchise's history.

Williams had managed the "Impossible Dream" Red Sox to the 1967 World Series. He managed the Oakland A's to a pair of

World Series championships in 1972–73. He also managed the Angels and the Expos before the Padres came calling.

General manager Jack McKeon said he believed Williams "provides us with the direction we need. I think the players are going to find that he's going to be tough."

The Padres were coming off a 41–69 season—shortened and split in 1981 by a midseason strike—under Frank Howard.

McKeon turned over the roster during Williams' first two seasons, which both ended with identical 81–81 records.

In 1984, everything came together for the first time in franchise history.

Williams had a mix of veterans—catcher Terry Kennedy, first baseman Steve Garvey, shortstop Garry Templeton, and third baseman Graig Nettles—and youngsters—second baseman Alan Wiggins and outfielders Carmelo Martinez, Kevin McReynolds, and Tony Gwynn—in the starting lineup.

He had a solid starting rotation in Eric Show, Tim Lollar, Ed Whitson, Mark Thurmond, and Andy Hawkins, two key middle relievers in Dave Dravecky and Craig Lefferts, and a future Hall of Famer to finish teams off in closer Goose Gossage.

In mid-May Williams found his Padres in a familiar spot—playing .500 baseball. They were 18–18 and in fourth place in the NL West.

It was during a seven-game losing streak that Williams said he'd been ranting and raving at players enough "that the clubhouse was in an uproar."

In his autobiography *No More Mr. Nice Guy*, Williams said, "I'd been confronting players on the field and in the dugout and in front of their lockers. And they were finally reacting....Just the way I like it: a team that was being pulled apart under my tension and would soon be pulling together with the common goal of revenge. A team on the verge of coming together just to show me up."

The wins started coming and by mid-August the Padres found themselves with a 69–47 record and a 10½-game lead in the division.

The timing coincided with one of the most memorable brawls in baseball history. It came against the Braves. The Padres didn't back down. Their manager wouldn't let them.

Atlanta pitcher Pasqual Perez had hit Padres leadoff hitter Alan Wiggins to open the game. It was a purposeful pitch.

"We know what we've got to do," was all Williams said as his team took the field in the bottom of the first inning.

And the bean brawl game was on. Williams, who was ejected along with Whitson in the fourth inning, wasn't around for the finish. The Padres spent most of the game trying to get back at Perez. Lefferts was finally the one who plunked him.

"The Braves, and hopefully all of baseball, had finally gotten the message," Williams said. "The Padres would no longer be intimidated."

The team carried that attitude with them the rest of the season. They struggled a bit down the stretch, but still cruised to their first division title with a franchise-best 92–70 record.

A memorable comeback against the Chicago Cubs followed in the National League Championship Series before the dream season ended with a World Series loss to the Detroit Tigers.

Expectations were high the following season, but the Padres didn't play up to them, finishing 83–79.

Williams met with team president Ballard Smith not long after the season ended, hoping to get a contract extension. He said he was blindsided when Smith said, "Dick, if you don't want to come back for the last year of your contract, I'll pay you off."

"What the hell are you talking about?" Williams said. "Hell no, I don't want to quit."

When Padres owner Joan Kroc got wind of Smith and McKeon trying to force the manager out, Kroc met with Williams and threw her support behind him.

The Padres called a press conference in December of 1985 to say it was all a "misunderstanding."

Two months later, Williams met with Kroc again. Something had changed. This time she, too, wanted him out.

As pitchers and catchers were assembling for the first day of spring training in Yuma, a press conference was being called in San Diego to announce that Williams and the Padres were parting company.

"For the past few weeks, I have been asking myself, 'Do I really want to manage the Padres another year?' My honest answer, finally, was 'No.'"

It was an emotional moment for Kroc, who said, "His [Williams'] leadership gave San Diego its first National League pennant. He taught us championship baseball, and he gave us the thrill of winning. Dick, I'll never forget that season we dedicated to Ray Kroc, the wonderful summer of 1984."

Williams' winning ways included rubbing many people—especially players—the wrong way.

"I'll say 23 out of 25 players don't like Dick Williams," said a Padres player who wished to remain anonymous. "I think it would be a benefit for a lot of guys (with a kinder, gentler manager) because Dick isn't the type of manager who pats you on the back when you do something well....If we get somebody who comes in and does that, a lot of guys will feel a lot more comfortable about playing baseball."

Said another Padres player: "I love playing for Dick, but when I get out of this game, I'm gonna run over him with a car. It's definitely a love-hate relationship."

That's how it went with Williams. But he got results. He is one of only two managers in baseball history—Bill McKechnie was the other—to lead three different franchises to the World Series.

Williams was inducted into the National Baseball Hall of Fame in 2008.

Rollie Fingers

Rollie Fingers' reputation preceded him when he was signed as a free agent by the Padres before the 1977 season.

Fingers was Oakland's closer for its three-time World Series champions in the early 1970s, earning MVP of the 1974 Series.

But it was a handlebar mustache that brought Fingers fame.

When Oakland outfielder Reggie Jackson reported for spring training wearing a mustache in 1972, it spawned an idea for a wacky promotion by A's owner Charlie Finley.

Finley would have a Mustache Night at the ballpark. To help with the promotion, Finley offered A's players $300 if they would grow mustaches. Hence, The Mustache Gang was born.

Who knew that the whiskers Fingers grew would make him one of the most recognizable faces in the game.

"Just being different," Fingers said. "Everybody else was just growing a mustache. I said, 'What the heck, I'll do a handlebar.' It was probably stupid, but then we win the World Series in '72 and then we win in '73 and then we win in '74—and it's kind of tough to shave it off after that. That's why I kept it."

Fingers brought along his catcher when he joined the Padres. Oakland's Gene Tenace also signed as a free agent with the team.

It was the first big splash Padres owner Ray Kroc made in the free-agent market. Fingers didn't disappoint.

He collected 108 of his 341 career saves during his four years with the Padres. He earned National League Fireman of the Year award, given to the league's top closer, three of those four seasons.

"A fellow has to have faith in God above and Rollie Fingers in the bullpen," said Alvin Dark, who managed Fingers in both Oakland and San Diego.

Fingers had 35 saves in 1977, then set an NL record with 37 saves in 1978. Fingers provided assistance that year for Gaylord Perry's Cy Young season, saving 11 of Perry's 21 victories. He was also a major factor in the franchise's first winning season.

"As far as closers go, I'd put Rollie Fingers up against anybody," said outfielder George Hendrick, who was Fingers' Padres teammate from 1977 to 1978. "If you took the greatest closer ever and gave me Rollie Fingers, I'd have no complaints."

Fingers was among the pioneer closers, moving into the role during an era when a pitcher may go three innings to earn his save.

"It's just the mindset of a relief pitcher—you just have to go maybe three innings, and I knew I could pitch every day," said Fingers, who was a starter at the beginning of his career before A's manager Dick Williams moved him into the bullpen. "I had decent command. I felt like I had more pressure on me during four days of waiting for a start than going into a game every day—I didn't even have to think about it."

As far as modern-day closers coming on in the ninth inning to get three outs, Fingers said, "I don't think I could have pitched that way. I needed a lot of work."

Fingers, who was inducted into the National Baseball Hall of Fame in 1992, was traded from the Padres to St. Louis following the 1980 season. Four days after that trade, the Cardinals moved him to Milwaukee.

In 1981, Fingers won the AL Cy Young and AL MVP awards with the Brewers. After four seasons with Milwaukee, Fingers had a chance to close out his career with the Cincinnati Reds. There was one problem. Reds owner Marge Schott enforced a no facial hair policy.

"Well, you tell Marge Schott to shave her Saint Bernard," Fingers said, "and I'll shave my mustache."

He retired instead.

Randy Jones

The applause would begin the moment Randy Jones emerged from the Padres dugout.

The cheers rose with each step the 6'0" left-hander made toward the bullpen for his warmup throws. And the crowd recognized Jones again when he returned to the dugout before that day's start on the mound.

"It seemed like I had an advantage for a couple of years because I got to share my success with an entire community," Jones said. "That's kind of unique. Not a lot of players get to do that. It seemed like the town just took me under its wing and I was their favorite for a couple of years."

Jones made his major league debut with the Padres in June of 1973, one year after being the team's fifth-round draft pick out of Chapman University.

He came along at a time when there wasn't much to cheer about in San Diego.

The Chargers were in the midst of seven straight losing seasons, Air Coryell still a couple of seasons away from taking flight. The

NBA's San Diego Rockets had moved to Houston in 1971. And the Padres? They were fortunate not to have followed the Rockets out of town.

Jones was the first Padres player to take the national stage (right fielder Dave Winfield soon would join him). Fans may have felt sorry for Jones initially. He led the National League in losses his first full season, going 8–22 in 1974 on a team that lost 102 games.

Everything turned around a year later. Jones became the first 20-game winner in franchise history—and still shares the honor only with Gaylord Perry (21 wins in 1978)—going 20–12 with a league-best 2.24 ERA over 285 innings. He finished second to right-hander Tom Seaver for the 1975 National League Cy Young Award. Seaver had gone 22–9 that season for the New York Mets.

"Not winning it last year was a big disappointment," Jones said the following season. "I thought I did more for my team than Tom did for his. That's what I was counting on."

The 1975 Padres were 71–91 with Jones. Imagine where they would have been without him. The 1976 season was more of the same, with the Padres going 73–89 on the way to fifth place in the NL West.

Jones couldn't be denied this time, though. He went 22–14 and led the NL in wins, complete games (25), and innings pitched (315⅓), was third in shutouts (5) and fifth in ERA (2.74). Jones received 15 of 24 first-place votes on the way to winning the 1976 NL Cy Young Award. He outpointed four other 20-game winners in the Mets' Jerry Koosman, the Dodgers' Don Sutton, the Phillies' Steve Carlton, and the Astros' J.R. Richard.

Jones tossed 43 complete games over two seasons—18 in '75 and 25 in '76—matching the total number of complete games the Padres compiled as a staff from 2001 to 2015.

"My proudest thing," Jones said years later, "was in the 70s, putting the franchise on the map."

Jones' starts were buzzworthy events. San Diegans seemed interested in just about anything that had to do with Jones.

An appointment to have his haired permed—getting what broadcaster Jerry Coleman once called the "Karl Marx hairdo" (apologies to curly-haired comedian Harpo Marx)—became a photo op for newspapers.

Randy Jones was the first 20-game winner among Padres pitchers, recording 20 wins in 1975 and 22 victories in 1976 when he won the National League Cy Young Award. (San Diego Padres)

And Jones accomplished all this with a fastball that couldn't break a pane of glass.

"His fastball has been timed at about 27 mph," Cincinnati's Pete Rose joked years ago. "Actually, it once was timed at about 75 mph, hardly fast enough to be arrested."

Said Jones: "Maybe that's why more people related to me. I wasn't a power pitcher. My abilities were more human than maybe some other pitchers you'd see out there in a major league game."

Jones had some velocity at Brea Olinda High before injuring his arm as a freshman at Chapman.

"I lost my balance on a pitch and something snapped," Jones said. "I had pulled some tendons. I wasn't that concerned about my future because I was going for a business degree in real estate and if my arm didn't come back, it didn't come back. But it came back enough for me to pitch in college....I'd lost my fastball, but I worked on my control. Most of the scouts disappeared after I hurt my arm, but a few stayed."

One scout who stuck around was from the Padres. Once Jones joined the organization, the left-hander came across a pitching instructor named Warren Hacker, who, Jones said, "taught me to throw a better sinker."

The sinker ball, complemented by a slider, became his bread and butter. Batters just beat balls into the ground. Scorecards were filled with notations reading 6–3 and 4–3, Jones keeping shortstop Enzo Hernandez and second baseman Tito Fuentes on their toes when he was pitching.

No one had more trouble with the sinker than Rose, a .303 career hitter and the game's all-time hit king with 4,256 hits.

So frustrated with the futility of facing Jones was Rose that the switch-hitter finally went against convention versus the lefty.

"I got up there on the mound and he stepped in left-handed," Jones recalled. "I looked at Pete like, 'Are you sure you want to do this?' He said, 'Shut up and pitch it.' I struck him out on three sliders.

"The third time up, I walked him on a 3–2 pitch right on the inside corner. His first step was back to the dugout because he knew I struck him out. Then the umpire called it a ball and Rose laughed at me all the way down to first base."

Rose batted .183 against Jones in 98 career plate appearances. That included a 1-for-26 stretch during the 1975–76 seasons.

"I just couldn't hit him," Rose said. "He had my number."

Walks were rare when Jones was on the mound. In 1976, he tied a record set by Hall of Famer Christy Mathewson 63 years earlier by going 68 straight innings without walking a batter.

Jones injured a nerve in his left arm near the end of that Cy Young season and was never the same. He would go 92–105 with a 3.30 ERA in his eight seasons with the Padres. He was traded to the Mets before the 1981 season. Jones spent two seasons in the Big Apple, made memorable only because he picked up the eight wins needed to conclude his career with an even 100 victories.

Jones was back in San Diego soon after the 1982 season ended. And he's been here ever since.

"Maybe it was the 'Tony Gwynn Syndrome,'" said Jones, who, like Gwynn, lived in Poway. "I loved where I lived and where I played. I always believed that one of those years it would click (for the Padres). It just never happened. But I had no desire to go play somewhere else."

Padres fans are thankful Jones returned. Whether as a restaurateur, pitching coach, broadcaster, or ambassador for the ballclub, Jones has remained among the most beloved figures in town for the past four decades.

36 Gaylord Perry

Gaylord Perry was 16 years into his Hall of Fame career when a 1978 trade sent him from Texas to San Diego.

Perry was getting by on guile and a smile, putting uncertainty in the minds of hitters not so much for what he had behind the ball as for what he put on it.

It was with more than a little surprise that Perry, whose 40th birthday arrived before the end of the season, put together one of his finest years.

He went 21–6 for the Padres with a 2.73 ERA and 154 strikeouts in 260⅔ innings, winning the 1978 National League Cy Young Award.

Perry became the first pitcher to win the Cy Young in both leagues, bookending this one with the one he won in the American League with the Cleveland Indians six years earlier.

"It was like the first one in a way," Perry said. "In '72, I had just been traded from San Francisco to Cleveland. In '78, I had just been traded from Texas to San Diego.

"But it was really a great experience in San Diego. The fact that I was still able to pitch that well when I was 40 was very satisfying. Probably the greatest thing I had going for me was having Rollie Fingers in the bullpen."

It also didn't hurt having a rookie named Ozzie Smith playing shortstop behind him.

Opposing hitters and managers used to watch closely when Perry was on the mound, hoping to catch him loading up the ball. Perry went so far as to title his 1974 autobiography *Me and the Spitter*.

In a *USA Today* story, Perry said: "I reckon I tried everything on the old apple but salt and pepper and chocolate sauce topping...

When my wife was having babies the doctor would send over all kinds of stuff and I'd try that, too. Once I even used fishing line oil."

Perry would try to get in the hitters' heads: "The day before I'd pitch, I'd put grease on my hands and go shake their hands just to get them thinking. Sometimes I'd roll a ball covered with grease into their dugout."

Perry seemed to invite suspicion, and he had honed his routine to a fine art by the time he joined the Padres. He touched his cap, his face, his glove, and his pants before every pitch. But he wasn't ejected from a game until August 23, 1982, the second-to-last season of a 22-year career that included 314 wins and enshrinement in Cooperstown in 1991.

One story goes that Perry wanted to be a pitchman for the makers of Vaseline. The company rejected the idea, supposedly sending him a postcard reading, *We soothe babies' (bottoms), not baseballs.*

Anyway, his performance in 1978 helped the Padres to the first winning season—84–78—in franchise history.

Perry's final outing of the '78 season included his 3,000th strikeout. He became only the third pitcher to reach the milestone, joining Walter Johnson and Bob Gibson.

Perry closed out the season with six straight wins.

"I really had a big September," he said. "I always had a good September. I wound it up the right way, and that put me up front in the (Cy Young) voting. I figured if I had a good September, I had a good chance to win it. There was nobody right behind me to sneak up on me."

The voting wasn't even close. Perry received 22 of 24 first-place votes. The Dodgers' Burt Hooton received the other two votes. Perry outpointed Hooton 116 to 38.

Perry became the oldest winner of the award.

"I'm dedicating this to all the people 40 or over," he said. "It was exciting when I won the first time, but this has more power and pleasure in it. This time I was 40, and it was the first time the Padres had played .500 ball or better."

How many of his pitches did Perry load up that season? He wouldn't say, not directly, anyway.

"I kept the slippery pitch ready all season, thinking they would probably legalize it sooner or later," he quipped.

Amid the celebratory mood the day the Cy Young Award was announced, Perry said, "I hope I'll be part of the San Diego franchise for a long time."

His tenure didn't even last another 52 weeks.

Perry went 12–11 in 1979, tossing seven shutout innings in a 3–0 win over the Giants to get over .500. The win came on September 3, giving him time for perhaps five more starts before the end of the year.

But Perry left the team with three weeks remaining in the season, heading back to his home in North Carolina. He said he would retire if he wasn't traded. The Padres obliged, sending him back to the Rangers.

When a reporter caught up with Perry a year later in Anaheim to ask what had happened, the pitcher said: "I went home."

Pressed further, Perry said: "For personal reasons."

37 Yuma

For the first 25 years of their existence, the Padres assembled before each season in Yuma, Arizona.

Yuma's most notable feature then was an 80-foot water tower with the city's name on it.

Yuma's most notable feature now is an 80-foot water tower with the city's name on it.

That's not to say it wasn't a popular place for the Padres to conduct spring training from 1969 to 1993 before they packed everything up for Peoria.

Yuma is just a three-hour drive from San Diego, which made it easy for Padres fans to get a glimpse of what was to come each season.

Part of Yuma's appeal was that there was pretty much nothing to do there—other than maybe golf in the morning or go to the greyhound races in the evening—so it was conducive to ballplayers preparing for a new season.

Or so it seemed.

The facility had just one field that first season, but the Caballeros de Yuma, a local civic group, led efforts to modernize. Four practice fields were built, along with a nice clubhouse.

It would come to be named the Ray Kroc Baseball Complex after the McDonald's magnate purchased the franchise in 1974.

Kroc visited frequently. One thing he enjoyed when he came to Yuma was making unannounced visits to the town's one McDonald's restaurant.

"Ray always expected to find a paper cup on the floor or something out of place," former Padres GM Buzzie Bavasi once recalled. "I finally said, 'Ray, how do you expect to sneak up on anybody in a town this small when you're getting around with a chauffeur in a white Rolls-Royce?'"

While the nightlife in Yuma may have left something to be desired, it wasn't without incident.

One evening, Padres coaches Roger Craig and Don Zimmer were coming out of a bar to head to the dog races. Craig went out to their cab while Zimmer settled up their bill.

"When he got into the cab," Craig recalled, "he said, 'Rog, I think I've broken my wrist.' I didn't know what he was talking about.

"It turns out some guy had challenged him as he was leaving the bar and Zim had flattened him," Craig said. "We had to leave the dog track and go to a hospital so they could put Zim's wrist in a cast."

Pitcher Gaylord Perry tried to cajole Kroc into buying the pitcher a tractor for his farm as a bonus for winning the 1978 Cy Young Award. Kroc declined.

But when Perry arrived for spring training the following year, he was greeted by a rusted-out tractor his teammates had rescued from a dump.

"In that town, you get to know your teammates real well," said pitcher Goose Gossage, who spent four springs in Yuma from 1984 to 1987. "You have no other choice."

Gossage recalled one bonding experience with pitcher Tim Stoddard and catcher Bruce Bochy when they found themselves in an establishment that featured female mud wrestling.

"I gave Bochy $200 to get Stoddard to wrestle," said Gossage, who didn't realize his teammates had put up an even greater sum to get him into the ring.

"I tried to get out of there, but four guys grabbed me," Gossage said. "They gave me shorts that were at least two sizes too small. But I was thinking to myself, *At least I'll get the chance to go out there and wrestle a pretty gal.*"

That's when a switch was pulled and the woman who stepped in opposite the pitcher was "some Amazon."

"She was a cross between Stoddard and Bochy," Gossage said.

It did not end well, although Gossage did emerge with a win.

Right fielder Tony Gwynn spent more time in Yuma than anyone, training there a dozen seasons.

Gwynn thought he knew everything there was to know about the place. But he was kicking himself that final spring in 1993 when he came across a little local knowledge that would have come in handy a decade earlier.

"In 12 years of coming to Yuma, I finally, just this year, realized there's bass over there on the golf course pond of (hole) 17," Gwynn recalled to a reporter during the team's final week in Yuma. "I've been complaining, 'Hey, maybe Peoria's got fish up there because I'm 0-for-Yuma.'"

Pitcher Kerry Taylor informed Gwynn of the golf course fishing hole. The outfielder headed out there with teammate Darrin Jackson and both players pulled fish out of the pond.

"Imagine that," Gwynn said. "They find bass within walking distance of the clubhouse and I've been going to the Colorado River, getting my shoes this thick in mud, car getting stuck out there. And now we're leaving. Amazing."

Gwynn said he would miss the place.

"I enjoyed my memories here," Gwynn said.

He wasn't alone.

38 Visit Peoria for Spring Training

The distance to spring training doubled for Padres fans when the team moved its Arizona complex from Yuma to Peoria before the 1994 season.

It remains worth the drive.

Visiting during February and March in the sunshine and laid-back atmosphere provides a unique baseball-watching experience.

Cozy Cactus League ballparks give fans up close looks at the players and opportunities for autographs and interaction that don't present themselves once the season begins.

Fans can get a glimpse of veteran players as well as minor league prospects on the six practice fields at the Peoria Sports Complex, which the Padres share with the Seattle Mariners. Practice field gates open each morning at approximately 9:00 AM and fans are welcome to watch warm-ups and workouts. Bleacher seating is available, but fans also can bring their own lawn chairs.

Parking is $5 per car and $10 for RVs.

Pitchers and catchers report in mid-February. They are joined by the remainder of the organization's players by month's end.

Half of the Padres' Cactus League games are played at the 12,000-seat Peoria Stadium.

When the Padres hit the road, fans can join them there as well. There are 15 teams training in the greater Phoenix area. That means virtually any game is within a 15- to 30-minute drive of the Padres' home base.

The spring training schedule is available at padres.com.

Fans also can get ticket, complex, and visitor information at peoriaspringtraining.com.

The Peoria Sports Complex includes a kids club called the Peanut Gang for those ages 14 and under.

Other information can be obtained by emailing sportscomplex@peoriaaz.gov or by calling (623) 773-8700.

Visit Cooperstown

The National Baseball Hall of Fame and Museum is a mythical place.

The Hall was established in 1936 and was dedicated on June 12, 1939, in Cooperstown, New York. The five-man inaugural Hall of Fame class included Ty Cobb, Walter Johnson, Christy Mathewson, Babe Ruth, and Honus Wagner.

Fittingly, Cooperstown comes with a myth of its own.

In 1905, a seven-man commission was formed to address the origins of the game. Sporting goods magnate Albert Goodwill Spalding, an outstanding pitcher in the game's formative years, claimed the game was invented in the United States. English-born journalist Henry Chadwick said it evolved from the English game rounders.

A Cooperstown cow pasture is said to be the birthplace of baseball. Abner Doubleday is credited with its creation. Evidence was dubious, but Spalding didn't let the facts get in the way of a good story.

After three years, the commission, led by National League present Abraham Mills, made it official: "The first scheme of

Padres Hall of Famers

Players in the Hall of Fame who spent at least part of their careers with the Padres:

Player	Position	(Years with Padres)
Roberto Alomar	2B	(1988–90)
Rollie Fingers	RHP	(1977–80)
Goose Gossage	RHP	(1984–87)
Tony Gwynn	OF	(1982–2001)
Rickey Henderson	OF	(1996–97; 2001)
Willie McCovey	1B	(1974–76)
Gaylord Perry	RHP	(1978–79)
Ozzie Smith	SS	(1978–81)
Dave Winfield	OF	(1973–80)

Manager	(Years with Team)
Dick Williams	(1982–85)

Broadcasters
Jerry Coleman (received in 2005)
Dick Enberg (received in 2015)

playing baseball, according to the best available evidence to date, was devised by Abner Doubleday at Cooperstown, N.Y., in 1839."

Further research completely discredited these findings. Doubleday never mentioned anything about the game and he was at West Point during the time it was supposedly invented.

But Cooperstown city fathers, seeking something to stimulate the local economy during the Depression, embraced the local legend.

Cooperstown welcomes nearly 300,000 baseball fans each year to the museum, which houses more than 40,000 artifacts, more than three million documents, and 130,000 baseball cards.

Notable Padres Artifacts at the Hall of Fame

Notable Padres artifacts at the National Baseball Hall of Fame in Cooperstown, according to Padres.com:

- Bat from first baseman Nate Colbert's record five-homer, 13-RBI game in a doubleheader on August 1, 1972
- Uniform worn by right-hander Gaylord Perry during the 1979 season
- Cap worn by first baseman Steve Garvey on April 16, 1983, when he set the NL record for consecutive games played
- World Series press pin from 1984
- Bats used by outfielders Marvell Wynne, Tony Gwynn, and John Kruk to homer in succession leading off a game on April 13, 1987
- Jersey worn by Gwynn during the 1994 season when he hit .394 to record his fifth NL batting title
- Bat used by third baseman Ken Caminiti to switch-hit home runs in consecutive games on September 16 and 17, 1995
- Bat and spikes used by Gwynn in 1997, when he achieved his record-tying eighth NL batting title
- Cap worn by Gwynn during the 1998 World Series
- Bat used by outfielder Greg Vaughn during his 50-home-run season of 1998
- Bat and uniform from final month of Gwynn's final season in 2001

The original five inductees have been joined by more than 300 other players, managers, umpires, and executives. There are nine players among them who played with the Padres as well as former Padres manager Dick Williams.

The motto for the Hall of Fame is "Preserving History, Honoring Excellence, Connecting Generations."

It does all that and more.

Visits to the three-story museum are self-guided. Some fans can get through the thousands of artifacts in a few hours, while others block out a weekend or more to take it all in.

The first floor of the museum includes the Hall of Fame Plaque Gallery, which includes the plaques of all the players, managers, umpires, and executives enshrined in Cooperstown. Also on the first floor is the Giamatti Research Center, which can be accessed by appointment for those wishing to conduct baseball research. Inquiries can be made by emailing research@baseballhall.org.

The town is approximately 90 miles from three New York airports—Albany International Airport, Syracuse Hancock International Airport, and Greater Binghamton Airport.

One of the most popular times to visit is Hall of Fame weekend, which takes place in late July each year. The event is held in a large open field outside the Clark Sports Center, on lower Susquehanna Avenue about one mile south of the museum. Admission to the ceremony is free.

Admission to the Hall of Fame is $23 for adults, $15 for seniors (65 and older), and $12 for kids (ages 7–12) and veterans. Active/career retired military and children under 6 are free. Tickets can be purchased ahead of time online or by calling (607) 547-0397. Rates are subject to change.

More information is available on the Hall's website at baseball-hall.org.

40 The Crowd in Cooperstown

It was Induction Weekend at Cooperstown and when the appointed hour arrived, they loaded the Hall of Famers on buses for the short trip across town to the stage where the ceremony takes place.

A record 55 of the 63 living Hall of Famers attended the 2007 ceremony in which Tony Gwynn and Cal Ripken Jr. were to be enshrined.

Ribbing from the veterans begins virtually the moment rookie Hall of Famers check into the Otesaga Hotel for the weekend. It continues Saturday during the morning's golf event and the evening's dinner. Then it resumes on the bus ride to the ceremony.

Gwynn thought some of the Hall of Famers were pulling his leg when it was suggested the largest crowd ever was assembled in the field adjacent to the Clark Sports Center.

He was already nervous enough, having learned shortly before boarding the bus that he would be batting leadoff. Gwynn was originally scheduled to be the third speaker at the ceremony. With rain and lightning in the forecast, however, the lineup was shuffled. Gwynn would speak first.

When Gwynn's bus turned the last corner to the ceremony he realized they weren't trying to get his goat. He saw the crowd.

Make that *the crowd*.

"I've been here so many times in the past," said John Boggs, Gwynn's longtime agent, "and you look out there (at the crowd) and it's like Woodstock."

Everybody else knew what was coming days ahead of time.

Fans began placing lawn chairs, blankets, cushions, and anything else they could find on the grass field to reserve their spots for an induction ceremony that was still three days away.

A day before the ceremony, the largest one-day crowd ever had visited the Hall of Fame.

To that point, the largest crowd for an induction day was the 50,000 who showed up to see Nolan Ryan, George Brett, Robin Yount, and Orlando Cepeda enshrined in 1999. The induction of Gwynn and Ripken didn't just surpass that, it smashed that.

An estimated 75,000—a figure since revised upward to 82,000—showed up to see the former Padres right fielder and former Orioles shortstop answer the call to the Hall.

It was affirmation for a pair of players—each amassing more than 3,000 career hits with just one team—who had performed with unusual class.

"I think that's about respect," Gwynn said. "I think that's about them feeling that I did the right thing."

Gwynn spoke for nearly 28 minutes, pausing on more than one occasion to look out at the sea of fans, many of them wearing the brown and yellow colors he wore early in his career or the blue and orange he wore over his last few seasons.

Gwynn's comments were periodically punctuated with chants of "To-ny! To-ny! To-ny!"

"I never really looked at what I did as being anything special," Gwynn said to the crowd. "I loved the game. I think that's why you (fans) are here today, because you love the game. You have a passion for it.

"I have a passion for it. I still have a passion for it. I just don't play anymore."

Maybe not, but he could still draw a crowd. And command the stage.

Jones vs. Kaat

Left-hander Randy Jones was always a favorite among Padres fans. Among stadium vendors, on the other hand….

Jones was known for working quickly. His brisk pace made it enjoyable to watch a game. But try making any money selling peanuts or Cracker Jack. Many a soda salesman watched the final out recorded with drinks still dripping in the rack carried at his waist.

Buzzie Bavasi, the Padres' original general manager, understood how they felt.

"Buzzie told me he wanted to save me for Fireworks Night on Saturday," Jones said. "We had a really good crowd, like Buzzie knew we would, and I got the game in in an hour-40. Problem was, it wasn't dark enough to start the fireworks and everybody had to wait around for darkness. Buzzie said, 'That's the last time you pitch Fireworks Night.'"

So imagine when Jones hooked up with Philadelphia Phillies left-hander Jim Kaat, who barely got the ball back from the catcher when he fired it again toward the plate.

"I had developed a quick motion in '75," Kaat said. "I didn't really have much of a windup, but (the quick pitch) was something that really frustrated hitters. As soon as I got the ball, my foot was on the rubber and I was ready to pitch. It kept hitters on the defensive."

Jones and Kaat tangled at San Diego Stadium on May 4, 1977.

The Padres won 4–1, notable because they were headed for a 93-loss season while Philadelphia was in the midst of a 101-win season.

But what really made the contest memorable was that it lasted only 89 minutes. Games were faster back then—averaging 2 hours, 28 minutes—but this was ridiculous.

It is the fastest nine-inning game in Padres history and, in fact, the second-fastest game in the major leagues in more than 50 years.

With the average game time these days virtually twice as long as the Jones-Kaat game, even pitching duels can be drawn out.

"It's probably one of the more frustrating or disappointing things to see—a pitcher's duel (that takes forever)," said Kaat, who became a broadcaster after his 25-year career ended. "People say it's the commercial breaks between innings (that) are longer, but for me, I think it's the hitters stepping out of the box, adjusting their wristbands....I timed it once, and that adds 30 minutes to a game.

"In the '60s and '70s the hitters never left the box."

Like Kaat, Jones didn't waste any time between pitches. Or waste any pitches, for that matter.

"I didn't lollygag around," said Jones, who was coming off his 1976 Cy Young season. "I grabbed the ball and threw it. Back in the old days, you got eight pitches between innings. I would only throw six. Kaat was even worse than me. I think he threw five. We would just start the inning and we would go."

There was barely time to catch your breath between innings.

"I remember taking my six (practice pitches), looking into the Phils dugout, seeing Jim talking to somebody and putting on his jacket," says Jones. "I'd get three outs before he'd buttoned up that jacket."

The crowd of 10,021 watched the Padres score four runs (three earned) on eight hits against Kaat over 6⅓ innings.

Padres center fielder Gene Richards had a two-run homer off Kaat in the seventh. After a flyout by Bill Almon and a single by Merv Rettenmund, Phillies manager Danny Ozark came to get the pitcher.

"I looked at Ozark and went, 'Man, what are you doing?'" said Jones, disappointed most perhaps because he had two hits off Kaat. "Jim was dealing. I was dealing. Bam! Bam! Bam! Jim worked even faster than me. Then Ozark went and slowed it down with relievers."

Kaat was replaced by Ron Reed, who checked the Padres on one hit over 1⅔ innings.

"Reed struck out three," Kaat said. "Those strikeouts really slow a game."

Jones pitched to just three batters over the minimum, allowing four hits, one walk, and one strikeout. Jones' sinkerball produced 18 ground-ball outs, one leading to a double play. There were three fly-ball outs, two lineouts, a pop-up, the strikeout, and a caught stealing.

The game ended so quickly that Kaat was in his seats at San Diego State for a concert two hours after the game started. And he didn't miss a song.

There's no way that happens these days. Kaat said he was watching a playoff game in 2010 and kept track of all the "lollygagging" as Jones might call it.

"I estimated the amount of time wasted at 30–35 minutes," says Kaat. "That's 15–20 seconds multiplied by the number of pitches, subtracting the hits and walks. If I threw a pitch to Mickey Mantle and he took it, his back foot always stayed in the box and he'd get right back in. Now hitters stand in the on-deck circle and listen to the music being played just for them.

"Add it all up, all those seconds and minutes. You see why it takes twice the amount of time that Randy and I needed."

Preston Gomez

Preston Gomez is the answer to a pair of Padres trivia questions:

Who was the first manager of the major league Padres?

Who pinch hit for Padres pitcher Clay Kirby after eight no-hit innings?

Gomez would never live up to expectations—how could he?—when it came to the first question.

Gomez would never live down the decision—how dare he!—when it came to the second question.

The Cuban-born Gomez served as third-base coach for the Los Angeles Dodgers from 1965 to 1968. When Padres GM Buzzie Bavasi moved to the Padres after three decades in the Dodgers' front office, Bavasi tabbed Gomez to come with him to manage the Padres.

"Preston is perfect for the kind of job we have to do here," Bavasi said.

Gomez was the second Latin American manager in baseball history. Cuban Mike Gonzalez served twice—in 1938 and 1940—as interim manager of the St. Louis Cardinals.

A 20-year playing career, all but eight games (with the Washington Senators) of it spent in the minor leagues, provided Gomez with plenty of baseball experience.

But how does anyone prepare for the challenges of guiding an expansion team?

That inaugural Padres team lost 110 games in 1969. They didn't do much better the next two years, losing 99 games in 1970 and 100 games in 1971, respectively.

Gomez was gone 11 games into the 1972 season—the quickest firing of a manager in modern history—and replaced by Padres assistant coach Don Zimmer. Gomez had a 180–316 record to show for his three-plus seasons at the helm.

"The meeting was very amicable," Bavasi said at the time. "I explained to Preston why I thought a change of managers was necessary at this time. After 12 years' association with Preston, I continue to consider him an exceptionally qualified baseball man."

Gomez's assistant coaches with the Padres were more notable than his players. His staffs included Hall of Fame manager Sparky Anderson as well as future managers Roger Craig and Bob Skinner.

San Diegan Dave Garcia got his first coaching job on Gomez's staff, joining the 1970 Padres. Garcia spent four years with the organization before moving on to managerial opportunities with the Angels and Indians.

"Preston was an outstanding baseball man," Garcia said. "He was a tough guy, a no-nonsense leader. He managed the game to win."

That was never more evident than on July 21, 1970, when Gomez pinch hit for Kirby after eight no-hit innings against the New York Mets in a game the Padres would lose 3–0.

"You play the game to win," Gomez said at the time. "I have to pinch hit there if we had a chance to win. Faced with the same situation, I'd do it again."

Gomez would go on to manage the Houston Astros (1974–75) and Chicago Cubs (1980). He joined the Angels in 1981 as third-base coach, became a special assistant to the GM in 1985, and would spend more than three decades with the organization.

43 Gwynn's World Series Homer off David Wells

Tony Gwynn once said he could specifically remember 2,000 of his 3,141 career hits.

One hit stands out above all the rest.

It was a home run on October 17, 1998. It came against left-hander David Wells. In Game 1 of the World Series. And it hit off the right-field facade in Yankee Stadium.

"That's the biggest game in the world, a World Series game," Gwynn said. "And the fact that it was in New York in Yankee Stadium. I'll remember that forever."

Several years later, ESPN interviewed Gwynn for a feature it called *10 Burning Questions With...* and one of the questions posed to the Hall of Famer was "What at-bat do you put in the VCR when it's 3:00 AM and you can't sleep?"

"The home run I hit in the World Series at Yankee Stadium," Gwynn said. "Without question. Poor David Wells. If he could see me at night looking at that over and over again, he'd probably get pissed off at me."

After the game that night, Wells had said: "I just hung one up there for him. You got to tip your hat to that guy. He's the best hitter in baseball."

Gwynn singled to left field in the first inning against Wells, then grounded out in the third. In the fifth inning, Quilvio Veras' two-out single to center field brought Gwynn to the plate again.

The Padres outfielder jumped on the first pitch from Wells and lined it deep to right field, where it ricocheted off the facing of a Bud Light sign on the upper deck.

So what was going through Wells' mind before he went into his windup?

"It's Tony Gwynn at the plate, and to figure out a guy like that, well, you're not going to figure it out." Wells said. "No strikes or one strike or two strikes, he's still going to put the bat on the ball 99 percent of the time.

"Pitch him down and away and he serves it into left. Down the middle, he comes right back at you. Flip a coin. So I tried to come in and obviously didn't get it down enough.

"I always knew he had pop, but behind in the lineup were two guys with tremendous pop, (Greg) Vaughn and (Ken) Caminiti. So you worried about Tony, but he's one guy you don't think home run, especially with those other two coming up."

Vaughn followed Gwynn to the plate. He, too, homered on the first pitch from Wells. It was the 12th time in World Series history teammates had gone back-to-back with home runs. It was the second homer of the game for Vaughn, staking the Padres to a 5–2 lead. The advantage was short-lived; the Yankees came back for a 9–6 win. It was the first of four straight wins in the Series for the Bronx Bombers.

Gwynn's home run remains the most memorable moment of the series for Padres fans.

Wells, who earlier in the season had pitched the 15th perfect game in major league history, would just as soon forget it.

The lefty from Point Loma High wasn't surprised Gwynn got his bat on the ball—only that the ball traveled so far once struck. After all, Gwynn only hit 135 home runs over his 20-year career.

"With a very educated hitter like Gwynn, the important thing was to not pitch in a pattern, 'cause he'll figure it out and hurt you," Wells said. "If you don't pitch him differently every time, he'll sit on a pitch and beat the (expletive) out of you. And he did. His eyes lit up like firecrackers when he saw that big beach ball coming in.

"Still, who expects Tony Gwynn to hit one off the facade?"

Jake Peavy

Right-hander Jake Peavy became a fan favorite seemingly moments after making his 2002 major league debut with the Padres.

Peavy was something seldom seen in San Diego, a homegrown player who not only made it to the majors but became a star.

Peavy was signed by the Padres in 1999 after being drafted in the 15th round out of St. Paul's Episcopal School in Mobile, Alabama.

He reached double digits in victories his first full season in the majors, going 12–11 in 2003. A year later, he led the National League with a 2.27 ERA. And the year after that he led the NL in strikeouts with 216.

Peavy put it all together in 2007, earning the NL's triple crown for pitching by leading the league in wins (19), strikeouts (240), and ERA (2.54). Peavy joined Arizona's Randy Johnson (2002) as the only NL pitchers over a 22-year span to accomplish the feat.

It was no surprise when Peavy was a unanimous choice for the 2007 NL Cy Young Award.

"As a small-town kid who has such a respect for the game of baseball, it's very humbling and you are in awe of that," Peavy said after joining Randy Jones (1976), Gaylord Perry (1978), and Mark Davis (1989) as Padres Cy Young winners. "It was just one of those seasons where everything came together.

"I'm dang proud to stand in front of the people and accept the award on behalf of this city and this franchise."

Peavy picked up a $100,000 bonus for winning the award. It also made his 2009 club option increase from $3 million to $11 million. That became a moot point a month later when Peavy signed a three-year, $52 million extension.

"I really have tried my best to stay away from the money issue because a lot of people in Semmes, Alabama, can't count that high," Peavy said at a news conference. "That's not saying that in an arrogant way at all. I mean, when people in Semmes see the kind of money we're talking about, they don't understand. I don't understand, to be honest with you. It's kind of crazy. I know how fortunate and blessed I am to be able to have the talent to play this game."

Peavy was looking forward to spending many, many years with the Padres, similar to teammate Trevor Hoffman and Padres Hall of Famer Tony Gwynn.

In fact, Peavy was making plans to move his family from Alabama to San Diego. The oldest of his two sons was just a year away from entering first grade.

"I've got to relocate because I want to be a daddy," he said. "I don't want to call and ask how the school day was, I want to tuck my boys in and ask them how their school day was. When you've got a 6-year-old in school, that's just all there is to it."

The long-term plans changed almost as fast as the Padres' fortunes. The team went from winning 89 games in 2007 to losing 99 games a year later.

Five years after moving into Petco Park, the Padres pivoted. Instead of trying to compete for division championships with a payroll on par with their rivals, they set about paring it to $40 million.

Peavy had followed up his Cy Young season by going 10–11 in 2008. The Padres began shopping their ace after the season, intent on trading him before his salary jumped to $11 million. That would make it 25 percent of the Padres' overall payroll. Some within the organization also had become increasingly concerned about his violent delivery.

Peavy was 6–6 midway through the 2009 season when the Padres shipped him to the Chicago White Sox at the trade deadline in exchange for pitchers Dexter Carter, Aaron Poreda, Clayton Richard, and Adam Russell.

The Padres had been trying to make the trade for two months, but Peavy originally balked at the idea.

"The ultimate decision," Peavy said, "was when the team you're playing for actively keeps telling you they need to move you, and one team comes after you like Chicago did, you're excited to play for a team where you know you're wanted."

Catfish Gets off the Hook

When Ray Kroc stepped up to purchase the Padres in January of 1974, saving the franchise from moving to Washington, D.C., Kroc pledged to make the team a winner.

His chance to live up to that promise came 11 months later when Oakland A's right-hander Catfish Hunter became baseball's first free agent.

A's owner Charles O. Finley had failed to make insurance payments as required by Hunter's contract. The pitcher's $100,000-a-year salary was to be paid half to Hunter and the other half in monthly payments directly to an annuity set up for him.

Finley did not follow the contract, missing several annuity payments. He tried to catch up with one lump-sum payment to Hunter, but the pitcher balked.

Said Hunter: "I told him, 'I don't want it that way. Pay the insurance like the contract read.'"

Marvin Miller, head of the Major League Baseball Players Association, saw an opportunity to take the case to an arbitrator.

"One thing worried me," Miller said. "The remedy was free agency. That was drastic. I thought it might be too drastic for an arbitrator."

It was not. Arbitrator Peter Seitz sided with Hunter, declaring him a free agent on December 16, 1974.

Hunter, 28, was not just any pitcher. He had led Oakland's pitching staff during the A's three straight World Series championships. In 1974, Hunter earned the AL Cy Young Award after leading the league in wins (25) and ERA (2.49).

After receiving word, Hunter said, "I hung up the phone, turned to my wife, and said, 'We don't belong to anybody.' I was scared. I didn't have a job. I didn't realize the implications."

He would soon enough.

Pretty much every team inquired about his services. A handful of them—the Padres included—were serious. Very serious.

Hunter lived in rural North Carolina, and he had teams come to him with their offers. His lawyer, a man named J. Carlton Cherry, handled the negotiations.

"Cherry didn't know what he had," Miller said. "He called me to say Finley had offered to forgive a loan and give Hunter a three-year guaranteed contract. He thought that was pretty good. As politely as I could, I explained that Hunter was the first free agent superstar. I told him, 'You haven't seen anything, yet.'"

Cleveland reportedly put a $2 million offer on the table. Kansas City offered to pay Hunter $50,000 a year for the rest of his life.

"What if I die?" Hunter asked. "They said, 'The contract is for you, not your wife and not your family.'"

The Royals were shown the door.

Padres GM Peter Bavasi was watching from the sidelines, waiting for his opportunity to jump in. Bavasi had come to North Carolina, staying at the Tomahawk Motel, with orders from Kroc to secure Hunter's signature on a contract.

"Ray asked what I thought it would cost," Bavasi said. "I told him Catfish made $100,000 the year before and from all indications, he wanted a long-term, guaranteed contract. I thought it would take $400,000."

Turns out, Bavasi wasn't even close.

An Associated Press story relaying events of the negotiations said that Bavasi waited for a late appointment so that other teams could come in and make their offers first.

Bavasi had purchased a new gray suit for the meeting. Hunter showed up in hunting clothes.

"It was the last day of the hunting season," Bavasi said. "He had his dogs in the truck, ready to go."

Hunter was chewing tobacco throughout the meeting and spitting the juice in a Styrofoam cup.

Not everything made it into the cup. Some spittle got on Bavasi's sleeve. He didn't flinch.

Bavasi was too busy focusing on Cherry's contract demands for his client.

"He wanted a variety of things that added up to $3,750,000," Bavasi said. "It was almost $4 million, a far cry from our $400,000."

When Cherry said, "Now, young man, does that scare you?" Bavasi answered: "It sure doesn't."

Bavasi asked for a break in the negotiations, went back to his hotel, and phoned Kroc, who was on a cruise. Through the static of a ship-to-shore line, the GM communicated the demand.

He said $4 million, but Kroc heard it as $400,000.

"That's great," Kroc said. "You brought it in right where you said. Four hundred thousand."

Replied Bavasi: "No, Mr. Kroc. The price is $4 million."

"Four million?"

Joan Kroc, the owner's wife, overheard the conversation, which started a ship-to-ship conversation.

But Ray Kroc, not to be dissuaded, provided his approval. Bavasi returned to the meeting and told Cherry he had a deal.

Unbeknownst to the Padres, the New York Yankees had entered the picture seemingly moments after the two sides had struck a deal.

The Yankees offered $3.75 million and convinced Cherry that New York would be a better place for Hunter.

But there was still the matter of getting out of the contract with the Padres. As lawyers were going over the deal line by line, Kroc's reps asked for one more thing: for Hunter to be a spokesman for McDonald's restaurants in the Southeast.

It amounted to a counteroffer.

"Cherry seized the opportunity to get out," Bavasi said. "Kroc went ballistic. I thought I would be fired. The lawyers understood what was going on, though."

Hunter signed with the Yankees, who made the announcement on New Year's Eve.

Reflecting on it all 20 years later, Bavasi said, "Isolate that signing and it tells you all you need to know about how baseball got in the mess it is in. All of this was created and sustained by the owners themselves. It was simply a complete lack of self-restraint.

"I saw Catfish Hunter with a Styrofoam cup in his hand. He didn't have a gun to my head."

The Padres would be used as leverage time and again over the next five years by free agents. The Players would get their prices bid up by the Padres, among others, then go sign somewhere else.

Pitcher Andy Messersmith teased San Diego fans in the spring of 1976 before signing with the Braves. So did slugger Reggie Jackson at the end of the year. And so did all-time hits leader Pete Rose in 1978 before signing with the Phillies.

The Padres did sign closer Rollie Fingers and outfielder Gene Tenace in 1976. Both had been Oakland teammates of Hunter's. Perhaps that was some consolation.

Draft Flops

In 2013, ESPN's Dan Szymborski declared the Padres the worst-drafting team in baseball.

Ever.

It's not too difficult to see how he reached that conclusion. The drafts in general have been bad from top to bottom. The first round specifically has been horrendous.

The Padres have struggled ever since making their first pick—high school first baseman Randy Elliott.

Elliott was the Padres' first-round pick (24th selection overall) in the 1969 draft. He reached the majors in 1972 and batted .207 in 27 games for the Padres.

At least he made the majors.

The Padres had the first overall pick in 2004 and used it on shortstop Matt Bush, a hometown star from San Diego's Mission Bay High.

Bush was involved in a bar fight in Arizona shortly after signing his $3.15 million bonus. Several incidents followed before the team released him. Bush never reached the major leagues, and the Padres often are reminded they passed on future All-Star pitchers Justin Verlander and Jered Weaver to take him.

The Sporting News rated Bush No. 2 among the worst first overall picks in history (behind only Yankees pitcher Brien Taylor in 1991).

Padres third baseman Dave Roberts, the first overall pick in 1972 out of the University of Oregon, was the No. 12 worst pick of all time on *The Sporting News* list.

Roberts signed the day after he was drafted by the Padres and made his major league debut the same day. Roberts batted .244

with five home runs and 33 RBIs that season. He had 21 homers the following season but never approached that figure again. In fact, he struggled to a .167 average in 1974 and spent much of the next four seasons going back and forth between the minors and the majors.

Like Roberts, high school catcher Mike Ivie also was a first overall pick in the draft. Ivie was a high school catcher out of Georgia who was selected in 1970. He was expected to be a catcher who hit for power, but Ivie developed a problem throwing the ball back to the pitcher. The team tried him as a corner infielder and even left field before finally giving up and trading him to the Giants in 1978.

He played in 403 games over parts of five seasons with the Padres. Ivie never did reach double figures in homers in San Diego, although he was a run producer with 70 RBIs in 1976 and 66 RBIs in 1977.

The Padres didn't fare any better with pitchers. In 1971, they selected right-hander Jay Franklin out of Virginia's James Madison High. Franklin received a September call-up at the end of the season and appeared in three games. He never pitched in the majors again.

The Padres had the second overall pick four years later and used it on Mike Lentz, a left-hander out of Washington's Juanita High. Lentz never reached the majors.

In 1977, outfielder Brian Greer from California's Sonora High was the Padres' first pick. His major league career lasted just five games. He had four at-bats. No hits.

Other first-round picks who never really panned out included Georgia college outfielder Jeff Pyburn (1980), Miami college catcher Frank Castro (1981), Texas high school left-hander Robbie Beckett (1990), Florida high school right-hander Greg Anthony (1991), Virginia high school shortstop Matt Halloran (1996), and Florida high school shortstop Kevin Nicholson (1997).

In 1999, the Padres had six first-round picks—outfielder Vince Faison; catcher Nick Trzesniak; and pitchers Gerik Baxter, Omar Ortiz, Casey Burns, and Mike Bynum—most of them coming as compensation for losing free agents off their 1998 World Series team.

Bynum is the only one who reached the major leagues. Baxter's life was cut tragically short two years after he was drafted when he died in a car accident.

The team continued to be snakebit into the 2000s.

Its most successful selection was Clemson shortstop Khalil Greene in 2002. He received a September call-up the following season and soon became a fixture at the position.

Greene spent six seasons with the team—setting a club record for a shortstop with 27 homers in 2007—but developed social anxiety disorder. He was traded to St. Louis after the 2008 season and was out of baseball a year later.

The Padres failed to sign right-hander Karsten Whitson, their first-round pick in 2010, and catcher Brett Austin, one of their first-round picks in 2011.

There were some occasions where the Padres identified and drafted talented players but couldn't get them to sign. First baseman Todd Helton was drafted in 1992 but went to college at Tennessee instead. He was drafted and signed by Colorado three years later and spent his entire 17-year career with the Rockies.

Third baseman Troy Glaus was drafted in 1994 out of Carlsbad High in north San Diego County. Glaus opted to attend UCLA instead and was drafted and signed by the Angels in 1997 before embarking on a 13-year big-league career.

It wasn't all bad.

Minnesota's Dave Winfield, selected by the Padres in the first round of the 1973 draft, did make the Hall of Fame.

47 Chris Gwynn's Big Hit

The Dodgers were done with Chris Gwynn after the 1995 season, but Chris Gwynn wasn't done with the Dodgers.

And for that, the Padres—and their fans—are eternally grateful.

The Padres were two games behind the Dodgers with three games to play coming into the final weekend of the 1996 season. That meant they needed to win each of the three games at Dodger Stadium to win the National League West championship.

"We went in there thinking we were going to sweep them," Gwynn said. "As it went on, they started to feel the pressure because they saw it slipping away."

The Padres opened the series with a 10-inning, 5–2 win compliments of a Ken Caminiti double. Tony Gwynn's eighth-inning single drove in two runs for a 4–2 win the following day.

"Then it's like, they're in trouble, and they know it," Chris Gwynn said.

That set up a winner-take-all game for the division. A sellout crowd of 53,270 Dodgers partisans watched the teams play 10 scoreless innings.

With Steve Finley and Caminiti on base in the 11th inning, Chris Gwynn was sent to the plate as a pinch hitter against Dodgers pitcher Chan Ho Park.

"I remember going to the plate, trying to relax," Chris said. "I knew Chan Ho from when he came up as a rookie when I was with the Dodgers. He had overpowering stuff at times.

"I was just going to be a situational hitter, relax and let my natural ability take over."

When Chris saw Park coming with a change-up, a great confidence came over him.

Wow, he thought. *I'm going to hit this ball awfully hard.*

And he did. Chris lined a double to right-center between center fielder Wayne Kirby and right fielder Raul Mondesi. Finley and Caminiti both scored for a 2–0 victory that completed a three-game sweep and delivered the second division title in the Padres' 28-year history.

Tony Gwynn wrapped up the season that day with a .353 average, giving him his seventh batting title. But after the game, he said, "Today, I'm just Chris Gwynn's anonymous brother."

It was a rare moment for the Gwynns to celebrate on the field. They were born nearly 4½ years apart, so Chris and Tony never played on the same team. Not in Little League. Not at Long Beach Poly High. Not at San Diego State.

Chris spent a decade in the Dodgers organization, beginning when they selected him in the first round of the 1985 draft out of SDSU. The Dodgers decided not to re-sign Chris after the 1995 season. The Padres picked him up three months before the 1996 season began.

"Being able to get that hit after playing there for so long was special for me," he said. "Deep down inside I think the Dodgers fans kind of gave me a pass because it was me."

It would be the final season of Chris' 10-year career. It didn't exactly go the way he might have envisioned. Chris came to the plate batting .169, his 99 plate appearances coming in a reserve role.

One swing of the bat set aside a season of struggles, setting off a celebration on the field that the Padres carried into the clubhouse.

As much as it meant to the franchise, it may have meant even more to the Gwynns.

"It's special because we were able to do something together," Chris said. "For once in our lives. For once."

Two decades later, it remains an unforgettable moment.

"Honest to God," Chris said, "when I go downtown in San Diego somewhere, somebody will recognize me and say, 'Thanks for the hit in '96.'

"They don't remember what I hit that season. They just remember that I got that hit. It's funny how that works."

48 Mark Davis

Mark Davis wasn't exactly an afterthought in the seven-player mid-season trade that sent him from the Giants to the Padres.

But when Davis came to the Padres in that 1987 deal, the names most people paid attention to were that of outfielder Kevin Mitchell and pitchers Dave Dravecky and Craig Lefferts.

Those were the players the Padres gave up to get third baseman Chris Brown and pitchers Keith Comstock and Mark Grant.

And Davis. Who?

The 26-year-old left-hander made 43 appearances out of the Padres bullpen the remainder of the 1987 season. Most of them were in middle relief, Davis hanging around just twice to pick up saves.

The following year, Davis emerged as the club's closer. He collected 28 saves and made the 1988 All-Star team.

In 1989, Davis took it to another level. His 44 saves (along with a 1.85 ERA and 92 strikeouts in 92⅔ innings) established a Padres record, one shy of Bruce Sutter's National League mark.

It was an emotional season for Davis, whose father was dying of prostate cancer. Winning the 1989 National League Cy Young Award provided some solace.

"The award means a lot to me, don't get me wrong," Davis said, "but more than anything, I wanted this for my father. He's been talking about it for a while, and I'm just so happy I was able to come through for him."

Davis was the third Padres pitcher to win the Cy Young Award, joining Randy Jones (1976) and Gaylord Perry (1978). Jake Peavy (2007) made it a quartet two decades later.

Davis was very emotional at a press conference to announce the award, holding back tears and pausing to compose himself.

"There are many people who share in this award for me," Davis continued, "but it's just that my father has seen me ever since I put my first glove on. It's nice for him to be here, or at least close by to know what's happening. It makes it very, very special."

Davis became the fourth closer to win the NL Cy Young, joining the Dodgers' Mike Marshall (1974), the Cubs' Sutter (1979), and the Phillies' Steve Bedrosian (1987). The Dodgers' Eric Gagne (2003) is the only closer to win it since.

Davis was a free agent following the 1989 season. He fully expected to re-sign with the Padres. His salary in 1989 was $600,000. He was due a substantial raise, but it went even beyond his expectations when the market for pitchers exploded.

Davis chose a four-year, $13 million deal with the Kansas City Royals. His $3.25 million annual salary was the highest in baseball history.

Things were never the same after his Cy Young season, however.

Davis was ineffective his first two months with the Royals, blowing four of nine save opportunities and losing the closer's role to Jeff Montgomery. Kansas City traded Davis to Atlanta two years later.

Davis, who returned to the Padres for the 1993–94 seasons, saved only 15 games over the last eight years—including the 1993–94 seasons back with the Padres—of his career.

49 A.J. Preller's 36-Hour Makeover

Hours before the first pitch of the 2015 season, Padres outfielder Matt Kemp sat in the visitors' dugout at Dodger Stadium wearing a T-shirt that read: "Rockstar GM."

The shirt also pictured the hair and eyebrows of A.J. Preller, the Padres' rookie general manager.

Kemp had used the "Rockstar GM" phrase during an introductory press conference at Petco Park.

The right fielder was the first piece in a massive makeover for the Padres. Much of it came during a 36-hour period in which Preller wheeled and dealed. He recruited five other teams in trades that included more than two dozen players.

The flurry of trades brought national attention to the Padres and rekindled the hopes of the fan base for the team to be a contender.

The Kemp trade was finalized on December 18, 2014, sending catcher Yasmani Grandal and right-handers Joe Wieland and Zach Eflin to the Dodgers for catcher Tim Federowicz and Kemp. Oh, and $32 million to offset the $107 million owed to the outfielder.

That same day, the Padres traded right-handers Jesse Hahn and R.J. Alvarez to Oakland for catcher Derek Norris, right-hander Seth Streich, and cash.

On December 19, a three-team trade was engineered, with the Padres sending right-hander Joe Ross and shortstop Trea Turner to Washington and catcher Rene Rivera and first baseman Jake Bauers to Tampa Bay. The Rays also got outfielder Steven Souza, right-hander Burch Smith, and left-hander Travis Ott from the Nationals.

The Padres got four players from the Rays—outfielder Wil Myers, catcher Ryan Hanigan, left-hander Jose Castillo, and right-hander Gerardo Reyes.

The Padres then traded Hanigan to Boston for third baseman Will Middlebrooks.

Preller still wasn't done dealing. He contacted Atlanta to acquire outfielder Justin Upton and right-hander Aaron Northcraft in exchange for left-hander Max Fried, second baseman Jace Peterson, third baseman Dustin Peterson, and outfielder Mallex Smith.

It was a dizzying display not seen in San Diego in two decades—when a 12-player trade with Houston brought Ken Caminiti and Steve Finley to the Padres.

The offseason euphoria was boosted again in February with the signing of free-agent right-hander James Shields, and still again on

Padres GM A.J. Preller (far left) made so many moves during the winter of 2014–15 that the stage got kind of crowded when Preller and manager Bud Black (far right) welcomed this quartet—(left to right) outfielder Justin Upton, catcher Derek Norris, third baseman Will Middlebrooks, and outfielder Wil Myers—to San Diego. (Kirk Kenney)

the eve of the 2015 season opener when closer Craig Kimbrel was acquired (along with outfielder Melvin Upton Jr.) from Atlanta.

But it was that 36-hour period in December that changed the face(s) of the franchise.

On Opening Day, the starting lineup included Upton, Myers, and Kemp from left to right in the outfield; Middlebrooks at third base; and Norris behind the plate.

The buzz translated into a 265,000 bump in attendance at Petco Park.

The Padres' overall record didn't receive a similar boost, however. In fact, the team's 74–88 record in 2015 was actually three games worse than the 77–85 mark it managed in 2014.

 # The Fire Sale

Pinching pennies is one thing.

But what about stringing Christmas lights along a bunch of potted plants in the lobby because you're too cheap to buy a tree?

That takes things to an entirely different level.

This was the backdrop for the Padres during the 1993 season, which would come to be referred to as the Fire Sale.

Television producer Tom Werner was part of a 15-person ownership group that purchased the Padres from Joan Kroc in 1990. Within two years the owners had gone about gutting the team to save money on payroll.

The Padres' 1992 Opening Day payroll was $29 million. It had been slashed to $11 million—the lowest in the majors—by the middle of the 1993 season. The team had 13 players making the major league minimum of $109,000.

The Padres, who had finished with winning records four of the previous five seasons, plummeted to 61–101 in 1993, and they finished 43 games out of first place.

"What we're doing isn't right, but there's nothing I can do about it," Padres right fielder Tony Gwynn said in the midst of the selloff. "I'm not bad-mouthing anyone. But when you make moves to save money, you don't send the right signals to the team or the fans. Then you're in scary territory.

"Everyone in baseball knows what's going on. The baseball vultures are flying above the Padres. They know we're not going to pay everyone, they know we don't have much leverage, so they're playing Pluck the Padres."

The selloff actually began late in the 1992 season when pitcher Craig Lefferts was traded to Baltimore for a pair of minor leaguers.

Closer Randy Myers and catcher Benito Santiago left as free agents after the season, not even receiving offers from the Padres.

Less than a month after the season ended, All-Star shortstop Tony Fernandez was traded to the New York Mets.

The Padres sent out a letter to season ticket holders over the winter promising to make every effort to keep outfielder Darrin Jackson, then traded him right before the 1993 season began. A class-action lawsuit resulted, and the Padres had to offer refunds to any ticket holders who wished to be reimbursed.

Padres GM Joe McIlvaine couldn't bear to preside over the dismantling of the team. He resigned in early June and was replaced by Randy Smith, who became the youngest GM in the baseball.

A month later, Smith traded third baseman Gary Sheffield and left-hander Rich Rodriguez to the Florida Marlins for three unknown pitchers, two minor leaguers, and a rookie with two wins and two saves.

Sheffield, the 1992 National League batting champion, was traded the same day he had been named to the Padres' 25th Anniversary Dream Team.

"To have to leave under these circumstances is tough," Sheffield said as he collected his things in the clubhouse. "It's not fair to the fans or the city. I figure if you can't afford a team, you should sell it and not use us as bait. Basically, that's what they're doing, and that's what I feel like, bait."

First baseman Fred McGriff, the 1992 NL home-run champion, was traded to Atlanta for three prospects. Only two of them reached the majors. Pitcher Donnie Elliott never won a game. Outfielder Melvin Nieves batted .207 with 17 homers and 45 RBIs over three seasons.

Finally, pitchers Bruce Hurst and Greg Harris were traded to Colorado. At least those received in return—catcher Brad Ausmus and pitchers Andy Ashby and Doug Bochtler—would prove to be productive.

The only star left in the lineup was Gwynn. The only remaining standout on the mound was right-hander Andy Benes.

"No, I do not think it was a baseball deal," Gwynn said after the Sheffield trade. "The decisions they make, they have to answer for. I'm as perplexed as anyone. To see Sheffield go just crushes you. He's 24. He's everything you're looking for in a franchise player."

Through it all, there was one saving grace.

One of those young pitchers acquired in the Sheffield trade turned out to be a right-hander named Trevor Hoffman.

51 Trevor Hoffman

The so-called Fire Sale in the early 1990s represented one of the darkest periods in Padres history.

There was one saving grace.

Trevor Hoffman.

The 25-year-old right-hander was acquired in 1993 when the Padres made a midseason trade with the Florida Marlins to dump the salary of All-Star third baseman Gary Sheffield.

The Padres sent pitcher Rich Rodriguez with Sheffield to the Marlins and received Hoffman and minor league pitchers Andres Berumen and Jose Martinez in return.

Berumen and Martinez won a total of two games for the Padres.

The way Hoffman's first appearance went for the Padres, it didn't look like he was going to do much better.

Who knew he would go on to a Hall of Fame–worthy career with 601 saves, second all-time in major league history?

Hoffman had two saves to his credit when he arrived in San Diego. And he heard boos from Padres fans the first time he walked off the mound at Jack Murphy Stadium.

A day after the trade, Hoffman came into a one-run game against Cincinnati in the eighth inning and gave up three runs. The Padres went from trailing 3–2 to losing 6–2.

"They had a right to boo," Hoffman said. "I didn't perform up to anyone's expectations, and I have to improve on that. It won't take much to improve on this performance."

Two days later, Hoffman blew his first save opportunity with the Padres, failing to hold a 1–0 lead against the Reds.

Hoffman had been the key piece in the trade.

Padres manager Jim Riggleman had requested Hoffman be part of the package for Sheffield.

"Above everybody else," Riggleman said.

Padres GM Randy Smith put a positive spin on it.

"Trevor Hoffman improves our bullpen immediately," Smith said. "With Hoffman and (Gene) Harris, I think we have one of the best bullpens in the league."

"It's flattering," Hoffman said, "but unless I do something to deserve it, it doesn't mean squat."

Added Hoffman: "Any time you're wanted, you feel good. I'm flattered—Gary was a great player here and earned all he got. All I can control is how I pitch. I'm here. I'm a Padre. I'm just glad I'm not a third baseman."

Hoffman was a shortstop much of his life before being converted to a pitcher. He grew up in Orange County and was a shortstop at Anaheim's Savanna High, then Cypress Junior College, then Arizona before being drafted by the Cincinnati Reds in the 11th round of the 1989 amateur draft.

The 6'1", 200-pound Hoffman was batting .212 at Class-A Charleston when Reds coaches asked him to become a pitcher. He had a mid-90s fastball then, and the request seemed reasonable.

Florida acquired Hoffman in the 1992 expansion draft. Though the Marlins thought highly of Hoffman, you pretty much give up whatever is necessary to get a power-hitting third baseman who will one day join the 500-homer club.

Harris was the Padres' closer when Hoffman arrived. Trevor was used as the setup man, making 39 appearances out of the bullpen. He picked up three saves for the Padres (blowing two other opportunities) that season.

Hoffman moved into the closer's role the following season—after Harris blew a save two weeks into the season in Pittsburgh and then blew a gasket about not having enough time to warm up—and quickly found his calling.

Padres closer Trevor Hoffman was quick with a smile, whether he was posing for picture day or greeting his catcher after recording another save, but he was all business during the ninth inning. (San Diego Padres)

Hoffman allowed only three runs over his first 22 appearances. He piled up 20 saves before the 1994 strike ended the season.

He would save at least 30 games—including a franchise-record 53 in 1998—in 14 of the following 15 seasons. The only season he didn't do so was in 2003 when his recovery from shoulder surgery limited him to nine September appearances.

It was an injury during the strike—while Hoffman was enjoying a day at the beach, of all things—that prompted the pitcher to develop the pitch that would become his no-so-secret weapon.

Hoffman admitted the fastball was his best pitch. Now it was gone. So he reinvented himself with a devastating change up that more than made up for diminished velocity.

"Most guys right there hit a wall," said former Padres GM Kevin Towers. "Most of it is mental. You have lost your ticket. But maybe because Hoffy really hadn't had that much time invested in pitching, he changed himself.

"When you look at what Trevor has done compared to what has happened to other pitchers in the same situation, it's all the more amazing."

Midway through his career, Hoffman began jogging to the mound with the sound of AC/DC's "Hells Bells" playing over the stadium speakers. It gave new meaning to the term *closing bell*.

When the Padres presented Hoffman with a mint condition 1958 Cadillac convertible years later during a jersey retirement ceremony, he said, "That thing's going to look so good driving around town." He added that "Hells Bells" "might be the only song played in it."

Hoffman climbed the career list for saves as he piled up one after another in a nearly unprecedented show of longevity.

The 53 saves he collected in 1998 tied the NL record. He converted 53-of-54 opportunities that year, including a record-tying 41 straight. His 88.8 save percentage ranked third all-time among players with at least 300 saves.

Hoffman's 479th save broke the major league record held by Lee Smith. Hoffman was the first closer to reach 500 and 600 saves. The second milestone came as a member of the Milwaukee Brewers, where he spent the last two seasons of his 18-year career.

Hoffman's career concluded with 601 saves, then a record and now second only to Mariano Rivera (652) in baseball history.

Those boos from his first appearance had long before been replaced with cheers by the time Hoffman walked off the mound for the last time. He has become one of the Padres' most celebrated and beloved players.

"To you fans...wow...you guys will always have my back," Hoffman said in 2011 during his jersey retirement ceremony. "I appreciated every opportunity I had to step on the mound for you. I can't describe the emotions one person can feel, sitting 450 feet away (in the bullpen), waiting to step out on the warning track and hear that first gong and feel the energy from you guys."

Hoffman established several team records in his 16 years with the Padres, becoming the franchise's career leader in appearances (902), saves (552), ERA (2.76), strikeouts/9 innings (9.72), and opponents' average (.211).

He had seven of the top eight single-season save totals in franchise history—ranging from 42 to his club-record 53 (in 1998)—when he was done. Mark Davis' 44 saves during his 1989 Cy Young season made him the only other closer on the list.

When Hoffman's jersey No. 51 was retired in 2011, it joined those of Steve Garvey (6), Tony Gwynn (19), Dave Winfield (31), Randy Jones (35), and Jackie Robinson (42) above the center-field batter's eye at Petco Park.

In a ceremony to honor Hoffman, Garvey, Gwynn, Jones, and Winfield walked out of a center-field gate to join the celebration.

"Seeing the other men together put it into perspective for me," said Hoffman, who is now a special assistant for the Padres. "I knew I'd soon be part of that group and share the biggest honor an organization can give you."

Hoffman came close to sharing in baseball's biggest honor in 2016 when he received 67.3 percent of the vote in his initial year of eligibility for the National Baseball Hall of Fame. Seventy-five percent is required for election. Hoffman didn't get in on his first crack at Cooperstown, but his strong showing suggested some certainty.

52 Sounding "Hells Bells"

For whom the bells toll.

Hells Bells.

The idea for entrance music for Padres closer Trevor Hoffman didn't come out of left field.

It came out of center.

Padres center fielder Steve Finley's rookie season was in 1989 with the Baltimore Orioles. It coincided with the release of the movie *Major League*. In the film, Charlie Sheen's character enters from the bullpen to the song "Wild Thing." The Orioles appropriated the music for rookie closer Gregg Olson.

Nine years later, Finley had that in mind when he suggested that an entrance song be used to stir the crowd when Hoffman entered in a save situation.

Padres vice president Charles Steinberg, who also had been with the Orioles back in 1989, took up the cause.

"I tried 'Wild Thing' and I was embarrassed," Steinberg said. "You feel like you're reaching into your old bag of tricks.

"I tried another song, the Fabulous Thunderbirds' 'Wrap It Up.' The crowd really wasn't getting it. I spread the word around the office—'We've got to come up with a song.'

"Chip Bowers, a young kid in corporate sales, said, 'You know that 'Hells Bells' by AC/DC?' "I said, 'Uh, no.' He said, 'You've got to give it a try.'"

It was an immediate hit.

Hoffman first entered to the song on July 25, 1998, before closing out a 6–5 win over Houston at Qualcomm Stadium.

Hoffman struck out the Astros' Moises Alou for the Padres victory, tying a major league record with his 41st consecutive save.

Appearances by Hoffman, accompanied by "Hells Bells," would forevermore be known as "Trevor Time."

The Australian hard rock band AC/DC released "Hells Bells" in 1980 as a tribute to lead singer Bon Scott, who had died earlier in the year of acute alcohol poisoning.

The song starts with the slow tolling of a one-ton bell, followed by the double-guitar intro music played by Angus Young and Malcolm Young.

The band originally planned to record the Denison Bell at the Carillon Tower and War Museum in Leicestershire, England. But each time the bell tolled, pigeons nesting in the bell tower would fly out. Their flapping wings ruined the sound of the bell.

Another bell—this one uninhabited by birds—was located and the song was completed.

Hoffman is forever grateful.

"The adrenaline starts to flow with the anticipation of the bells," he said.

53 Trevor's 500th Save

They say one of the beauties of baseball is that every time you go to a game there's the possibility of witnessing something that's never been done before.

That was the case when the Padres beat the Dodgers 5–2 at Petco Park on June 6, 2007.

The occasion was Padres closer Trevor Hoffman's 500th career save, a moment 15 years in the making.

"It's been a long time, hasn't it?" Hoffman said to the cheering crowd of 31,541 after the game. "I'm honored to put this uniform on and perform in front of y'all."

Hoffman had become baseball's all-time saves leader with his 479th save the previous year. It came in the Padres' final home game of the 2006 season, when Hoffman closed out a 2–1 win over Pittsburgh to eclipse Lee Smith's record 478 saves.

Hoffman added three more saves by the end of the season, giving him 482 coming into the 2007 campaign.

Hoffman, who saved at least 30 games in a season 14 times, could get 18 saves with his eyes closed. So it was no surprise that he was moving in on the milestone before midseason.

He was at 499 when the Dodgers came calling. The Padres had a three-run lead entering the ninth inning. "Hells Bells" sounded to summon Hoffman from the bullpen.

He allowed a leadoff double to Nomar Garciaparra before retiring Jeff Kent and Luis Gonzalez on ground-outs.

That brought the Dodgers' Russell Martin to the plate. Hoffman ended the game by striking out Martin looking with a low fastball, setting off a celebration.

Padres catcher Josh Bard came out from behind the plate and gave Hoffman a hug.

Heading into the big moment, Padres left-hander David Wells had said: "It's going to be awesome to see that five-zero-zero up on that board. I'm just going to stare at him and see how he takes it in."

Wells had a good view for the occasion. He and outfielder Mike Cameron hoisted Hoffman on their shoulders surrounded by teammates as cheers rained down from the stands.

"It's cool," said Padres starting pitcher Greg Maddux, who picked up his 338th career victory in the game. "I had a chance to witness history. The guy's doing something nobody in baseball has ever done. For me personally, I felt privileged to see it."

A few days earlier the question had been raised about how 500 saves compared with 500 home runs.

"Well, nobody's gotten 500 saves," Maddux said. "A lot of people have 500 homers. He's setting the bar."

Hoffman raised the bar to 600 saves—601 to be exact—before his career concluded in 2010 with the Brewers. Only the Yankees' Mariano Rivera (652) saved more games.

Atta Baby!

A crowd of 31,137 showed up for a Giants–Padres game at Petco Park late in the 2015 season.

Make that 31,138.

Petco welcomed its first baby in the ballpark's 12-year history during the Padres' 5–4 walk-off win on September 24, 2015.

A baby boy was born in the third inning in the Palm Court Plaza—now the Bud Selig Hall of Fame Plaza—beyond the left-field stands.

Jaime Stiles said she was in labor for 28 hours with her first son, Grayson, so she wasn't concerned about going to the ballgame when contractions began 90 minutes before the game started. In fact, she viewed it as a welcome distraction.

So Stiles and her mother, Estelle Stiles, drove downtown and purchased tickets. The contractions started getting stronger as they entered the ballpark.

"Honestly, we didn't even make it to our seats," Jaime said.

They thought about going back to the car and heading to the hospital, but that wasn't an option.

"All of the sudden, it was go time," Jaime said. "It happened so fast I didn't really have time to think about it. It was seriously from zero to 60 in like 30 minutes. I was in total shock. It was the craziest thing that I could've ever imagined. There it was, me having a baby at Petco Park."

Donna Borowy, an on-call nurse at Petco Park who is also a midwife, assisted with the delivery.

"She was asking if she would make it to the hospital, and I checked her cervix and I said, 'Probably not,'" Borowy said. "I said, 'Your bag of water breaks, you're gonna have that baby here.' Bag of water broke within minutes, had the baby three minutes later. This is the youngest Petco fan that we'll ever have."

Levi Michael Stiles—whose key stats were 6 pounds, 14 ounces, 20.5 inches—was a big hit in his major league debut.

"It was fast. He was crying—he was pink and perfect," Jaime said. "Everybody was cheering. It was really kind of funny. It was an out-out-body, very surreal experience."

Stiles was taken to the hospital after the birth. Members of the Pad Squad and the Friar mascot visited the family there the following day. They brought gifts that included a No. 15 Padres camouflage jersey with LEVI on the back and stuffed animals, among other things.

It was some story, and will be for years to come.

After all, how many people can say they attended their first major league game the day they were born?

The 5.5 Hole

Wee Willie Keeler said "hit 'em where they ain't" more than half a century before Tony Gwynn stepped to the plate.

Gwynn definitely had that thought in mind, though, when he created an updated term based on the same theory.

Tony called it the "5.5 hole."

Those familiar with scoring a baseball game are aware that the third baseman is number 5 and the shortstop number 6 in scorekeeping shorthand. Logically, the 5.5 hole would be midway between them.

It is the spot where Gwynn lined so many of his 3,141 hits during a Hall of Fame career.

Gwynn even had 5.5 stitched onto the tongues of his cleats.

On the day Gwynn retired, the Padres etched the number 5.5 into the infield dirt between third and short at Qualcomm Stadium.

While he would turn on more pitches later in his career, Gwynn made his living stroking the ball into left field past the outstretched gloves of those left-side infielders.

"My bread and butter," he would say.

Years later, when Gwynn was working as a Padres broadcaster, he was in the booth one evening when the Padres' Kevin

Kouzmanoff stepped to the plate. Kouzmanoff hit a liner to the third baseman for an out.

Gwynn's broadcast partner said: "Kouz hit it hard, can't ask anything more of him there, right Tony?"

"He hit it hard," Gwynn said, "but they've had a man there for 200 years."

Gwynn realized that better than anyone. Padres fans have a constant reminder.

The bronze statue of Mr. Padre located in Petco's Park at the Park captures Gwynn in midswing, the bat head dropped to carve a ball into left field.

It's obvious that Gwynn is sending another pitch the other way through the 5.5 hole.

56 Prop C Gets an Aye

There were plenty of speeches filled with persuasive arguments, but it was deeds, not words, that paved the way for Petco Park.

The Padres picked the right year to win a team-record 98 games. They picked the right year to beat Houston and Atlanta in the National League playoffs. They picked the right year to reach the World Series.

Yes, 1998 was a very good year.

A four-game sweep by the Yankees did nothing to diminish it.

Election Day came two weeks after the Series ended.

At Election Central in downtown San Diego's Golden Hall, a large board tracks local, state, and federal elections. Of particular interest to baseball fans on this night was Proposition C.

Here's how it appeared on the board:

PROP C–CITY OF SAN DIEGO–DOWNTOWN
REDEVELOPMENT AND CONSTRUCTION
OF A BALLPARK.
YES (x) 195,490 59.64
NO 132,272 40.36

The measure had passed in a landslide.

After the results were final, ballpark supporters gathered at the U.S. Grant Hotel two blocks away.

Their cheers were not as deafening as the ones that carried the Padres through the 1998 postseason. Of course, there were probably 58,000 fewer people in the ballroom than the ballpark.

Those present were no less euphoric than the fans had been during the playoffs.

Padres owner John Moores and CEO Larry Lucchino were overjoyed.

"I owe a lot of people a lot of gratitude," Lucchino said. "I'm really excited about what lies ahead. A large cross-section of people endorsed us."

Moores was equally ecstatic.

"It was just a remarkable, remarkable experience," he said. "A glorious, glorious payoff. We're clearly on the road to making this one of the great cities for baseball in the Western Hemisphere."

The vote basically saved baseball for San Diego.

Aging Qualcomm Stadium was now more suitable for football and lacked the modern amenities baseball fans had come to expect.

The project still had to survive 19 legal challenges that were responsible for delaying funding and causing a two-year delay in construction. But the $450 million ballpark opened to rave reviews in 2004.

57 Benito's 34-Game Hitting Streak

Trivia question: Who holds the Padres record for longest consecutive-game hitting streak?

Tip: It's not Tony Gwynn.

Gwynn held the record with a 25-game streak in 1983. It was broken four years later by rookie catcher Benito Santiago, who put together a 34-game streak from August 25 to October 2 during the 1987 season.

It was the 15th longest streak in major league history and the longest by a rookie, a catcher, or a Latin player.

Gwynn, for one, was impressed by the streak.

"Every player but the catcher gets to rest and contemplate his next at-bat," Gwynn said.

The streak was icing on the cake for a season in which Santiago batted .300 with 18 homers, 79 RBIs, and 21 stolen bases. He was a unanimous choice for National League Rookie of the Year.

The streak began with a three-run homer off Neal Heaton in a 5–1 home victory over Montreal.

Santiago broke Gwynn's team record with a fourth-inning single at Cincinnati.

"I think it's great," Gwynn said after that game. "It's a great capper to the kind of season he is having. I hope he keeps it going. I really think he's going to hit in the rest of the games, so when the season starts next year everyone is still going to be talking about it."

Santiago claimed the modern-day rookie record two games later with a 2-for-4 performance against the Dodgers in Los Angeles.

He passed Guy Curtright, who set the mark with the 1943 Chicago White Sox.

"This is very exciting. I don't know what to say," Santiago said.

Santiago's streak reached 32 games with his most unusual hit—an eighth-inning bunt that caught Cincinnati on its heels. It's no wonder. It was the first bunt hit of Santiago's career.

A first-inning double off the Dodgers' Fernando Valenzuela extended the streak to 34 games.

The streak ended the following game against the Dodgers' Orel Hershiser, who got Santiago on a strikeout, ground-out, and fly-out in his first three at-bats.

"I bore down each time he came up," said Hershiser. "Every time he batted the fans went nuts, and I knew this was all the writers had to write about."

Said Santiago: "Orel Hershiser is one of the toughest pitchers I see. He gave me nothing good enough for base hits."

Santiago never got a fourth chance that night. The Padres won the home game 1–0, so they didn't bat in the ninth inning. Santiago was due up second.

"I'm glad it is over," Santiago said. "I am happy for everything. We win...it is better for the team. Sooner or later, someone gets me out. It was a quick game...only three at-bats, but that is all right.

"I feel great inside; I am happy for the year."

58 Tony's 3,000th Hit

Tony Gwynn was a student of the game when he was still a student. Baseball milestones were among the things that got Gwynn's attention.

"As a kid growing up, I remember seeing Roberto Clemente get his 3,000th hit and seeing Lou Brock get his 3,000th hit," Gwynn said. "In my case, that always seemed unreachable.

"But as you start playing you ask yourself if that's a number that you could shoot at."

Nearly 1,300 major league players have collected at least 1,000 career hits. Getting to 2,000 hits pares the list to 276 players.

And reaching the 3,000-hit milestone? Only 15 players had accomplished the feat when Gwynn reached the major leagues in 1982.

"My dad was really big on it," Gwynn said. "He said, 'If you want to do it, you can do it.'"

The comments came not long after Gwynn collected his 2,000[th] hit in 1993. Charles Gwynn Sr. passed away the following year.

In 1995, sitting in the Padres dugout on a summer afternoon before batting practice, Gwynn took a moment to consider what it would mean to collect 3,000 hits.

"Getting there is important because I know a lot of people would like to see me do it," Gwynn said. "I know my dad would have loved to see me do it. My dad is still my driving force to want to get there. But if I don't get there, I don't think there's many people who could say I wasn't very consistent and, in my time, in my era, in my league, one of the best."

There was no way Gwynn wouldn't make it, although he had to travel to another country to get there.

Gwynn admitted pressing in the run-up to the big hit during the summer of 1999.

He was 13 hits away when the Padres began a six-game homestand at the end of July. *No problem*, Gwynn thought. He got seven hits, so he was still six hits away when the Padres hit the road. First there were three games in St. Louis.

Gwynn got five hits in the series against the Cardinals, leaving him at 2,999. He had a chance to get No. 3,000 in the same game that the Cardinals' Mark McGwire belted his 500th home run.

It wasn't to be.

So the Padres continued their road trip, heading north for Canada. This time, Gwynn got things out of the way without delay.

Gwynn looped a first-inning single off Expos right-hander Dan Smith before 13,540 fans at Olympic Stadium in Montreal to reach 3,000 hits.

Longtime Padres broadcaster Jerry Coleman had the call: "There's a drive, right-center field, base hit. And there it is. Ohhhhhh, doctor! You can hang a star on that, baby. A star for the ages for Tony Gwynn. No. 3,000."

Gwynn hugged first-base coach Davey Lopes as Padres teammates and coaches ran out to first base to congratulate him.

Gwynn also received a hug from the first-base umpire, which may have seemed odd to many observers. But the ump was Kerwin Danley, who was one of Gwynn's college teammates at San Diego State.

Gwynn also hugged his wife Alicia and mother Vendella when they came out to first base to congratulate him.

"Happy birthday," Gwynn whispered in his mother's ear.

"August 6," Gwynn said. "On the same day six years apart, I got 2,000 and 3,000, both of them on my mom's birthday. It just kind of worked out."

Gwynn was the 22nd player to reach the milestone. Notably, Gwynn was the first National League player in 20 years to reach the milestone. St. Louis' Lou Brock did it in 1979, followed by seven American League hitters before Gwynn.

The ranks had swelled to 29 players by the time the Yankees' Alex Rodriguez joined the club during the 2015 season.

"This is the one sport that really tracks how well the guys of today do with the guys of yesterday," Gwynn said a few years after his 2001 retirement. "When you get to 3,000, you're tied with Roberto Clemente.

The 3,000-Hit Club

Hits	Player	3,000th Hit Details
4,256	Pete Rose, Reds	Single off Montreal's Steve Rogers, at Cincinnati, May 5, 1978
4,189	Ty Cobb, Tigers	Single off Red Sox's Elmer Myers, at Detroit, August 19, 1921
3,771	Hank Aaron, Braves	Single off Reds' Wayne Simpson, at Cincinnati, May 17, 1970
3,630	Stan Musial, Cardinals	Double off Cubs' Moe Drabowsky, at Chicago, May 13, 1958
3,514	Tris Speaker, Indians	Single off Senators' Tom Zachary, at Cleveland, May 17, 1925
3,465	Derek Jeter, Yankees	Homer off Rays' David Price, at New York, July 9, 2011
3,420	Honus Wagner, Pirates	Double off Phillies' Erskine Mayer, at Philadelphia, June 9, 1914
3,419	Carl Yastrzemski, Red Sox	Single off Yankees' Jim Beattie, at Boston, September 12, 1979
3,319	Paul Molitor, Twins	Triple off Royals' Jose Rosado, at Kansas City, September 16, 1996
3,315	Eddie Collins, White Sox	Single off Tigers' Rip Collins, at Detroit, June 3, 1925
3,283	Willie Mays, Giants	Single off Expos' Mike Wegener, at San Francisco, July 18, 1970
3,255	Eddie Murray, Indians	Single off Twins' Mike Trombley, at Minneapolis, June 30, 1995
3,252	Nap Lajoie, Indians	Double off Yankees' Marty McHale, at Cleveland, September 27, 1914
3,184	Cal Ripken Jr., Orioles	Single off Twins' Hector Carrasco, at Minneapolis, April 15, 2000

Hits	Player	3,000ᵗʰ Hit Details
3,154	George Brett, Royals	Single off Angels' Tim Fortugno, at Anaheim, September 30, 1992
3,152	Paul Waner, Braves	Single off Pirates' Rip Sewell, Boston, June 19, 1942
3,142	Robin Yount, Brewers	Single off Indians' Jose Mesa, at Milwaukee, September 9, 1992
3,141	Tony Gwynn, Padres	Single off Montreal's Dan Smith, in Montreal, August 6, 1999
3,110	Dave Winfield, Twins	Single off Athletics' Dennis Eckersley, at Minneapolis, September 16, 1993
3,070	Alex Rodriguez, Yankees	Homer off Tigers' Justin Verlander, at New York, June 19, 2015
3,060	Craig Biggio, Astros	Single off Rockies' Aaron Cook, at Houston, June 28, 2007
3,055	Rickey Henderson, Padres	Double off Rockies' John Thomson, at San Diego, October 7, 2001
3,053	Rod Carew, Angels	Single off Twins' Frank Viola, at Anaheim, August 4, 1985
3,023	Lou Brock, Cardinals	Single off Cubs' Dennis Lamp, at St. Louis, August 13, 1979
3,020	Rafael Palmeiro, Orioles	Double off Mariners' Joel Pineiro, at Seattle, July 15, 2005
3,011	Cap Anson, Colts	Unknown
3,010	Wade Boggs, Devil Rays	Homer off Indians' Chris Haney, at Tampa Bay, August 7, 1999
3,007	Al Kaline, Tigers	Double off Orioles' Dave McNally, at Baltimore, September 24, 1974
3,000	Roberto Clemente, Pirates	Double off Mets' Jon Matlack, at Pittsburgh, September 30, 1972

"I think it's a wonderful thing. Only a few guys have the opportunity to get to where Roberto Clemente had gotten to. And once you're there, you're in select company. That's a big deal to me and I hope those other guys feel like it is, and I hope the guys playing today feel like they have something to shoot for."

Rickey's 3,000th Hit

Rickey Henderson offered to sit out the game.

Tony Gwynn wouldn't hear of it.

It was the last day of the 2001 regular season, and the final game of Gwynn's 20-year career.

There were 60,103 fans at Qualcomm Stadium for Gwynn's sendoff.

They got a bonus.

Coming into the game, Henderson was one hit away from becoming the 25th member of one of baseball's most exclusive clubs.

"Of all the things I wanted to have happen today, Rickey getting his 3,000th hit was at the top of the list," Gwynn said.

Henderson got it out of the way in the bottom of the first inning on the first pitch he saw from Colorado's John Thomson, hitting a high fly ball to right field. It fell in between three converging Rockies players just five feet from the foul line.

"It was a miracle to me," Henderson said. "As I'm running, I'm remembering that the hit I got for 3,000 is the same exact hit I got for my first hit."

In Oakland 22 years earlier, Henderson's first hit had been a bloop single to right field off Texas' John Henry Johnson.

Henderson took an extended look toward right field as he made his way between first and second on the hit.

"I wanted to stop and run out and get the ball," Henderson said. "Then I decided to run to second."

Padres teammates and coaches ran out to second base after the hit and manager Bruce Bochy presented the Hall of Famer with a commemorative plaque.

"I wasn't going to play today out of respect to Tony," Henderson said. "But he asked me to do it today."

"I'm so proud of you, Rickey," Gwynn said during postgame remarks to the fans. "I'm so happy for you. And you (fans) had a chance to witness some history. I had wanted to get my 3,000th hit here and couldn't get it done." (He got it in Montreal.) "Rickey did it. What a night. Rickey cruising into second and the guys all running out to him."

Henderson had a history of sharing his big moments with others.

In 1991, he stole the 939th base of his career to pass Lou Brock for career steals. It happened the same day that Texas' Nolan Ryan threw his seventh no-hitter.

Cobb's run-scoring record was tied by Henderson on the very day the Giants' Barry Bonds broke the single-season walks record.

Henderson eclipsed the runs record on the day Bonds hit his 70th homer, which tied the record set three years earlier by the Cardinals' Mark McGwire.

Henderson added another 55 hits the following two seasons before calling it a career.

It was the 3,000th he would remember the most, of course.

Gwynn had pulled Henderson aside hours before the game for some BP, one session in the stadium's indoor cage before taking their turns on the field.

"It was a very sweet thing," Henderson said. "Tony just wanted me and him to go together. We had some fun."

Reaching the milestone made Henderson and Gwynn the second pair of 3,000-hit teammates. They joined Cobb and Tris Speaker, who played together for the 1928 Philadelphia Athletics.

60 12 Hours in Philly

Padres left fielder Phil Plantier was sitting in the visitor's clubhouse at Philadelphia's Veterans Stadium.

Dawn was on the horizon.

"You know when you're a little kid and you talk about playing baseball all night long," Plantier said. "You just want to play until the sun comes up....Well, now that I've done it, I don't ever want to do it again."

The Padres were in Philadelphia for a twi-night doubleheader that became something out of the Twilight Zone.

It was July 2, 1993, and the first game at Veterans Stadium was scheduled to begin at 4:35 PM.

Rain forced the teams to sit around for 70 minutes, pushing first pitch to 5:45. It wasn't clear sailing from there, however.

Two more rain delays came, this time totaling 4:44. The game resumed shortly before midnight.

The Padres posted a 5–2 victory over the Phillies in Game 1, which ended at 1:03 AM. The actual game was played in a brisk 2:34, only to be slowed by rain delays totaling 5:54.

Game 2 began at 1:28 AM.

After Padres starting pitcher Andy Benes threw his first pitch, catcher Kevin Higgins glanced up at home-plate umpire Larry Poncino and said, "Ponce, you want a shot and a beer? It's last call."

Of course the game went extra innings, going into the 10th before Philadelphia earned a split with a 6–5 victory.

Phillies reliever Mitch Williams singled in the winning run, exactly 12 hours, 5 minutes after the day's first pitch.

The game-winning run scored at 4:40 AM, making it the latest—earliest?—a major league game ever ended.

At midnight (and each hour afterward), the sound of bells tolling was played over the PA system to mark the top of the hour.

There were two runners on base in the sixth inning when the bells rang at 3:00 AM. The batter just happened to be the Padres' Derek Bell.

"We thought for sure Derek was going to hit a three-run bomb," Padres right fielder Tony Gwynn said.

But Bell popped out.

About 5,000 people from an original gathering of 54,617 stuck around until the final pitch.

"You've got to have a sense of humor about this," said Gwynn, who watched the second game from the bench because of an abdomen strain. "Sure, we were tired and we were bitching and we didn't feel we should have been out there after the long rain delay. We should have had one win and playing two today. That's how it should have been. All of a sudden we have to play; we've got to finish the first game the next day."

The Padres began getting loopy about 2:00 AM.

"That's when you began to hear comments like, 'That's the best slide I've ever seen at 2 in the morning.' 'Best curveball I ever saw at 3,'" Gwynn said.

The 4:40 AM finish broke the record set by the Mets–Braves game played in 1985 on the Fourth (and 5th) of July. The Mets won 16–13 in a game that went 19 innings, ended at 3:55 AM—and was then followed by fireworks.

61 Rocky Mountain Low

There are those who are still waiting for Colorado's Matt Holliday to touch home plate.

Unfortunately, Tim McClelland is not among them.

The umpire signaled safe, Holliday sliding home with the run that gave Colorado a 13-inning, 9–8 victory in the wild-card tiebreaker game.

Replays were inconclusive on the play at the plate. Even Holliday wasn't sure if he scored after banging into Padres catcher Michael Barrett.

"I don't know," Holliday said afterward. "He hit me pretty good. I got stepped on and banged my chin."

Regardless, the Rockies were headed to the playoffs and the Padres were headed home.

One of the lowest moments in Padres history came in the Mile High City in the 163rd game of the 2007 season. It was the final touch on a promising season that ended painfully, the Padres' post-season plans going poof.

A one-game playoff for the National League wild-card berth was required after San Diego and Colorado finished with identical 89–73 records. The Rockies had won a coin flip some weeks earlier, giving them the right to host a tiebreaker if one was needed.

It wouldn't have come to this had the Padres played better than .500 baseball over the last four weeks of the season.

It wouldn't have come to this had the Rockies not won 13 of 14 games to close out the regular season.

It wouldn't have come to this had Padres closer Trevor Hoffman gotten the last strike in Milwaukee in the second-to-last game of the season. Tony Gwynn Jr., of all people, lined an RBI triple in the ninth to extend a game the Brewers won in extra innings.

And it wouldn't have come to this if the Padres had beaten the Brewers on the last day of the regular season.

But here they were at Coors Field for one deciding game.

Fate still looked like it would favor the Padres. They had ace right-hander Jake Peavy rested and ready.

Peavy was the unanimous choice for the National League Cy Young Award that season, winning pitching's triple crown by leading the league in victories (19), strikeouts (240), and ERA (2.54).

No matter. The Rockies knocked Peavy around like he was pitching BP, scoring six runs on 10 hits in 6⅓ innings.

"This is the best team in baseball right now," Peavy said of Colorado. "They have been for the last month. They've just got something going. Somebody is looking out for that bunch over there."

Colorado scored three runs in the first two innings before Padres first baseman Adrian Gonzalez hit a third-inning grand slam to help the team to a 5–3 lead.

The Rockies scored single runs in the third, fifth, and sixth innings to get back on top 6–5. An RBI double by the Padres' Brian Giles knotted the score 6–6 in the eighth.

It stayed that way until the Padres' Scott Hairston hit a two-run homer in the top of the 13th to provide an 8–6 lead.

Padres manager Bud Black summoned Hoffman, who earlier in the season had become the first pitcher to record 500 saves, to get the final three outs.

"I knew we would fight back," said Rockies first baseman Todd Helton. "But we were going against the greatest closer of all time."

The swiftness with which the Rockies responded was head-spinning.

Leadoff hitter Kaz Matsui doubled. Teammate Troy Tulowitzki doubled him home. Holliday then hit a triple that scored Tulo to tie the game 8–8. Helton was intentionally walked, setting the stage for Jamey Carroll's sacrifice fly to right field.

Giles threw a one-hopper home, but Barrett couldn't handle it. The ball bounced away as Holliday slid in. Barrett retrieved the ball and tagged Holliday. Too late.

"I'm having a hard time expressing myself right now," Hoffman said later. "I wish I could, but I can't after what happened tonight."

He wasn't the only one left speechless.

Wear Camo to a Game

San Diego is a military city, so it makes sense that the Padres would take the lead among major league teams in honoring veterans.

The most visible representation of this is the military-inspired camouflage uniforms worn by Padres players for each Sunday home game at Petco Park. The uniforms have proven popular with fans, too, with many of them wearing camo in the stands for home games in general and the Sunday contests in particular.

The organization created a Military Affairs Department in 1995 and became the first professional sports team to have a military appreciation event a year later. The Padres are the only MLB team to host a Military Opening Day during the first homestand of each season.

Part of the Padres' inspiration for saluting veterans was the daily presence of a war hero in their midst.

Broadcaster Jerry Coleman was a Marine aviator who flew 120 combat missions in World War II and the Korean War.

Coleman was the only active major league player to serve in both wars.

"I can say this again and again," Coleman said when the team unveiled its camouflage uniforms in 2000, "anytime you honor the military, it's all right with me."

The Padres honored World War II and Korean War POWs that same year by awarding them lifetime passes to home games during the regular season. The organization continues to honor other veterans with military appreciation pricing.

"There's such a population of military here, I think it's a great gesture to the people who protect us," said Padres left-hander Sterling Hitchcock, who was the starting pitcher when the team wore camo for the first time.

The Padres dedicated an area beyond right field at Petco called the Flight Deck that honors former major league and Negro League players who served in the military.

According to the Padres, their Director of Military Affairs, Captain John C. (Jack) Ensch, USN, Ret., researched and developed the Military Honor Wall. The centerpiece of the Flight Deck area is a large-scale representation of the USS *Midway*, a decommissioned aircraft carrier moored just a couple of miles from the ballpark at Navy Pier. It serves now as a museum that draws nearly one million visitors a year.

The Padres' Sunday camouflage uniform tradition began in 2008. The players also wear camo for games on Memorial Day, Independence Day, and Labor Day.

The Padres honor active and former military members each game before the second inning, asking those in attendance to stand and be recognized for their service. Padres players and coaches join fans in applauding the men and women who have made such sacrifices for our country.

63 Before It Was the Q

What's in a name?

When it comes to the Padres' first major league home, the name of the stadium depends on the particular year in question.

The minor league Padres played first at Lane Field downtown before moving to Westgate Park in what now is Fashion Valley.

The ballclub moved into San Diego Stadium in 1968 for its final season as the Triple-A Pacific Coast League Padres.

And it was San Diego Stadium where the major league Padres debuted in 1969.

The stadium's first name change came in 1980, when it was renamed San Diego Jack Murphy Stadium, in honor of the *San Diego Union* sports editor.

Murphy wrote columns in the mid-1960s to champion building a 50,000-seat, multipurpose stadium that would provide a larger arena for the Chargers to perform and pave the way for Major League Baseball to come to the city.

Voters approved a ballot measure in 1965 to build the stadium, which opened two years later.

Murphy died of cancer in September of 1980. Within weeks of his death, Mayor Pete Wilson and the San Diego City Council voted to rename the stadium in honor of Murphy. Voters approved the idea the following year.

The stadium was affectionately called "The Murph" for years. Murphy's brother, Bob Murphy, a broadcaster for the New York Mets, continued to call it Jack Murphy Stadium even after the stadium name again was changed in the late 1990s.

When a cash shortfall occurred during a stadium expansion project in 1997, Qualcomm, one of the largest companies in San

Diego, agreed to pay $18 million to bridge the difference. The company received naming rights to the stadium for 20 years in exchange for its contribution.

It ranks among the best naming-rights deals in history. Qualcomm Stadium gave the company tremendous exposure. And it gave the fans another idea for a nickname: they affectionately call the place The Q.

Matt Kemp's Cycle

Matt Kemp must have been the only one who didn't know.

Padres third-base coach Glenn Hoffman was waiting with a smile when the outfielder tripled in the ninth inning off Colorado Rockies reliever Justin Miller.

The triple—along with a home run, single, and double earlier in the game—completed the cycle for Kemp.

"That's the first one," Hoffman said after Kemp slid into third base.

"Yeah, that is my first one," Kemp said.

"No," Hoffman said. "That's the first one for the Padres."

Mark it down.

Padres 9, Rockies 5.

Coors Field.

August 14, 2015.

The first cycle in Padres history. It only took the better part of 47 years and 7,444 games to do it.

"Anytime you make history, it's special," Kemp said.

It seemed like everyone but Kemp knew the Padres were the only team in the majors that never had a batter hit for the cycle or a pitcher throw a no-hitter.

Check one item off the list.

It was the 307th cycle in major league history, 141 of them coming since the Padres joined the National League in 1969.

Cycles by Franchise

(Through 2015 season, original season in parenthesis)

23—Pittsburgh Pirates (1882)
23—San Francisco Giants (1883)
21—Boston Red Sox (1901)
19—St. Louis Cardinals
17—Oakland Athletics (1901)
15—New York Yankees (1901)
14—Minnesota Twins (1901)
11—Chicago Cubs (1876)
10—Detroit Tigers (1901)
10—New York Mets (1962)
10—Texas Rangers (1961)
9—Baltimore Orioles (1901)
9—Cincinnati Reds (1882)
9—Los Angeles Dodgers (1883)
8—Houston Astros (1962)
8—Philadelphia Phillies (1883)
8—Washington Nationals (1969)
7—Cleveland Indians (1901)
7—Colorado Rockies (1993)
7—Los Angeles Angels (1961)
7—Milwaukee Brewers (1969)
6—Arizona Diamondbacks (1998)
6—Atlanta Braves (1876)
6—Kansas City Royals
5—Chicago White Sox
4—Seattle Mariners (1977)
2—Toronto Blue Jays (1977)
1—San Diego Padres (1969)
1—Tampa Bay Rays (1998)
0—Miami Marlins (1993)

The Miami Marlins now are the only active major league team that has never had a player hit for the cycle.

Kemp began his day with a first-inning home run, launching an 0–1 pitch from Rockies starting pitcher Yohan Flande over the center-field fence.

Kemp singled to center off Flande in the third inning. He doubled off reliever Rafael Betancourt in the seventh, the ball sailing over the head of Rockies center fielder Charlie Blackmon.

All Kemp needed coming into the last inning was a triple. Much easier said than done. The Padres had a player come within a hit of the cycle 361 times. The triple was the missing hit in 258 of those occasions.

In the ninth, Kemp hit a 1–0 slider from Miller that appeared headed out of the ballpark. It stayed in, barely, hitting the wall in right-center and caroming back to center into the spot Blackmon had just vacated.

Kemp rounded second base as Blackmon rounded up the ball and threw it to second baseman D.J. LeMahieu, who didn't even attempt a relay throw.

And there it was.

Kemp was initially slow to get out of the batter's box.

"I was actually looking at the ball because I thought I hit a home run, but I didn't get as much as I thought I did," Kemp said.

Rockies third baseman Nolan Arenado had a question for Kemp after he reached third base in the ninth: "Would you rather it have been a home run or a triple?"

Kemp related the question to reporters after the game in the Padres clubhouse.

His answer: "I like home runs, but it was my first cycle…so I think the cycle would be better."

Padres fans couldn't have agreed more.

65 See a Padres Player Pitch a No-No

The website nonohitters.com includes virtually everything anyone would want to know about no-hitters.

And, in the case of Padres fans, something of which they would rather not be reminded.

When the last out of the 2015 season went into the books, a counter on the site clicked once again.

It read 7,490. And counting.

As if the Padres needed to be told that they are the only team in the major leagues that has not had a pitcher throw a no-hitter.

The franchise had three no-hitters during its minor league existence in the Pacific Coast League—getting one from Russ Heman against Vancouver in 1959, Allan Worthington against Hawaii in 1961, and Sam Ellis against Tacoma in 1962.

The Padres have had 28 one-hitters in their history, one of them broken up in the ninth inning and four others that ended in the eighth.

The Montreal Expos, the Padres' National League expansion partner in 1969, got their no-hitter out of the way quickly—in the team's ninth game of existence.

Showoffs.

Right-hander Bill Stoneman did the honors, holding the Phillies hitless in a 7–0 win at Philadelphia. Stoneman threw another no-hitter for the Expos—in a 7–0 home win over the Mets in 1972—for good measure.

The Kansas City Royals and Seattle Pilots joined the American League the same year the Padres and Expos debuted in the National League.

No-Hitters by Team

(Former nicknames/locations of franchise in parenthesis)

25—Dodgers
(Brooklyn Atlantics/Brooklyn Grays/Brooklyn Bridegrooms/Brooklyn Grooms/Brooklyn Superbas/Brooklyn Trolley Dodgers/Brooklyn Robins/Brooklyn Dodgers)

18—Red Sox
(Boston Americans)

18—White Sox
(Chicago White Stockings)

17—Giants
(New York Gothams/New York Giants)

16—Reds
(Cincinnati Red Stockings/Cincinnati Redlegs)

14—Indians
(Cleveland Bluebirds/Cleveland Naps)

14—Braves
(Boston Red Caps/Boston Beaneaters/Boston Doves/Boston Rustlers/Boston Bees/Boston Braves/Milwaukee Braves)

14—Cubs
(Chicago White Stockings/Chicago Colts/Chicago Orphans)

13—Phillies
(Philadelphia Quakers)

11—Astros
(Houston Colt .45's)

11—Athletics
(Philadelphia Athletics/Kansas City Athletics)

11—Yankees
(New York Highlanders/Baltimore Orioles)

10—Angels
(California Angels/Anaheim Angels)

10—Cardinals
(St. Louis Browns/St. Louis Perfectos)

9—Orioles
(Milwaukee Brewers/St. Louis Browns)

7—Twins
(Washington Senators)

7—Tigers

7—Nationals
(Montreal Expos)

6—Pirates
(Pittsburgh Alleghenys)

5—Rangers
(Washington Senators)

5—Marlins
(Florida Marlins)

5—Mariners

4—Royals

2—Diamondbacks

1—Brewers
(Seattle Pilots)

1—Blue Jays

1—Rockies

1—Rays
(Tampa Bay Devil Rays)

1—Mets

0—Padres

The Royals got a no-hitter from Steve Busby in 1973 with a 3–0 victory over Detroit. Busby repeated the feat the following season in a 2–0 win over Milwaukee.

The Pilots moved after one season, becoming the Milwaukee Brewers in 1970.

A generation passed before the team had its first no-hitter, with Juan Nieves performing the feat in 1987 during a 7–0 win over Baltimore.

An 18-year wait for a no-hitter seems substantial, but who are Brewers fans to complain when Padres fans have now waited three decades longer?

The Padres' misery had company until 2012, when Mets pitcher Johan Santana beat St. Louis 8–0 without allowing a hit. That ended a 50-year no-hitter drought for the Mets (whose counter stopped at 8,019), leaving the Padres all to themselves.

There have been 293 no-hitters (including 23 perfect games) in major league history through the 2015 season. In the Padres' 47-year history there have been 126 no-hitters.

Pretty amazing.

Padres fans can go on complaining that the franchise has never had a no-hitter. Or they can look at it another way—maybe they'll have the good fortune to be in attendance on the day a Padres pitcher tosses a no-hitter for the first time.

Why the Padres?

Minor league baseball came to town in 1936, when owner Bill Lane moved his Hollywood Stars south to San Diego.

Lane tired of annual rental disputes at little Wrigley Field, where the Stars shared the ballpark with owner William Wrigley Jr.'s Los Angeles Angels. The Stars' rent was going to be doubled following the 1935 season, prompting Lane to pick up stakes. He relocated the Pacific Coast League team to a downtown San

Diego site located on Broadway between Harbor Drive and Pacific Highway along San Diego Bay.

The San Diego Stars wouldn't have been a bad name, but Lane left it in Hollywood. He held a newspaper contest to come up with a new nickname.

Among the submissions were Aviators, Balboas, Blues, Dons, Don Juans, Flyers, Friars, Gaels, Gobs, Gorillas, Pilots, Sandies, Skippers, Tars, Tunas, Twilers, and Vaqueros.

Eight people entered the name Padres. Don Blackwell was among them, receiving two season tickets for the suggestion.

The name traces to San Diego's origins in 1769, when Spanish Franciscan friars, notably Father Junipero Serra, founded the Mission San Diego de Alcalá. It was the first of the 21 California missions and, in fact, the first settlement in the state.

The major league Padres came along exactly 200 years later. Interestingly enough, Qualcomm Stadium, where the Padres played their first 36 seasons in the majors, is located about a mile west of the mission.

The Padres weren't alone in assuming the name of a minor league team. The Baltimore Orioles (International League), Detroit Tigers (Western League), Los Angeles Angels (Pacific Coast League), and Milwaukee Brewers (American Association) did likewise when they hit the big time.

67 The Swinging Friar

The Swinging Friar is among the best mascots in baseball.

It was the inspiration of San Diego High graduate Carlos Hadaway. He was a 19-year-old seaman apprentice in 1961 when the minor league Padres had a contest to come up with a mascot.

Hadaway came up with some sketches of a brown-robed friar swinging a bat. His superior chose two of them to submit for the contest.

When he was informed that he won, Hadaway was asked to create a larger version and he presented it to Padres general manager Eddie Leishman.

"I wanted to do something with a Padre swinging a bat," Hadaway said.

He had some background, drawing a comic strip called *Square dat Hadaway* for a Navy newspaper called the *Hoist*.

Hadaway received a small fee for his creation.

The major league team used the logo from its inception in 1969 through its World Series season of 1984. It was resurrected in 1995 and has been a fixture ever since. A costumed Swinging Friar is popular in the stands at games and at promotional events. Animated versions appear on the Petco Park video board.

As a child, Hadaway was blinded twice and had six operations to regain his sight. Not long thereafter he began to embrace his art, with the encouragement of his third-grade teacher.

Living now in Fountain Hills, Arizona, Hadaway has fashioned a notable career in Western art.

He remains very proud of his contribution to the Padres. On his website—thearizonakid.com—the first thing he mentions about his art is creating The Swinging Friar.

"It belongs to the fans of San Diego," Hadaway said. "I think it's the neatest emblem for a baseball team. I wasn't in it for the money...I've always had a place in my heart for the Padres."

68 The 1968 Expansion Draft

San Diego was awarded a Major League Baseball franchise on May 27, 1968, when National League owners voted unanimously to expand.

All the Padres needed were players to fill the roster.

That task was undertaken in the 1968 National League expansion draft. The Padres and Montreal Expos, who came into being the same season, took turns picking from among those made available.

Both teams drafted 30 players. They selected from among the NL's 10 existing teams, who were each allowed to protect 40 players in their organization.

The draft was conducted October 14, 1968. The Padres went first. They selected outfielder Ollie Brown, who would become known as the Original Padre.

Brown, who had 52 home runs and 208 RBIs in three-plus seasons with the team, was among several players selected who would make a significant impact for the franchise.

First baseman Nate Colbert and outfielder Cito Gaston both played six seasons with the team. Catcher Fred Kendall's eight years with the club made him the longest-tenured member of the original players.

Colbert was a three-time All-Star for the Padres. He remains the franchise's all-time home-run leader (163) and is sixth in RBIs

(481). Gaston made one All-Star team. He collected 77 homers and 316 RBIs with the team.

Clay Kirby (1969–73) and Steve Arlin (1969–74) were the two pitchers who made the biggest impact. Kirby went 52–81, just outside the team's all-time top 10 in victories. He still ranks sixth all-time in strikeouts (802) and sixth in starts (170). Arlin, who was 32–62, still ranks second all-time in shutouts (11).

Pitcher Dick Selma had the distinction of pitching the team's first game—beating Houston 2–1—but was traded less than three weeks later to the Chicago Cubs.

Padres president Buzzie Bavasi oversaw the Padres' expansion draft. Bavasi came down to San Diego after spending 18 years as GM of the Dodgers.

While Bavasi knew the Dodgers as well as anyone, the three Dodgers players the Padres selected—outfielders Al Ferrera and Jim Williams and shortstop Zoilo Versalles—were not the ones Bavasi originally had in mind.

Ferrera was productive during the Padres' first two seasons while Williams played sparingly. Versalles didn't even make it to spring training, getting traded to the Indians nearly two months after the Padres selected him.

In a twist that would appear to be an incredible conflict of interest, Dodgers owner Walter O'Malley called Bavasi before the draft and asked him to help decide which 40 players the Dodgers should protect.

Bavasi explained in his autobiography *Off the Record* that O'Malley had called on him after Fresco Thompson, who replaced Bavasi in Los Angeles, had been hospitalized with cancer.

Bavasi visited Thompson in the hospital and was asked: "Who are you going to take in the draft?"

"Bill Russell, Jeff Torber, and Jim Brewer," Bavasi said, naming three players the Dodgers were not planning to protect.

The 1968 National League Expansion Draft

Pick	Player, Pos.	Selected From	Selected By
1	Ollie Brown, OF	San Francisco Giants	San Diego Padres
2	Manny Mota, OF	Pittsburgh Pirates	Montreal Expos
3	Dave Giusti, RHP	St. Louis Cardinals	San Diego Padres
4	Mack Jones, OF	Cincinnati Reds	Montreal Expos
5	Dick Selma, RHP	New York Mets	San Diego Padres
6	John Bateman, C	Houston Astros	Montreal Expos
7	Al Santorini, RHP	Atlanta Braves	San Diego Padres
8	Gary Sutherland, 2B/SS	Philadelphia Phillies	Montreal Expos
9	José Arcia, 2B/SS	Chicago Cubs	San Diego Padres
10	Jack Billingham, RHP	Los Angeles Dodgers	Montreal Expos
11	Donn Clendenon, 1B	Pittsburgh Pirates	Montreal Expos
12	Clay Kirby, RHP	St. Louis Cardinals	San Diego Padres
13	Jesús Alou, OF	San Francisco Giants	Montreal Expos
14	Fred Kendall, C	Cincinnati Reds	San Diego Padres
15	Mike Wegener, RHP	Philadelphia Phillies	Montreal Expos
16	Jerry Morales, OF	New York Mets	San Diego Padres
17	Skip Guinn, LHP	Atlanta Braves	Montreal Expos
18	Nate Colbert, 1B	Houston Astros	San Diego Padres
19	Bill Stoneman, RHP	Chicago Cubs	Montreal Expos
20	Zoilo Versalles, 2B/3B	Los Angeles Dodgers	San Diego Padres
21	Maury Wills, SS	Pittsburgh Pirates	Montreal Expos
22	Frank Reberger, RHP	Chicago Cubs	San Diego Padres
23	Larry Jackson, RHP	Philadelphia Phillies	Montreal Expos
24	Jerry DaVanon, SS/2B	St. Louis Cardinals	San Diego Padres
25	Bob Reynolds, RHP	San Francisco Giants	Montreal Expos
26	Larry Stahl, OF	New York Mets	San Diego Padres
27	Dan McGinn, LHP	Cincinnati Reds	Montreal Expos
28	Dick Kelley, LHP	Atlanta Braves	San Diego Padres
29	José Herrera, OF	Houston Astros	Montreal Expos

"Oh, you can't do that," said Thompson, "particularly Russell and Brewer. Russell's a fine prospect."

"That's why I'm taking him," Bavasi said.

"You can't do that," Thompson said. "Buzzie, don't do that to me, really."

"Who do you want me to take?" Bavasi asked.

Pick	Player, Pos.	Selected From	Selected By
30	Al Ferrara, OF	Los Angeles Dodgers	San Diego Padres
31	Mike Corkins, RHP	San Francisco Giants	San Diego Padres
32	Jimy Williams, 2B/SS	Cincinnati Reds	Montreal Expos
33	Tom Dukes, RHP	Houston Astros	San Diego Padres
34	Remy Hermoso, 2B/SS	Atlanta Braves	Montreal Expos
35	Rick James, RHP	Chicago Cubs	San Diego Padres
36	Mudcat Grant, RHP	Los Angeles Dodgers	Montreal Expos
37	Tony González, OF	Philadelphia Phillies	San Diego Padres
38	Jerry Robertson, RHP	St. Louis Cardinals	Montreal Expos
39	Dave Roberts, LHP	Pittsburgh Pirates	San Diego Padres
40	Don Shaw, LHP	New York Mets	Montreal Expos
41	Ty Cline, OF	San Francisco Giants	Montreal Expos
42	Ivan Murrell, OF	Houston Astros	San Diego Padres
43	Garry Jestadt, 3B/2B	Chicago Cubs	Montreal Expos
44	Jim Williams, OF	Los Angeles Dodgers	San Diego Padres
45	Carl Morton, RHP	Atlanta Braves	Montreal Expos
46	Billy McCool, LHP	Cincinnati Reds	San Diego Padres
47	Larry Jaster, LHP	St. Louis Cardinals	Montreal Expos
48	Roberto Peña, SS	Philadelphia Phillies	San Diego Padres
49	Ernie McAnally, RHP	New York Mets	Montreal Expos
50	Al McBean, RHP	Pittsburgh Pirates	San Diego Padres
51	Rafael Robles, SS	San Francisco Giants	San Diego Padres
52	Jim Fairey, OF	Los Angeles Dodgers	Montreal Expos
53	Fred Katawczik, LHP	Cincinnati Reds	San Diego Padres
54	Coco Laboy, 3B	St. Louis Cardinals	Montreal Expos
55	Ron Slocum, 3B	Pittsburgh Pirates	San Diego Padres
56	John Boccabella, C	Chicago Cubs	Montreal Expos
57	Steve Arlin, RHP	Philadelphia Phillies	San Diego Padres
58	Ron Brand, C	Houston Astros	Montreal Expos
59	Cito Gaston, OF	Atlanta Braves	San Diego Padres
60	John Glass, RHP	New York Mets	Montreal Expos

Wherupon Thompson suggested Ferrera, Williams, and Versalles.

Bavasi agreed.

"I had spoken with the doctor, who had told me that Fresco was dying and that he wasn't going to make it. I knew I had to keep my promise.

"…I went to Dodger Stadium and met with Walter O'Malley and (manager) Walter Alston. I said, 'You can't leave Brewer on the unprotected list. If you leave him there and I don't draft him, people are going to crucify me."

"Brewer had had 14 saves in 1968. I talked them into including Brewer on the protected list, which took the heat off me. Leaving Russell unprotected was OK, because nobody knew him at the time."

Russell would make a name for himself soon enough. He debuted with the Dodgers in the outfield in 1969. He became the team's starting shortstop three years later and was a fixture there for the next 15 years.

The Padres, meanwhile, spent their first decade searching for a capable shortstop before Ozzie Smith's arrival in 1978.

The First Game

The Padres hosted Houston on April 8, 1969, in the first game in franchise history.

After 32 years as a minor league team competing in the Pacific Coast League, San Diego came of age. While everyone in town was excited to have a major league team, hopes were not especially high.

Hanging from a San Diego Stadium balcony before the game was a sign that read: "Wait Till Next Year."

They didn't have to wait for a win. Dick Selma pitched a five-hitter with 12 strikeouts in a 2–1 victory over the Astros.

Houston scored once in the first inning, but Selma put up zeros the rest of the way. Third baseman Ed Spiezio scored the first run in Padres history. It came in the fifth inning on the first home run

Padres manager Preston Gomez handed the ball to right-hander Dick Selma to pitch the franchise's inaugural game. The starting lineup produced just two runs, but it was enough to bring home a victory. (Kirk Kenney)

in franchise history, a liner into the left-field bleachers off Houston starting pitcher Don Wilson.

Right fielder Ollie Brown drove in the winning run with a sixth-inning double against Wilson that went off the left-field wall. It scored teammate Roberto Pena, who had reached base when he was hit by a pitch.

The Padres collected only four hits in the game. Two of them were by Selma. The right-hander came into the game with a sizeable chip on his shoulder.

When Selma bumped into Wilson at a dinner a night earlier, the Houston hurler said. "You know, don't you, that you're going to lose tomorrow night?"

A crowd of 30,000 was expected for the game, although only 23,370 showed up at the half-filled stadium. Among them were

First Padres Game

April 8, 1969, at San Diego Stadium
Padres 2, Astros 1

Houston	AB	R	H	BI
Alou, RF	4	1	3	0
Morgan, 2B	4	0	0	0
Miller, CF	4	0	0	0
Rader, 3B	4	0	1	1
Blefary, 1B	4	0	1	0
Watson, LF	4	0	0	0
Menke, SS	3	0	0	0
Edwards, C	3	0	0	0
Wilson, P	2	0	0	0
Geiger, PH	1	0	0	0
Billingham, P	0	0	0	0
Totals	32	1	5	1

San Diego	AB	R	H	BI
Robles, SS	4	0	0	0
Pena, 2B	3	1	0	0
Gonzalez, CF	4	0	0	0
Brown, RF	4	0	1	1
Davis, 1B	3		0	0
Colbert, 1B	0	0		0
Stahl, LF	3	0	0	0
Spiezio, 3B	3	1	1	1
Cannizzaro, C	2	0	0	0
Selma, P	2	0	2	0
Totals	28	2	4	2

HOUSTON 100 000 000—1 5 1
SAN DIEGO 000 011 00x—2 4 0

E—Morgan (1). LOB—Houston 6, San Diego 5. 2B—Brown (1). 3B—Alou (1). HR—Spiezio (1), off Wilson. RBIs—Rader (1), Brown (1), Spiezio (1). SB—Alou (1), Robles (1). SF—Selma.

HOUSTON	IP	H	R	ER	BB	SO
Wilson, L (0–1)	6	3	2	2	1	4
Billingham	2	1	0	0	0	3
SAN DIEGO	IP	H	R	ER	BB	SO
Selma, W (1–0)	9	5	1	1	2	12

PB—Cannizzaro. HBP—Pena, by Wilson
Umpires—Home, Shag Crawford; First, Chris Pelekoudas; Second, Doug Harvey; Third, Frank Dezelan.
T—2:14. A—23,370.

Louis Tamagni and his girlfriend, Gayle Wallace, who were sitting in the last row of the upper deck in left field.

"All I had was $1.50," Tamagni said. "She wanted to go to the top so I came to the top. It's a good view."

A fan named Eldon Mower considered putting some money on the Padres to win their division.

"I saw where the odds are 300-1," he said. "Somebody bet on the Red Sox when they were 100-1 and I heard he won $30,000.

"After all, there are only six teams in the division and that's pretty good odds."

Hopefully, Mower saved his money.

Padres manager Preston Gomez did not exactly come into the season with lofty expectations. He was hoping for a fifth-place finish, one spot ahead of Houston.

The Padres swept the three-game series with the Astros. Reality set in soon enough, however. San Diego followed that series with a six-game losing streak and never got back over .500 again in a season that included 9-, 10-, and 11-game losing streaks.

The Padres finished the season with a 52–110 record and the first of six straight last-place finishes in the NL West.

For one night, at least, anything seemed possible.

"We didn't look like any expansion team tonight—we looked like the old Dodgers," Padres left-hander Johnny Podres said.

In fact, all four 1969 expansion teams—San Diego, Montreal, Seattle, and Kansas City—all won their season openers.

According to the newspaper game story, Spiezio's home run earned him a gift certificate from the *San Diego Union* and *Evening Tribune*. Selma also received a gift certificate for being named the Padres' outstanding player of the game.

Selma may not have had time to cash in.

He was traded to the Chicago Cubs three weeks later.

70 Dock's No-No

A crowd of 9,903 assembled at San Diego Stadium on the evening of June 12, 1970, for a doubleheader between the Pittsburgh Pirates and the Padres.

They would witness something no one had ever seen in San Diego—a no-hitter. It included something else no one had ever seen—a pitcher on acid throwing a no-hitter—although it would be more than a decade before that part of the story came to light.

The Padres were still in their infancy, barely a year old, when they were no-hit for the first time.

Pittsburgh right-hander Dock Ellis struck out six, walked eight, and hit a batter, but he did not allow the Padres a hit. The game's only runs in the Pirates' 2–0 victory came on a pair of solo home runs by Willie Stargell off Padres left-hander Dave Roberts.

"Ellis had a fastball that sailed," said Padres second baseman Dave Campbell, who batted leadoff in the game. "I always thought that when he was at his best, his stuff was as good as any pitcher in the league."

It was the first game of the doubleheader, and Ellis could have been aided by an earlier than normal start time.

"The game was played in the twilight, which made it tough to see," Padres catcher Chris Cannizzaro said.

It was more than a decade later when Ellis revealed he was under the influence of psychedelic drugs while he was on the mound.

The right-hander said he was tripping on LSD.

"When I went out there, I was out to lunch," Ellis said.

Ellis almost didn't make it to the stadium in the first place. The Pirates had arrived in San Diego on a Thursday, which was an off-day. Ellis was given permission to visit a friend in Los Angeles, although he was to pitch Friday in the first game of the doubleheader.

In an interview with National Public Radio shortly before his death in 2008, Ellis explained how everything unfolded. At least how he remembered it.

"I took some LSD at the airport because I knew where it would hit me," said Ellis, who then rented a car and drove to L.A. "I'd be in my own little area that I know where to go, so that's how I got to my friend's girlfriend's house.

"She said, 'What's wrong with you?' I said, 'I'm high as a Georgia pine.'

Ellis partied into the night. He said he dropped some more LSD the following morning and was going to go back to sleep when his friend's girlfriend said, "You better get up. You've got to go pitch."

"I pitch tomorrow," Ellis said. "What are you talking about?

"She grabbed the paper, brought me the sports page, and showed me. Boom. I said, 'Wow, what happened to yesterday?'

No-Hitters Against the Padres

There have been nine no-hitters pitched against the Padres:

June 12, 1970 at San Diego: Dock Ellis (Pirates 2, Padres 0)

Sept. 2, 1972 at Chicago: Milt Pappas (Cubs 8, Padres 0)

Aug. 5, 1973 at Atlanta: Phil Niekro (Braves 9, Padres 0)

Sept. 11, 1991 at Atlanta: Kent Mercker, Mark Wohlers, and Alejandro Pena (Braves 1, Padres 0)

May 12, 2001 at San Diego: A.J. Burnett (Marlins 3, Padres 0)

Sept. 3, 2001 at San Diego: Bud Smith (Cardinals 4, Padres 0)

July 10, 2009 at San Francisco: Jonathan Sanchez (Giants 8, Padres 0)

July 13, 2013 at San Diego: Tim Lincecum (Giants 9, Padres 0)

June 25, 2014 at San Francisco: Tim Lincecum (Giants 4, Padres 0)

"She said, 'I don't know, but you better get to that airport.'"

Ellis took the short flight from Los Angeles to San Diego, then a taxi ride to the stadium, arriving about 90 minutes before he was supposed to pitch.

It was just enough time, Ellis said, to get some pills from a woman he knew sitting along the rail in the field-level seats.

"So I got the bennies (slang for the stimulant Benzedrine), went back to the clubhouse, took them," Ellis said. "The game started and the mist started, misty rain. So all during the game was a little mist.

"The opposing team and my teammates, they knew I was high, but they didn't know what I was high on. They had no idea what LSD was, other than what they saw on TV with the hippies."

Ellis said Pirates catcher Jerry May put tape on his fingers so that the pitcher could see the signals.

"I didn't see the hitters," Ellis said. "All I could tell was if they were on the right side or the left side."

Added Ellis: "I didn't know if I was facing Hank Aaron, Willie Mays, or Mickey Mantle. I was just out there throwing a baseball and having a great time."

At one point, Ellis said he saw President Richard Nixon behind the plate calling balls and strikes. And one of the batters was Jimi Hendrix, who was swinging a guitar at the plate.

"We had a rookie on the team at that particular time named Dave Cash," Ellis said. "He kept saying after the first inning, 'You got a no-no going.' A no-hitter."

"Yeah, right," Ellis said.

"Then around the fourth inning he said it again," said Ellis. "'You got a no-no going.'"

It was true.

"I could also feel the pressure from the other players wanting to tell him to shut up," Ellis said. "It's a superstition thing where you're not supposed to say nothing if somebody's throwing a no-hitter."

Ellis made three putouts in the game, but he said he had difficulty with his depth perception.

"There were times when the ball was hit back at me I jumped because I thought it was coming fast, but the ball was coming slow," Ellis said. "The third baseman come by and grabbed the ball and threw somebody out."

On one play, Ellis said, "I covered first base and I caught the ball and I tagged the base all in one motion. I said, 'Oooh, I just made a touchdown.'"

Ellis struck out pinch hitter Ed Spiezio with a curveball to end the game, setting off a celebration among his teammates.

Nothing seemed amiss in the immediate aftermath.

"Dock has always been a real live, active personality," Padres first baseman Nate Colbert said. "He acted the same in that game as he always did, and he had great stuff."

Ellis had issues with drugs and alcohol throughout his career, which ended in 1980. He went to rehab shortly thereafter and later became a drug counselor and motivational speaker.

He died in 2008 from liver disease.

Ellis said the LSD no-hitter wasn't something that he bragged about. In fact, a decade passed before he mentioned that aspect of the event. Ellis said he had just come out of drug treatment "and the honesty was just flowin'."

71 The Curse of Clay Kirby

The Padres are the only team in the major leagues to have never thrown a no-hitter.

Longtime fans have come to call it The Curse of Clay Kirby.

Baseball superstition being what it is, this seems as good an explanation as any for no no-no.

It was a summer night in 1970. July 21, to be exact. The Padres were hosting the New York Mets. Hall of Fame baseball writer Phil Collier began his story this way for the *San Diego Union*:

"Barring a miracle, the San Diego Padres will finish last in the National League West again this season and the 10,373 who turned out to watch them last night will still be wondering if Clay Kirby would have pitched a no-hitter against the New York Mets.

"They will always wonder because Preston Gomez, the San Diego manager, believes one more victory by a team that is floundering is more important than box office."

The Padres already were 20 games under .500 (38–58) and on their way to a 99-loss season.

Fans had nothing to hope for and little to cheer for, so the possibility of witnessing a no-hitter meant everything to them.

Kirby, 22, had not allowed a hit through eight innings, but the Padres trailed 1–0.

The Mets scored in the first inning without the benefit of a hit. Kirby walked Tommy Agee and Ken Singleton, a double steal followed, then an infield out by Art Shamsky scored Agee from third.

Mets starter Jim McAndrew was shutting out the Padres on three hits—a third-inning double by Ed Spiezio, a fourth-inning double by Al Ferrera, and a fifth-inning single by Bob Barton.

The Mets nearly scored another run in the eighth inning without a hit, but Joe Foy, who had walked leading off the inning and moved to third, was thrown out at the plate by Padres first baseman Nate Colbert.

On to the bottom of the eighth.

With two outs and no one on base, Gomez chose to send Cito Gaston to the plate to pinch hit for Kirby.

Protests came from the crowd.

"I knew the fans would be upset, but I play to win," said Gomez, who made a similar move when he managed in the minors. "I know the Kid (Kirby) feels bad, but it was a decision I had to make. It (the booing) won't bother me. I would rather take a chance on winning than to lose on a no-hitter."

Kirby would like to have stayed in, but he knew Gomez would not be swayed in the matter.

"I was a little surprised when he took me out," Kirby said. "I never like to come out of a game, even if I'm 100 runs behind, but he (Gomez) had his mind made up.

"A no-hitter would have been special, but I would rather have won the game than to have pitched one."

Within a minute of the move, the switchboards lit up at both the stadium and the *San Diego Union*.

The fans in attendance didn't take it so well, either. In fact, one jumped a field-level railing when Gaston came out to pinch hit for Kirby.

The right-hander happened to be standing in the path of the trespasser when he came into the dugout.

"He was looking for Preston and I figured he wouldn't recognize him," Kirby said. "I wasn't going to let him get to Preston."

The Padres still could have had a combined no-hitter, but reliever Jack Baldschun allowed three hits and two runs in the ninth inning of what became a 3–0 loss to the Mets.

More than 100 Padres fans stood at the field-level railing after the game chanting "Gomez must go. Gomez must go."

Kirby pitched a one-hitter at San Francisco the following season, losing his no-hitter in the eighth inning on a Willie McCovey home run.

And so it went.

Several closer calls have followed through the years.

In 1972, Steve Arlin took a no-hitter into the ninth inning against Philadelphia. Denny Doyle broke it up with a single.

In 1997, Andy Ashby's no-hit bid ended when Atlanta's Kenny Lofton led off the ninth with a single.

In 2006, Chris Young took a no-hitter into the ninth against Pittsburgh. A one-out walk was followed by Joe Randa's two-run homer.

In 2011, five Padres pitchers had combined to hold the Dodgers hitless for 8⅔ innings before Luke Gregerson allowed a double to Juan Uribe.

The Padres have pitched 28 one-hitters over the first 47 years of the franchise.

But never a no-no.

Curses.

72 Nate Colbert's Big Day

In 1954, St. Louis first baseman Stan Musial set a major league record when he hit five home runs in a doubleheader against the visiting New York Giants.

After the second game, an eight-year-old boy sitting in the Sportsman's Park stands turned to his father and said: "No one will ever do that again."

Oh, yeah?

Nate Colbert was that eight-year-old boy. Colbert was playing first base for the Padres 18 years later.

It was August 1, 1972, and the Padres were in Atlanta for a doubleheader against the Braves that they would sweep on 9–0 and 11–7 scores.

Colbert hit a record-tying five home runs against the Braves.

"Stan Musial was my idol," Colbert said. "I used to imitate his stance. I put (Musial's) number six on everything....To tie him, it meant a lot."

Colbert collected 13 RBIs to set a major league record (tied by St. Louis' Mark Whiten in 1993). Colbert also had two singles on the day, giving him 22 total bases, which is a record that still stands.

Colbert got his day off to a fast start, hitting a three-run homer in the first inning off Braves starting pitcher Ron Schueler. He added a solo home run in the seventh inning off reliever Mike McQueen.

Two singles made Colbert 4-for-5 in the game with five RBIs.

"Great game, big guy," Padres manager Don Zimmer told Colbert between games.

Colbert told the manager, "I'm not done yet."

And he wasn't. Not by a long shot.

Braves starting pitcher Tom Kelley walked Colbert when he came to the plate in the first inning. Kelley wasn't around when Colbert came to the plate again in the second inning. Reliever Pat Jarvis, who replaced Kelley, wished he wasn't, either. Colbert hit a grand slam.

Colbert added a two-run homer off Jim Hardin in the seventh.

The slugger needed help from a teammate to come to the plate in the ninth. Colbert was due up fourth. When Derrel Thomas and

Nate Colbert holds the Padres career record for home runs with 163. Five of them came in Atlanta on the most memorable day of Colbert's career.
(Fantography.com/Kevin Plant)

Dave Roberts made infield outs, it was left to left fielder Larry Stahl to keep the inning alive. Stahl singled to right field.

That brought Colbert to the plate to face submariner Cecil Upshaw, who had been very successful against Colbert in previous meetings.

Nate had collected just four hits in 17 at-bats against Upshaw, who, on this day, decided to throw Colbert an overhand fastball.

Colbert launched a two-run homer to left field on the first pitch.

"Why did you do that?" Colbert asked Upshaw later.

"You were so hot, I thought I'd surprise you with something," Upshaw said.

Some surprise.

It completed Colbert's day with this line: 7-for-9, 7 runs, 5 HR, 13 RBIs. He finished the season with 38 homers and 111 RBIs, marking it the best season of his 10-year career.

Already a fan favorite, Colbert's autograph was even more sought after following his big day. This, too, reminded Colbert of Musial.

When he was a kid, Colbert met Musial after a game.

"I waited outside one night and I followed Stan to his car," Colbert said. "And everybody had left and…it was time to go and he says, 'Can I do this some other time?' and I said, "Well, you know, I've been trying to get your autograph for (several days)."

Musial caught himself and said, "I apologize. Don't ever do what I just did."

"What's that?" Colbert asked.

"Well, you're a ball fan," Musial said. "You going to play in the big leagues?"

Colbert said that was his plan.

"Well, let me tell you this," Musial said. "Whenever you give somebody your autograph, you be nice to them because you won't remember it, but they will."

KIRK KENNEY

"That has stuck with me all the way through," Colbert said.

It was a story Colbert could have related to Musial when the pair posed for a photo two decades later.

"After I hit my five," Colbert said, "Stan came to San Diego and congratulated me and presented me with the plaque at the ball club, which was just completely awesome."

73 Collect Washington Padres Cards

In 1974, a kid could go to the grocery store, put a dime on the counter, and walk out with a pack of Topps baseball cards.

Imagine the surprise of Padres fans when unwrapping packages and seeing their favorite players listed not from SAN DIEGO but from WASHINGTON.

When the Topps Company starting rolling the presses on its 1974 card set in December 1973, the card company—like everyone else—was convinced of the Padres' imminent departure to Washington, D.C.

Padres owner C. Arnholdt Smith's financial troubles led to him putting the team up for sale midway through the 1973 season.

On December 6, 1973, National League owners unanimously approved the sale of the Padres to businessman Joseph Danzansky, who planned to move the team to Washington, D.C.

Topps produced 15 cards depicting the "Washington" Padres, including first basemen Nate Colbert and Willie McCovey, outfielders Johnny Grubb and Cito Gaston, and pitchers Randy Jones and Bill Greif.

In addition to the player's name and position, the cards were printed with WASHINGTON in the upper left corner and

204

Printing deadlines forced Topps to make a decision with its 1974 set—what city to put for the Padres. Ray Kroc's 11th-hour purchase of the team saved it from moving to Washington, D.C., and made these cards a collector's item.
(Kirk Kenney)

"NAT'L LEA." instead of the team's nickname in the bottom right corner. But player photos were from the 1973 season, so they were pictured wearing the Padres' brown and gold uniforms with SD on their hats.

Sports Collectors Daily values most of the cards at $8 apiece. Jones' card is $12 since it is his rookie card. The card for McCovey, who went into the Hall of Fame in 1986, is the most expensive at $50.

Outfielder Dave Winfield also is in the set, although he appears only as a San Diego player. The card is still valued at $75 because it is the first card for Winfield, who joined the Padres in the middle of the 1973 season after playing at the University of Minnesota.

Had there been a Washington variation for Winfield, who was elected to the Hall of Fame in 2001, it would have been worth hundreds of dollars because it is his rookie card.

On January 25, 1974, McDonald's owner Ray Kroc purchased the Padres for $12 million, saving baseball for San Diego.

With the team staying in San Diego, Topps put out corrected versions of the 15 Padres cards later in the season. Those cards are valued at about one-quarter of their Washington versions.

The Washington Padres cards remain popular in the card collecting hobby and are most commonly found for sale on eBay.

Collect Them, Trade Them
The "Washington" Padres from the 1974 Topps set:

No. 32 Johnny Grubb	No. 226 Padres team card
No. 53 Fred Kendall	No. 241 Glenn Beckert
No. 77 Rich Troedson	No. 250 Willie McCovey
No. 102 Bill Greif	No. 309 Dave Roberts
No. 125 Nate Colbert	No. 364 Cito Gaston
No. 148 Dave Hilton	No. 387 Rich Morales
No. 173 Randy Jones	No. 599 Ron Diorio
No. 197 Vincente Romo	

74 "I've Never Seen Such Stupid Ballplaying"

San Diegans knew little about Ray Kroc, other than that he was the owner of McDonald's, when he bought the Padres on January 25, 1974, and saved the baseball team from moving to Washington, D.C.

That all changed three months later when Kroc took to the public address system during the eighth inning of the home opener between the Padres and the Houston Astros at San Diego Stadium and said: "I've never seen such stupid ballplaying in my life."

With those words, Kroc forever endeared himself to the fans and the city.

The Padres, who opened the season with three straight losses on the road to the Dodgers, were on the way to an embarrassing 9–5 loss to the Astros when Kroc cleared his throat.

"I have some good news and some bad news," he began. "The good news is you loyal fans have outstripped Los Angeles. They had 31,000 on opening night. We have nearly 40,000 [39,083 to be exact]."

Just then Kroc was interrupted when a streaker ran across the field.

"Get him out of here," he yelled. "Take him to jail."

Kroc continued: "The bad news is I've never seen such stupid ballplaying in my life."

The crowd loved it. Of course, the players and coaches for both teams had a different reaction.

"In my 19 years in baseball I've never been called stupid in the middle of a game by an owner," said Padres first baseman Willie McCovey. "That statement is going to be ringing in guys' ears."

Said Houston third baseman Doug Rader: "He thinks he's in a sales convention dealing with a bunch of short-order cooks."

Baseball commissioner Bowie Kuhn told Kroc to apologize. He did the following day, saying, "I used a bad choice of words and I'm sorry. I was bitterly disappointed and embarrassed before....I meant to say we were playing lousy ball. It was nothing personal. I'm afraid I talked without thinking."

The Padres players accepted Kroc's apology and put the incident behind them. But it wasn't forgotten. Not by a long shot. It was perhaps the defining moment for baseball here, with the fans realizing the owner was one of them (give or take a few hundred million dollars).

The Padres would pass the 1,000,000 mark in home attendance for the first time, drawing 463,573 more fans than in 1973. This despite the team finishing last for the fifth straight season, with a 60–102 record.

Ray Kroc transformed baseball here. It wasn't always easy to watch what was going on down on the field, but Kroc's ownership made it fun to be at the ballpark.

And it all began that night when Kroc took the mic.

75 Short-Order Cook at Third

When Padres owner Ray Kroc got on the PA microphone in the 1974 home opener and admonished his team for "stupid ball-playing," Houston third baseman Doug Rader was among those offended by the remark.

Rader said Kroc was treating the baseball players like "a bunch of short-order cooks."

Ever the promoter, Kroc took advantage of Rader's statement from that infamous night.

When Houston returned to San Diego Stadium in June, the Padres had Short-Order Cooks Night. Short-order cooks throughout San Diego and Imperial counties were invited to the game for free.

Rader had an active sense of humor and joined in the spirit of the day. He put on a cook's hat and apron before the game, delivered the lineup card to the home-plate umpire on a frying pan, and flipped it with a spatula.

"Boys," he said to them, "what's your pleasure: rare, medium, or well done?"

Rader must have made a good impression on Kroc. The Padres traded for him following the 1975 season and made him their everyday third baseman.

Rader played 191 games for the Padres over the next year and a half—batting .261 with 14 homers and 82 RBIs—before moving on to the Toronto Blue Jays midway through the 1977 season.

After he retired, Rader began his coaching career with the 1979 Padres on Roger Craig's staff. Rader began a three-year stretch as manager of the Padres' Triple-A Hawaii affiliate a year later.

He was the Islanders manager in July of 1982 when he called Tony Gwynn into his office to tell the young outfielder he was going to the big leagues.

Rader went on to manage in the major leagues for the Rangers, White Sox, and Angels, where he presented the lineup card in a more routine manner.

76 Big Mac Sundays

When the Padres traded with the San Francisco Giants for Willie McCovey during the 1973 offseason, the franchise acquired more than a future Hall of Fame first baseman.

It also got a ready-made promotion.

McCovey's nickname was Big Mac. It was an apt description for both the player's stature and standing as one of the game's premier home-run hitters. He would collect 521 career home runs (52 of them for the Padres over two-plus seasons). St. Louis pitcher Bob Gibson called McCovey "the scariest hitter in baseball."

McCovey's nickname matched up nicely with the prominent menu item sold by Padres owner Ray Kroc at his McDonald's restaurants. The Big Mac sandwich had been hugely popular since its introduction in 1968.

During the 1975 season the Padres marketing department came up with Big Mac Sundays. All fans in attendance could take their ticket stubs following a Padres win and each would be redeemed for a free Big Mac.

Tremendous idea. In theory.

Of course, the Padres went out and lost 11 straight Sunday home games. They would go 2–13 at home on Sundays that season.

The promotion was revised way before the streak reached double digits, however.

And that's how Guaranteed Big Mac Sundays was born. Win or lose, everyone got a free Big Mac.

This created another issue.

There were nearly two dozen McDonald's restaurants in San Diego at the time, but it was the location three miles or so from the stadium that found itself inundated with baseball fans immediately after the game.

The sign on the McDonald's marquee may tout how many burgers are served, but it's pretty much impossible for one location to crank out thousands of the things at a moment's notice. The location was overwhelmed.

That explains why many such giveaways now do not begin until the day after the event when people have dispersed throughout the city.

Padres first baseman Willie McCovey, pictured with former Padres executive Andy Strasberg, brought some much-needed star power to the lineup when the Padres acquired him from the San Francisco Giants following the 1973 season.
(Fantography.com/Andy Strasberg)

77 History from the Other Dugout

Padres fans witnessed no shortage of history, although too often it was achieved by someone in the visitors' dugout at the stadium.

Here are three examples:

Willie Mays' 600th HR

On September 22, 1969, Willie Mays stepped to the plate in the seventh inning as a pinch-hitter for the San Francisco Giants.

The Say Hey Kid belted the first pitch he saw from Padres pitcher Mike Corkins into the left-center field bleachers for a two-run homer in a 4–2 Giants victory.

Mays was congratulated by all of his teammates as he touched home plate, joining Babe Ruth as the only two players to reach the 600-homer milestone.

"Why did it have to be me?" Corkins asked.

Why not? Mays' first career home run was against Hall of Famer Warren Spahn.

The Adirondack Bat Co. awarded Mays an Italian sports car and one share of stock for each foot the 391-foot homer traveled.

A crowd of just 4,779 witnessed the milestone. The stands were empty where the ball landed.

The Padres had planned a promotion to let general admission fans sit in the left-field seats. Whoever caught the 600th home-run ball was to be awarded two box seats for every home game for the 1970 season. One problem: the promotion wasn't until the following night.

Al Frolander Jr., 15, of Carlsbad came up with the ball. Frolander received an autographed baseball from Mays in exchange for the 600th homer ball, which was sent to the Hall of Fame.

Mays would finish his career with 660 homers. The figure still ranks fifth on the all-time list, behind Barry Bonds, Hank Aaron, Ruth, and Alex Rodriguez.

Lou Brock Breaks Steals Record

On August 29, 1977, St. Louis outfielder Lou Brock broke Ty Cobb's 49-year-old major league record for career stolen bases.

Brock came into the game with 891 career steals, one shy of the record. He wasted no time tying Ty, walking in the first inning and stealing second base on the next pitch from Dave Friesleben. The game was halted briefly and the base was removed from its moorings and presented to Brock.

In the seventh inning, Brock reached first base on a fielder's choice. The crowd of 19,656 anticipated what was to come next.

Brock stole second again off Friesleben, sliding in ahead of the throw from Padres catcher Dave Roberts—again—for career steal No. 893.

"I gave it my best shot," Roberts said. "I didn't rush that one, but it was to the right side of the bag and he slid under it.

"I'm happy for the man. I think Lou Brock's a great guy. There's nothing personal in him stealing the record off me."

Brock's Cardinals teammates ran out to second base to congratulate him for breaking the record. As in the first inning, the base was removed and presented to Brock, this time by Padres player representative Randy Jones.

Brock held the bag from the record-breaking steal over his head and received a standing ovation from the crowd.

Brock led the National League in steals eight times during his career. That included 1974, when he broke Maury Wills' single-season record with 118 steals. Brock retired with 938 career stolen bases.

In 1982, Rickey Henderson pushed the single-season record to 130. Henderson also shattered Brock's career mark, finishing with 1,406 career steals.

Orel Hershiser's Shutout Streak

On September 28, 1988, the Dodgers' Hershiser completed a streak that is even more amazing when placed in contemporary context.

The Dodgers' right-hander completed a major league record streak of 59 consecutive scoreless innings, breaking the record 58 innings compiled by another Dodgers great, Don Drysdale. While some pitchers these days have approached the mark, pitching in relative bits and pieces, Hershiser's streak included five consecutive shutouts, topped off by 10 shutout innings against the Padres. Matching him inning for inning was Padres starting pitcher Andy Hawkins, who also tossed 10 shutout innings.

The game remained scoreless until the 16th inning when the Dodgers finally pushed across a run. But the Padres won 2–1 on pinch hitter Mark Parent's two-run homer in the bottom of the 16th.

Hershiser had the idea of leaving the game after nine innings tied with Drysdale at 58 innings.

"I didn't want to break the record," said Hershiser. "Out of respect for Don Drysdale, for who he is and what he accomplished, I just wanted to tie it, be part of it. I wanted two Dodgers to hold that record. But my mind was changed for me by a higher Dodgers source—my manager."

Dodgers manager Tommy Lasorda told pitching coach Ron Perranoski: "No way he's coming out. He's going all the way. I know he wants to stay even with Drysdale. He's a wonderful young man. But he's going back out."

Through the first nine innings Hershiser allowed a one-out single in the first, a two-out single in the fourth, a one-out single in the seventh, and a two-out single in the eighth.

"Orel is just unbelievable," said Padres right fielder Tony Gwynn, who was 0-for-5 in the game. "I'm going to have dreams about his sinkerball tonight. He worked me over like a rookie. He broke a record I never thought would be touched. But the way he's throwing, you can see how he did it."

When he came off the mound after tying the record, Hershiser was congratulated by teammates, as well as Drysdale, who was in the Dodgers dugout.

In the 10th, Hershiser got into a bit of a predicament. He struck out Marvell Wynne leading off the inning, but the ball skidded past the catcher for a wild pitch that allowed Wynne to get to first base.

A sacrifice bunt by Benito Santiago and an infield out by Randy Ready moved Wynne to third base with the potential game-winning and streak-ending run.

But Keith Moreland, pinch hitting for Hawkins, flied out to right field and Hershiser walked off to a standing ovation from the crowd of 22,596.

"There were some catcalls (early in the game)," Hershiser said. "But the closer I got to the record, the more they warmed to and rooted for me. I could feel that. In the end, I think they appreciated what happened."

Hershiser was asked afterward why he didn't want the record all for himself.

"Because I think Don was a better pitcher than I am," Hershiser said. "He is a Hall of Famer and one of the finest human beings I've ever met."

Drysdale, then a Dodgers broadcaster, couldn't believe Hershiser wanted to stop with them tied at 58 innings.

"I would have grabbed him, kicked him in the butt, and told him to get back out there and go as far as he can," Drysdale said. "I was rooting all the way for him. I'm terribly proud of him. It was great fun for me to watch. I loved it. But through it all, I tried pretty much to stay away from him. I didn't want to jinx him."

78 Alvin Dark's Spring Cleaning

The Padres didn't enjoy many firsts in their first decade of existence, but here was one: in 1978, owner Ray Kroc fired manager Alvin Dark during spring training.

It marked the earliest a team had ever fired its manager and was only the second time in baseball history that a manager had been dismissed in spring training (the 1954 Cubs replaced Phil Cavarretta with Stan Hack).

"We were getting a lot of feedback from the players," Kroc said. "When you see something like that fomenting and feel it is festering, you have to do something.

"We decided to act quickly. We want relaxed, happy ballplayers."

Dark had been hired to manage the Padres during the previous year when Kroc dismissed John McNamara in midseason.

Dark, who was coaching with the Chicago Cubs when the Padres came calling, had a history of managerial success.

Dark was a standout shortstop in the majors during his 14-year career. He began his managerial career with the San Francisco Giants in 1961 and took them to the World Series a year later.

He also managed in Kansas City and Cleveland before going to Oakland, where he guided the A's to the 1974 World Series title. Dark was fired just a year later when Oakland was swept by Boston in the 1975 American League Championship Series.

Dark seemingly wanted control over everything by the time he arrived in San Diego.

"He wanted to be the pitching coach, the batting coach, and the infield coach," Kroc said.

None of this made Dark very popular with his coaches. The players weren't too fond of him, either.

Dark had become a born-again Christian, and he pushed his religious beliefs on the players. He started Bible study sessions. He also banned alcohol in the clubhouse.

Getting on the field provided no respite from their manager.

"He put in so many trick plays and had so many signs that everybody was uptight," catcher Gene Tenace said. "There were too many things to worry about."

Pitching coach Roger Craig became Padres manager after Dark was dismissed. Craig led the Padres to an 84–78 record, the first winning season in franchise history.

Two years after he was dismissed, Dark wrote his autobiography. Its title: *When in Doubt, Fire the Manager.*

Jerry—Not Gary— Coleman Hired

Child actor Gary Coleman starred in the movie *The Kid from Left Field*, where the plot had the 12-year-old Coleman becoming manager of the San Diego Padres.

The movie's television debut was September 30, 1979.

A day later, the Padres did something that seemed just as improbable. They brought broadcaster Jerry Coleman down from the booth to the dugout. He was hired to replace Roger Craig as manager.

"I think (owner) Ray Kroc told 'em to give the job to Gary Coleman and they misunderstood him," noted one observer after Jerry Coleman was introduced.

When he was approached about the idea, Coleman himself said: "You're kidding."

The idea still hadn't sunk in when Coleman was introduced to the media.

"I'm probably more surprised by this than you are," he said.

Coleman played nine years with the Yankees. The Associated Press named him American League Rookie of the Year in 1949 and he was MVP of the 1950 World Series. But Coleman's playing career had ended in 1957 and he had no managerial experience.

"I'll have to gain the respect of the players in spring training," Coleman said. "I know there will be some credibility gap."

Padres president Ballard Smith had several reasons for tabbing Coleman as the sixth manager in the Padres' 11-year history.

"He's had experience as a player," Smith said. "In the front office, he is familiar with our players and the rest of the National League, he knows how to communicate with people."

Added Smith: "We knew some experienced managers would be looking for jobs this fall, but why should we hire somebody else's reject. We believe Jerry will do a better job than we've been getting in the past."

After giving the idea some thought, Coleman agreed to take the job.

"I'm 55 years old," he said. "I've never had an opportunity to manage. I said, 'Damn, why not?' This is my last challenge. I relish it. I grasp it. I'm going to run with it."

Player reaction was favorable—at least publicly—to the selection.

"I think he can do it," left-hander Randy Jones said. "I believe Jerry will have a good effect on the team. It will be interesting. He's a very positive person."

Said outfielder Jay Johnstone: "There'll be a lot on his shoulders, but I think he's capable of doing it."

The Padres had finished 68–93 in 1979 under Craig. Coleman improved on that, going 73–89. It was the second-best record in franchise history, but it wasn't enough to get him a second season.

Coleman never really did win over the players. He also lost support in the front office in midseason when Fontaine was replaced as GM by Jack McKeon.

Coleman was fired as manager after the season and replaced by Frank Howard.

"My disappointment is that I didn't do a better job," Coleman said. "It was a great experience and it's over, the book is closed."

Coleman returned to the broadcast booth, where he would serve the Padres for another 33 years.

80 Hang a Star on That, Baby!

"You can hang a star on that, baby!"

An outstanding defensive play by a Padre didn't receive official confirmation until broadcaster Jerry Coleman made it so.

Coleman, who was born in San Jose and grew up in Northern California, was often asked how he came up with his signature phrase.

"Back in grade school, we had a spelling test every Friday," Coleman said. "If you got all 20 right, you got a gold star. I never got a gold star."

Coleman never forgot what it meant for those who did receive one, however.

"Kids in the class would be talking about hanging stars on their tests and that always stuck with me as the epitome of excellence," he said.

It stuck with fans, too.

If it was a home game, those in attendance would glance back to the broadcast booth in anticipation of seeing an oversized gold star dangle from the window.

Padres engineer Tommy Jorgensen was the first person given star-hanging duties.

"I told him I would make him famous as the guy who threw out the star, which somebody made for us on the end of a broomstick," Coleman said.

Responsibilities for the star were passed along to future engineers and/or broadcast partners through the years. The cue came with Coleman's exclamation.

In 1972, Coleman began a 42-year run as Padres play-by-play man—interrupted for a year when he came down from the broadcast booth to manage the 1980 Padres—that made him one of the city's most beloved figures.

Coleman had one other catchphrase—"Oh, doctor!"—that many believe he borrowed from a former Yankees broadcaster who Coleman worked with in the mid-1960s. Not so.

"Everyone thinks I picked up 'Oh, doctor' from Red Barber," Coleman said. "Red was a great teacher and really helped me when I was starting out in New York. But 'Oh, doctor' really originated with manager Casey Stengel. I never heard Red say it."

81 Finishing Last Twice in '81

The Padres finished last in the National League West in each of the franchise's first six seasons.

In 1981, they outdid even themselves. The Padres had the distinction of finishing last not once but twice that year.

Baseball's fifth work stoppage in 10 years created the unusual circumstances. The strike led to the cancellation of 713 games, more than one-third of the season.

The strike started June 12 and lasted until July 31. Games did not resume until August 10, one day after the belated All-Star Game—catcher Terry Kennedy and shortstop Ozzie Smith represented the Padres—was played in Cleveland.

Owners decided the season would be split into two halves, with the winner of each half in each division meeting in the first round of the playoffs.

The Padres didn't have to concern themselves with any of that. They went 23–33 before the strike and 18–36 after the strike. That was good for sixth place in the NL West. Again and again. Overall, the Padres were 41–69 (.373). The franchise hasn't finished with that low of a winning percentage ever since.

The Toronto Blue Jays were just as bad, finishing last twice in the AL East.

The strike caused some crazy results:

- Most of the teams didn't play the same number of games. Pittsburgh played the fewest (102). San Francisco played the most (111).
- Cincinnati won more games (66) than any team in the majors, but the Reds didn't make the playoffs.
- Kansas City made the playoffs despite the Royals having a losing overall record (50–53).
- The Expos reached the playoffs for the only time in their 36 years in Montreal, beating the Phillies in the League Division Series before losing to the Dodgers in the National League Championship Series.
- The Dodgers defeated the Yankees in the World Series. Neither team would have made the playoffs in a normal year.

The season was pretty forgettable for the Padres.

Juan Eichelberger was the Padres' top starting pitcher, going 8–8 with a 3.50 ERA. Steve Mura (5–14), Chris Welsh (6–7), and Rick Wise (4–8) rounded out the then four-man rotation.

Kennedy was the only .300 hitter on the team. He batted .301, with two homers and 41 RBIs. Gene Richards led the club with 42 RBIs. Joe Lefebvre had a team-high eight homers.

Home attendance was 519,161, the lowest in the National League.

Padres manager Frank Howard was dismissed after the season. He was replaced by Dick Williams. And better days were ahead.

Of course they were; what could be worse than finishing last twice in the same season?

82 Gwynn's Debut

It is a handshake as much as a hit that Tony Gwynn remembered most vividly from his major league debut.

Perhaps that is because congratulations came from the man who collected more hits than anyone who ever played the game.

Gwynn's major league debut was July 19, 1982, in a game against the Philadelphia Phillies at San Diego Jack Murphy Stadium.

"I wasn't nervous or anything," said Gwynn, whose debut came just 14 months after being drafted in the third round out of San Diego State. "I did want to get a hit in my first game—and I ended up getting my first hit in the eighth inning."

It was a double to center field off Phillies reliever Sid Monge.

"I got a fastball out over the plate and just kind of carved it in to left-center field," said Gwynn. "You get to second base, you're kind of basking in the glory of getting a hit....I'm standing on second base, kind of looking around and see them flash on the board that I got my first big-league hit. And as I turned back around, there's Pete Rose standing in front of me."

Rose, the Phillies' first baseman, had been trailing the play.

"First big-league hit, huh?" said Rose.

"Yes, Mr. Rose," said Gwynn.

That's when Rose stuck out his hand. Gwynn accepted it with a big grin on his face.

"Shaking Pete Rose's hand is what sticks out for me," said Gwynn, reflecting on the moment 30 years later. "It was an era when veteran guys didn't say a whole lot to young guys. He didn't have to do that, but he did. That always resonated with me."

So did this:

After shaking hands, Rose took a few steps back toward first base, stopped, turned, and said, "Congratulations, kid. Don't catch me in one night."

A day earlier, Gwynn had no idea he was about to be promoted to the major leagues. In fact, when he was called into the office of Doug Rader, Gwynn's manager at Triple-A Hawaii, the outfielder assumed he was about to be scolded for a base-running blunder the previous game.

"The night before I had been thrown out at the plate to end the game, and we lost," said Gwynn. "Doug called me into his office, he closed the door, and before he could sit down, I said, 'Doug, I know I should have picked up my third-base coach a little sooner, and that was my fault.'

"He said, 'Yeah, you're right, but that's not why I called you in here.' Then I didn't have any idea what he was going to talk about."

Rader told Gwynn he wouldn't be playing in that night's game because there was a plane to catch for the mainland. Gwynn thought Rader was pulling his leg.

"No, I'm serious," said Rader.

"I called my wife, Alicia, who was six months pregnant at the time, and told her," said Gwynn. "I can still hear the scream out of the phone in my ear of how happy she was that we were going to get to go back to San Diego."

They flew all night, touching down midmorning at Lindbergh Field.

"My wife slept on the plane, but I couldn't," said Gwynn.

Once at their hotel, Gwynn remained restless. So he went to the ballpark—five and a half hours before the start of the game. Gwynn's wife and his parents, who drove down from Long Beach, would settle into their seats somewhat closer to first pitch.

In the clubhouse, Padres equipment manager Ray Peralta directed Gwynn to his locker. Longtime clubhouse man Whitey Wietelmann brought Gwynn his jersey.

"When he handed it to me it was No. 19," said Gwynn. "When I looked at it, I was just happy it was lower than 53, which is the number I wore in spring training."

Gwynn said Wietelmann told him that only a few players had worn No. 19—including Wietelmann for the minor league Padres—and concluded by saying, "So don't disgrace it."

"I'll try to do the best that I can, Mr. Wietelmann," said Gwynn.

The rookie was warmly welcomed in the Padres clubhouse by second baseman Tim Flannery, catcher Terry Kennedy, and outfielder Ruppert Jones, among others.

Gwynn did receive some needling. Someone put stickpins along the bottom edge of his jersey. That was the extent of his hazing. That, and one player pretending to throw the ball from

Gwynn's first hit into the stands. It remains safely behind glass in Gwynn's trophy case.

Gwynn had been anxious on the flight from Hawaii wondering if he would play in the game and whether Hall of Fame left-hander Steve Carlton would be on the mound for the Phillies.

Gwynn was in. Carlton wasn't (Mike Krukow was the starting pitcher). Padres manager Dick Williams penciled Gwynn into the starting lineup in center field. He batted fifth in the order.

"Just play the game like you've been playing it," Gwynn said Williams told him.

Gwynn was surprisingly calm for his first plate appearance.

"I wasn't nervous in the on-deck circle," said Gwynn. "As I walked up to the plate, obviously you could hear the crowd cheering for you, but when you're playing you just try to focus in on what you're trying to do."

The first-inning at-bat produced a sacrifice fly to center field for his first RBI. A lineout to shortstop and a strikeout followed before the eighth-inning double. Gwynn added a single in the ninth, giving him a 2-for-4 performance in his debut.

Rose also had two hits in the 7–6 Phillies win, giving him 3,800 for his career. Gwynn, who finished with 3,141 hits, didn't catch Rose, who retired four years later with 4,256. He made a pretty good go at it, however. No one had more hits than Gwynn over the next 20 years.

Skunks in the Tarp

Tarping the field doesn't seem like the most difficult task.

You gather a couple of dozen guys together, get them to unroll the square piece of canvas off its coil, then have each person grab a handhold and place the thing over the infield.

Of course, when you only practice once every three years the results can be kind of comical. Members of the Padres grounds crew have been known to struggle with the tarp through the years.

In fact, on one occasion the tarp pretty much disintegrated in their hands when the crew tried to pull it over the field after years of being rolled up.

That wasn't the most memorable incident, however.

It was 25 years ago at then–Jack Murphy Stadium when a family of skunks scattered after the grounds crew disrupted them while unrolling the tarp, which had seemed like a nice, dry place to take up residence.

The skunks were released along the San Diego River, although they always seemed to find their way back to the ballpark.

It's no wonder they made themselves at home. The odds of the tarp being touched were extremely remote.

Through the 2015 season, the Padres had only 17 rainouts in their 47-year history. Only two of them came during the 12 years they had occupied Petco Park.

It was an unprecedented summer storm in 2015 that forced the postponent of a July 19 game against the Rockies. That ended a nine-year stretch without a rainout that covered 770 games.

Before that, the Padres had just two rainouts from 1983 to 2006, covering a span of 1,802 games.

All-Time Padres Rainouts

Date	Opponent	Date	Opponent
July 19, 2015	Rockies	April 9, 1975	Giants
April 4, 2006	Giants	April 8, 1975	Giants
May 12, 1998	Mets	June 6, 1972	Pirates
April 20, 1983	Braves	June 5, 1972	Pirates
April 29, 1980	Braves	May 28, 1971	Mets
April 28, 1980	Braves	May 7, 1971	Reds
April 15, 1978	Giants	April 14, 1971	Cubs
May 8, 1977	Expos (DH)	April 27, 1970	Expos
Sept. 10, 1976	Astros (DH)		

The number of rainouts might not even be in double figures had it not been for Buzzie Bavasi, the Padres' first president.

Bavasi believed that doubleheaders drew better crowds, so he would call a game at the drop of a raindrop.

Six of the team's rainouts came within the franchise's first four years of existence.

84 Beanballs with the Braves

Pascual Perez was a lanky right-hander whose 11-year career in the major leagues is remembered as much for off-the-field incidents as on-the-field achievements.

Perez once circled Atlanta's Interstate 285 three times looking for Atlanta-Fulton County Stadium before running out of gas and missing his start.

Padres fans wish that was the case on August 12, 1984, when Perez served as the instigator in a Padres-Braves game that is still regarded among the most memorable bean-brawl games in baseball history.

Blood was set to boiling virtually as soon as the umpire said, "Play ball!" The Padres had beaten Atlanta two of three games in the series—and eight of 11 meetings on the season—dropping the second-place Braves 9½ games out of first place.

To make matters worse, Padres leadoff hitter Alan Wiggins had bunted twice for hits the night before, which the Braves took as showing them up moreso than playing to win.

And so the stage was set.

Perez—who had hit only two batters in 135⅔ innings—drilled Wiggins in the side with the game's first pitch.

What ensued over the next nine innings would have been comical if it weren't so concerning. The game would include three hit batters, four brawls, the ejection of 14 players and coaches, and the arrest of five fans at Fulton-County Stadium.

In the dugout after Wiggins was hit and before the Padres went out for the bottom of the first inning, manager Dick Williams said, "We know what we've got to do."

San Diego was on its way to the first pennant in Padres history, and the team wasn't going to back down or be intimidated.

Padres starting pitcher Ed Whitson tried to retaliate when Perez came to the plate in the second inning. Perez somehow deflected the ball with his bat, which he then held up as a weapon as he ran around behind the plate after both benches emptied.

Warned after the first incident, Whitson was ejected when he threw at Perez again in the fourth inning (Perez anticipated the inside pitch and backed out of the way). Williams was ejected with Whitson.

The Padres finally hit Perez in his fourth at-bat, when Craig Lefferts got him in the elbow in the eighth inning. That set off a brawl highlighted—lowlighted?—by the Padres' Champ Summers running in a rage over to the Atlanta dugout, where the Braves'

Bob Horner stopped him (side note: Horner had a cast on his arm and was in the press box when tensions rose but came down to the clubhouse and put on his uniform so he could be a more active participant).

At this point, one Braves fan threw beer on Summers while two others came on the field—one of them jumping on Summers' back.

The last brawl came in the ninth inning when Braves reliever Donnie Moore hit Padres third baseman Graig Nettles, who then charged the mound.

The ensuing melee was most notable for the wild punches being thrown by the Padres' Kurt Bevacqua—who wasn't even in the lineup and later ended up mixing it up with fans in the stands after being showered with beer.

Atlanta won the game 5–3 and the Padres went just 23–22 over the remainder of the regular season. But San Diego's 92–70 record was good enough to win the NL West. The Padres went on to upset the Chicago Cubs in the National League Championship Series and reach the World Series for the first time.

Umpire John McSherry said the game "set back baseball 50 years."

Atlanta manager Joe Torre called Williams an "idiot" and said, "It was obvious he was the cause of the whole thing."

Added Torre: "Precipitating a thing like that was inexcusable. It was stupid of them, period, to take four shots at Perez. It was gutless. It stinks. It was Hitler-like action. I think [Williams] should be suspended for the rest of the year."

"Tell Joe Torre to stick that finger he's pointing," said Williams, who wrote in his autobiography, "I meant it. How dare he get on his high horse and rip me for something he did just two innings later? And something he probably started by ordering Perez to throw at Wiggins in the first inning?

"I've been sorry for many things in my career. But my only regret about the 'Battle of Atlanta,' as one newspaper called it, is that Torre wound up looking like the good guy."

Williams was fined $10,000 and suspended 10 games. Torre was suspended three games.

"We had some honor to defend," Williams said. "Perez is a headhunter. There's no question we went after him. I'm responsible for it. I'll accept the penalty."

Padres catcher Terry Kennedy summed things up: "It would've been a lot simpler if we'd hit Perez his first time up."

85 Eric Show Sits Down on Mound

When Tony Gwynn approached 3,000 career hits in the summer of 1999, the Padres did several things to recognize the achievement.

One of the most visual examples was ringing the upper deck of Qualcomm Stadium with a banner for each member of the 3,000-hit club. The group numbered 22 players when Gwynn joined it. Membership has expanded now to 29, the Yankees' Alex Rodriguez joining this past June.

What I came to find out while researching some stories at the time was that six members of the 3,000-hit club—Cap Anson, Ty Cobb, Eddie Collins, Nap Lajoie, Tris Speaker, and Honus Wagner—have career hit totals that are in dispute.

I revisit this now as we observe the 30th anniversary of one of baseball's most celebrated feats from the 1980s—Pete Rose passing Ty Cobb to become baseball's all-time hits leader.

It occurred with the Padres in town. Or did it? There is no doubt the celebration took place during a Padres–Reds game.

Here's how it unfolded:

It was September 11, 1985, and Cincinnati was hosting the Padres at Riverfront Stadium. Right-hander Eric Show was on the mound for the Padres and Bruce Bochy was catching when Rose singled to left-center field on a 2–1 slider for the 4,192nd hit of his career.

Fireworks go off. Reds first-base coach Tommy Helms and Padres first baseman Steve Garvey congratulate Rose. Padres short-stop Garry Templeton throws the ball to him.

"As outfielders, we talked before the game about running the ball back into the infield, and maybe having a chance to give it to him," Gwynn said. "But Pete came around first like he was going for two, and (left fielder) Carmelo (Martinez) had to turn and wheel and get it in. That was Pete Rose."

Show also congratulates Rose, but what most people remember about Show is that he sat down on the mound while waiting for all the festivities to conclude at first base.

Overhead a lighted sign on the Goodyear Blimp blinks: *Pete Rose, 4,192* and on the field a red Corvette rolls out with the license plate PR 4192. The crowd of 47,237 gives Rose a seven-minute standing ovation.

Rose looks to the sky and sees the visions of his father and Cobb. In the book *Pete Rose: My Story*, he says: "Ty Cobb was in the second row. Dad was in the first." Rose hugs his son, Petey, a Reds batboy, and cries.

A memorable, emotional scene.

There's one problem with all of it—Cobb's hit total, amassed from 1905 to 1928, has been revised to 4,189.

That means Rose actually broke the record three days earlier at Chicago's Wrigley Field with hit No. 4,190, a first-inning single to left-center off Chicago Cubs right-hander Reggie Patterson.

Cobb's total was revised downward after research revealed a box score from a game in 1910 that was counted twice (the revision also costing Cobb that year's AL batting title).

Most sources now list 4,189 hits as Cobb's correct total.

The Society for American Baseball Research (SABR), *Total Baseball*, baseball-reference.com, baseball-almanac.com, and retrosheet.org are among those listing 4,189 hits.

Major League Baseball and the Elias Sports Bureau still recognize Cobb with 4,191 hits. Cobb's Hall of Fame plaque still lists 4,191 as well, mostly because Cooperstown takes its cue from MLB.

This is where it gets good. Or absurd, depending on your point of view.

Total Baseball is MLB's official encyclopedia and historical record. Elias is MLB's official statistician. And they don't agree. What the heck?

MLB does not move quickly on such matters. A researcher discovered in 1977 that Hack Wilson's record 190 RBIs in 1930 should actually have been 191 RBIs. MLB—after exhaustive review—didn't make the change in its record book until 1999.

According to a *New York Times* story, the statistical database for MLB.com was purchased from *Total Baseball*. It included hundreds of statistics that MLB would dispute, Cobb's hit total among them. MLB then manually changed Cobb's hit total to 4,191.

MLB was aware of the 4,189/4,191 controversy in the early 1980s, well before Rose broke the record.

Here's what commissioner Bowie Kuhn said when he addressed the issue in 1981:

"The passage of 70 years, in our judgment...constitutes a certain statute of limitation as to recognizing any changes in the records....The only way to make changes with confidence would be for a complete and thorough review of all team and individual statistics. That is not practical."

Not practical? Several baseball historians—led by SABR—have taken it upon themselves to sift through box scores and scoresheets and set the records straight.

"A statute of limitations on the truth?" said John Thorn, co-editor of *Total Baseball*. "When you discover truth, you have to report it."

At this point, MLB still isn't budging.

Rose is said to have changed his jersey before each at-bat on the night he collected No. 4,192 in Cincinnati. The jerseys were sold for a generous sum to memorabilia collectors.

Bet they want Ty Cobb to have 4,191 hits, too.

86 LaMarr Hoyt Trade Goes South

LaMarr Hoyt was going to be the piece to the Padres pitching staff that made the franchise a playoff contender for years to come.

Hoyt won the 1983 Cy Young Award with the Chicago White Sox, fashioning a 24–10 record with a 3.66 ERA and 148 strikeouts while walking only 31 hitters in 260.2 innings. After slumping to 13–18 with a 4.47 ERA in 1984, Hoyt was available.

The Padres were looking for a big-time pitcher to add to a team coming off its first World Series appearance. This looked like just the opportunity GM Jack McKeon was looking for at the Winter Meetings.

So Trader Jack dealt pitchers Tim Lollar and Bill Long and infielders Luis Salazar and Ozzie Guillen to Chicago for Hoyt and pitchers Kevin Kristan and Todd Simmons.

"We came to the Winter Meetings looking for a premier pitcher and we got one," McKeon said.

The Padres gave up a good player, too.

Guillen launched a 16-year major league career by earning 1985 AL Rookie of the Year honors with the White Sox.

Hoyt did make McKeon look good that year, though, going 16–8 with a 3.47 ERA. He was the starting pitcher for the 1985 All-Star Game, was the game's winning pitcher, and earned MVP honors.

Everything began to unravel after the season, however.

Hoyt had two brushes with the law in eight days in February of 1986. The first incident came at the San Ysidro border checkpoint, where Hoyt was in possession of marijuana, Valium tablets, and Quaaludes. The drugs were confiscated and he received a $620 fine. San Diego Police stopped him the next time, again with marijuana as well as a switchblade knife. The misdemeanor offenses came with similar punishments.

Within days, Hoyt was checked into a rehabilitation facility to deal with drug and alcohol issues. Padres president Ballard Smith was among those who had pushed Hoyt into rehab.

The right-hander returned to the Padres just as the season was starting.

"Ballard expressed an interest in me," Hoyt said. "He said he'd like to see me pitch here for the next 10 years....

"It seems like everyone in life ought to be able to mess up one time....Now, it's just a simple matter of taking it one day at a time, maybe even taking it an hour at a time, or a minute at a time."

Hoyt struggled again on the mound, going 8–11 with a career-high 5.15 ERA.

No one realized it at the time, but Hoyt would never pitch in the big leagues again.

One month after the season, Hoyt was arrested for drug possession at the United States–Mexico border. That led to a 45-day jail sentence. When he got out, Hoyt was suspended by Commissioner Peter Ueberroth. That suspension ended midway through the 1987 season, but Hoyt was released by the Padres as soon as he was eligible to play.

The White Sox signed him again with the hope of giving Hoyt a second chance. He wasted that opportunity during the offseason when he had a fourth drug arrest.

Hoyt paid quite a price for his addiction. So did the Padres.

87 Jimmy Jones' One-Hitter

Jimmy Jones made everyone forget that the Padres selected him ahead of Dwight Gooden in the baseball draft.

For a day, anyway.

The Texan made his major league debut on September 21, 1986, in Houston, with several friends and family members making the drive down from Dallas for the occasion.

"All these people were here," Jones said. "I didn't want to go out there, pitch four innings, and shower up. I didn't want to disappoint them."

He didn't. Not by a longshot.

Jones came within one pitch of baseball history, tossing a one-hitter in a 5–0 win over the Astros. The only hit was a third-inning triple by Houston pitcher Bob Knepper.

Knepper was also the Astros' only base runner, meaning Jones had come within a pitch of a perfect game.

"I guess I'm on cloud nine right now," said Jones, who struck out five and did not walk a batter.

Center fielder Kevin McReynolds and right fielder Tony Gwynn were kicking themselves for not catching the ball Knepper hit. They may have gotten to the ball if it hadn't been the pitcher at the plate.

"Aw, the darned thing should have been caught," Gwynn said. "I was playing Knepper (who is left-handed) to pull, even though he's hit the ball the other way a couple of times. Mac was playing him more the other way. If I'd have been moved over just a step or two toward center, I'd have caught that ball."

Knepper's hit went to the gap in right-center field.

"I just wish real bad there was some way I could have caught that ball, or they could have given me an error on it, or something," McReynolds said. "If it was any other hitter, I'd have caught that ball, but I was playing the pitcher toward the left-center alley. I just missed it by about a step."

Knepper was a career .137 hitter who was batting .093 coming into the game.

"I don't think I've ever broken up a no-hitter before," he said. "But I swing the bat OK. It's no shame to lose it to me."

Jones' performance was the greatest pitching debut in baseball history. It was the 11th one-hitter in Padres history.

He never would approach such success again. Jones went 9–7 in 1987 and 9–14 in 1988, then was traded to the Yankees. The mid-90s velocity Jones displayed out of high school had disappeared and never returned. He also pitched for Houston and Montreal before his eight-year career came to a close.

Jones was selected by the Padres with the third overall pick in the 1982 draft. Gooden was chosen two picks later by the New York Mets. Gooden won the 1985 Cy Young Award and he helped the Mets to the 1986 World Series title.

"People have criticized us for picking Jones ahead of Gooden," a Padres official said. "Well, Gooden didn't pitch a one-hitter in his debut."

Jones' performance was certainly something to crow about.

For a day, anyway.

88 The Feeney Finger

Padres president Chub Feeney had an odd way of showing his appreciation to the fans on Fan Appreciation Night.

He gave two of them the finger.

People loving alliteration as they do, the incident would forevermore be known as The Feeney Finger.

The 1988 season was approaching its conclusion. The Padres were headed for an 83–78 record and third place in the National League West, a disappointment after high expectations when the year began.

Manager Larry Bowa had been fired two months into the season and replaced by General Manager Jack McKeon.

But that wasn't enough change for some Padres faithful.

Many in the crowd of 21,252 cheered during the seventh-inning stretch of the game against Houston when two men walked around with a sign that read "Scrub Chub."

At one point, they stopped below the owner's box. Feeney ran down from his seat to a railing, flipped them off, then waved and returned to his seat. The gesture drew boos from the crowd.

TV cameras captured the incident, and Padres broadcaster Ted Leitner didn't miss a beat, saying, "Chub says we're No. 1."

Feeney was unaware cameras were on him at the time. After the game, he denied doing anything improper.

"I ran down and waved to them," Feeney said. "What's the big deal? I would never give an obscene gesture. That's ridiculous. I deny giving an obscene gesture."

Lines lit up with angry fans during the Padres' postgame radio talk show.

Television, radio, and print media had a field day with the incident. A newspaper cartoonist even drew a Feeney Finger with a dotted outline that readers could clip and save. A popcorn vendor did brisk business while giving away photocopied cutouts of the cartoon.

Padres shortstop Garry Templeton, upon hearing of Feeney giving the finger, said, "Tell (Chub) that's a $5,000 fine."

That was the amount Templeton was fined seven years earlier when he acted similarly, flipping off St. Louis fans who had been heckling him. That incident led the Cardinals to trade Templeton to San Diego in exchange for Padres shortstop Ozzie Smith.

Feeney announced his resignation at a news conference fewer than 24 hours after the incident. A statement handed out to assembled media read:

"I would like to take this opportunity to offer my sincerest apology for the incident that occurred at last night's Astro–Padre game. A totally inappropriate gesture was made by myself—even though it was not intended to be public—in a moment of frustration and anger which I wish with all my heart had never occurred.

"My deepest regret is the reflection such conduct has on the Padres, Mrs. Joan Kroc, and the game of baseball. My adult life has been devoted to baseball, and of utmost importance to me has been the positive effect it has on our society and the young people who follow and love the game.

"I am gravely upset with myself for allowing my anger to get the better of me where the game I care for so much is involved. I cannot undo what has been done, but again I apologize for the incident."

Feeney reluctantly answered a few questions, then excused himself.

It was a crushing blow for the longtime baseball executive. Feeney spent 24 years running the Giants' front office, then 17 years as president of the National League before becoming Padres president in 1987.

After a distinguished career, this was no way to leave the stage.

Feeney was asked about the incident when a reporter caught up with him the following year at spring training.

"It's one of those things that happens," Feeney said. "I was laughing at those guys who had the sign and made the gesture.

"Obviously, I had no idea it was going to be on television. I thought that was kind of a dirty pool trick, too. I just hope that that's forgotten."

Though six months had passed since the incident, Feeney said he still did not find any humor in it.

"No," he said. "I can't laugh about it. I wish it hadn't happened. I certainly felt very uncomfortable for the next couple of days. It's something I have more or less forgotten. It's certainly not the high point of my career."

89 Clark vs. Gwynn— '89 Batting Title

There were no Twitter updates in 1989, so one of the closest batting races in National League history had to be updated by hand.

The Giants were in town for a three-game series that would conclude the regular season. San Francisco first baseman Will Clark and the Padres' Tony Gwynn were battling neck-and-neck for the batting title.

Clark led Gwynn by a point—.333 to .332—coming into the series. He still led by a point—.334 to .333—coming into the last game.

San Diego fans had held out hope for an NL West title until the team was eliminated from the race in the season's final week.

In lieu of a postseason berth, the batting race created tremendous excitement for the fans at Jack Murphy Stadium. 24,031 people showed up for the final game, which is why the Padres were able to go over 2,000,000 in attendance for the year.

A Padres fan in the stands had a white eraser board with him. After each at-bat, he would update averages and hold the board up for everyone to see.

Clark batted .287, .308, and .282 his first three seasons in the majors before challenging Gwynn for the title. Tony said he had his eye on Will back in spring training, noticing how Clark had begun to use the whole field and go with the ball where it was pitched.

"Usually it takes hitters two or three years of learning, and then they blossom," Gwynn said. "Will likes to hit, no question about it. He's always watching and asking questions. He's probably going to be one of the best hitters in baseball for a long time, because he works hard at his craft and is willing to learn."

Gwynn learned a little more about Clark when the two sat next to each other on the bench at the 1989 All-Star Game.

"For two innings, all we did was watch hitters and talk about what we thought they were trying to do at the plate," Gwynn said. "It was, 'Watch his foot. Look at his stride. It looks like he's uppercutting everything, but he hits the ball hard. How does he do that?' Just hearing what he said gives me a good idea of what he's thinking about when he hits. I don't like to be a pest, but if they want to talk hitting, I'll fire questions forever."

There was no question on Gwynn's mind who was going to win this challenge.

The future Hall of Famer went 7-for-13 in the series—6-for-8 the last two games—while Clark went 4-for-12.

Clark managed only a sixth-inning single in the final game, going 1-for-4.

Gwynn lined a single to right field in the first inning before grounding out to second base in the third.

There was some controversy when Gwynn beat out an infield single on a close play in the fifth inning. A Giants coach was ejected after arguing the call from the dugout.

Gwynn added another single in the eighth, making him 3-for-4 on the day, to remove any doubt.

The 1989 National League batting championship came down to the last game of the regular season. A fan at San Diego Jack Murphy Stadium updated the averages of the Padres' Tony Gwynn and Giants first baseman Will Clark after each at-bat. (Fantography.com/Jan Brooks)

Clark's reaction: he took off his first baseman's glove and offered his hand.

"He said congratulations," Gwynn said. "But the way it turned out doesn't take anything away from the year Will had. He had a great year and I had a pretty good year, too."

Gwynn won his third straight batting title with a .336 average to Clark's .333.

"I gave it my best run and lost to the best," said Clark. "Tony's been through this (a batting race) before. It was all new to me."

Clark said Padres pitchers had Gwynn's back in the series.

"They pitched me tough every game," Clark said. "You could see they had one goal...to do all they could to help Tony win the batting championship...change-ups on 2–0 counts, sliders on 3–1, curveballs on 2–1. I saw it all."

Padres rookie Greg Harris threw seven shutout innings before turning things over to the bullpen in the Padres' 3–0 victory in the finale.

"Will seemed to be looking for hits, instead of driving the ball," Harris noted after the game. "I pounded him with fastballs inside the first couple pitches, then tried to get him out with something away."

The championship made Gwynn the first player to win three straight batting titles since Stan Musial from 1950 to 1952. Gwynn would repeat the feat—going one better, in fact—when he won four straight titles from 1994 to 1997.

90 Barr-Strangled Banner

Roseanne Barr had the No. 1-rated TV show in the country in 1990.

Tom Werner was the executive producer of the *Roseanne* show.

Werner also was among a group of 15 investors who in June of 1990 completed the purchase of the Padres from owner Joan Kroc.

Soon after the sale, Werner had a question: "What do you think about Roseanne singing the national anthem?"

The idea was to have Barr sing the Star-Spangled Banner between games of a Reds–Padres doubleheader on July 25, 1990, which was declared as Working Women's Day at Jack Murphy Stadium.

One of the people the new owner asked about the idea was Andy Strasberg, then the Padres' vice president of public relations.

Strasberg remembers the first thing he said to Werner was "Great. Can she sing?"

"Don't worry about it," Werner told him.

"Why don't we have her sing 'Take Me Out to the Ballgame?'" Strasberg suggested.

"She wants to sing the anthem," Werner said.

"Why don't we have her prerecord it so she can just enjoy herself and lip-sync like everybody else?" Strasberg asked.

"No, she wants to sing it live," Werner said.

The Padres were purchased for $75 million by the Werner group. The *Roseanne* show on ABC—then the top-rated program in the country—was worth five times that much to the network.

Barr's performance is still one of the most memorable moments in Padres history. For all the wrong reasons.

Whitney Houston's rendition of the national anthem before Super Bowl XXV remains the gold standard. Barr lowered the bar quite a bit, her version generally regarded as the worst of all time.

July 2015 marked the 25th anniversary of the "Barr Strangled Banner," as a headline put it in the *San Diego Tribune*. Others put it in less printable terms.

Barr still gets asked about the incident all the time, although she is very reluctant to discuss it for the record. She did release a transcript on her website roseanneworld.com from a recent interview she gave to the *Washington Post*.

"I meant no disrespect to the country and (people) fighting for the safety and freedoms of old loudmouth Jewish women," Barr said. "I'm sorry some saw it that way."

No one has butchered it like Barr. Not even close. It wasn't just the off-key screeching or the fingers in her ears as boos rang out from the crowd of 27,285. To top it off, Barr made an obscene gesture and spit as she stepped away from the microphone.

Outrage was immediate.

"I was embarrassed as a person and I was embarrassed for them [the Padres]," Padres pitcher Eric Show told reporters afterward. "I can't believe it happened. It's an insult. There are people who died for that song."

Teammate Tony Gwynn had similar feelings: "I thought it was a disgrace. When they said she was going to sing the national anthem I thought something like this was going to happen."

So did Strasberg.

Five days before she was to sing, Barr made an appearance on *The Tonight Show* with Johnny Carson.

During the interview, Carson said, "I understand in a couple days you're going to be doing the national anthem. I didn't know you could sing."

"Of course, I can," Barr said.

Asked to give the audience a sample, Barr sang "Kung Fu Fighting."

It was not good.

"I realized she can't sing," Strasberg said. "We've got a problem here."

Said Werner: "Don't worry, she's a professional."

Um, yeah.

A professional comedian. Barr had planned to ham it up a little for the crowd, which wasn't a bright idea. Things snowballed from there.

The Padres welcomed television star Roseanne Barr on the scoreboard when she came out to sing the national anthem between games of a doubleheader with Cincinnati—then Barr opened her mouth. (Fantography.com/Jan Brooks)

"It was a series of unfortunate circumstances," Strasberg said.

On *The Tonight Show,* Carson had warned her, "Don't start too high. Robert Goulet started too high and it was a disaster."

"The echo and no musical support caused me to do just that—I started too high," Barr said. "I knew about six notes in that I couldn't hit the big note, so I just tried to get through it. But I couldn't hear anything with 50 thousand drunk [expletive] booing, screaming you fat [expletive], giving me the finger and throwing bottles at me, during the song they 'respect' so much."

She quickly had a problem with the split-second delay in the audio over the stadium sound system. So Barr put her fingers in her ears.

"But the perception in the stands is that people are booing and she doesn't want to hear the boos," Strasberg said. "And her voice gets louder and now she's screeching."

Boos began almost as soon as Barr opened her mouth. Perhaps it was the comedian's instinct, when things went south, to take it over the top. Maybe she was going for a laugh when she made it so shrill, stretching out and screeching the word "free" toward the end of the song.

But that's not what you do with this song, and certainly not in this town.

Barr's performance didn't end with the music. She grabbed herself and spit on the ground before walking off the field. It was supposed to imitate a ballplayer, but from the stands it appeared more as a gesture to the crowd. Blame Padres catcher Mark Parent. A newspaper account the next day said Parent was sitting next to Roseanne in the dugout beforehand and provided the inspiration for that little portion of the incident.

"Hey, why don't you grab your crotch," Parent had suggested.

"Yeah," Barr said. "Just like a player. And I'll spit, too."

They laughed about it.

"I'll do it after I sing," Barr had said. "You know how people are about the anthem."

She had no idea.

Barr spoke to reporters briefly after she left the field with new husband Tom Arnold, who had thrown out the first pitch.

"I thought it was great," she said. "I did well, I think. You can tell they wanted more."

Asked about all the booing, Barr said: "That's just because they weren't sitting in front."

The incident drew national attention, providing fodder for radio shows, TV commentators, and newspaper columnists for weeks to come. Even President George Bush chimed in, calling it a "disgrace."

"Had it gone better," Barr said in her website comments, "I would have taken a longer beat between singing and the 'tribute' to baseball players. But at that point, I just wanted to get out of there—my kids were sitting in the audience and I was concerned that they would be hurt. I sent cops to retrieve them. Luckily they got out OK, and we flew home in the Padres' private jet. 'We've got your back, don't worry' is the last thing the Padres and Tom Werner said, and I never heard anything from the Padres or Tom Werner after that."

Reporters tried to get to Werner in his luxury box for a comment after the incident, but he refused to come out. The team issued a statement: "The Padres understand that many people were concerned about Roseanne Barr's rendition of the national anthem. She was doing the best she could under the circumstances of the audio delay, and she certainly meant no disrespect for the national anthem."

The *Roseanne* show drew 21 million viewers a week during the 1989–90 television season, making it the No. 1-rated show in the country. The audience dropped to fewer than 17 million viewers a week the following season. There's no telling whether any of the dropoff was due to Barr's singing, but it couldn't have helped.

Asked if she had any regrets, Barr said: "Do I regret that the next day all of my projects were cancelled and I had to have LAPD stand on my roof and protect my life and my kids for two years? Do I regret not being able to go out in public for about one full year without being spit on in restaurants, 7–11, etc? Do I regret *Rolling Stone* selling T-shirts with my picture in the middle of a gun target during Desert Storm? Do I regret that every 'feminist' in Hollywood ran the other way when they saw me at Hollywood functions, to avoid taking a picture with me? Do I regret my cartoon, little Rosey, the only female protagonist for children being cancelled despite good ratings and replaced with *Teenage Mutant Ninja Turtles*? Do I regret President George Bush 1 calling me disgraceful on television as he unleashed Desert Storm? Do I regret not one person in Hollywood defending me? Do I regret becoming aware of the toxic anti-Semitism in this country through the dozens of death threats I received?

"Actually, no, I don't regret any of it. It was the catalyst I needed to re-connect to my Creator, who is my Source. Two years later, I was able to escape from a horrible marriage, and was in a new marriage and pregnant with my youngest son. I have sung the national anthem much better since then at various baseball games around the country. I also recorded a kids' album. I'm glad that I still love to sing and that I improved as a singer since 1991."

Barr has been through several ups and downs since, but it's obvious she never completely put the incident behind her.

Barr took another crack at the national anthem in 2011. She received voice instruction from a friend, singer Bonnie Bramlett, before belting it out at a girls' softball game near her home in Hawaii. This rendition drew cheers after Barr finished the final note.

She had it all chronicled for TV in an episode of her Lifetime reality show *Roseanne's Nuts*.

During an interview on the show, Barr said, "Singing the 'Star Spangled Banner' the first time ruined everything." But she wanted her grandkids to know you can always try to make things right.

"Even if you've made a bad mistake, nobody can stop you from trying to correct it," Barr said. "I'm a patriot of this country. I have a right to sing the 'Star Spangled Banner,' and I'm going to do a much better job than the last time."

That, she did.

Of course, she couldn't do any worse.

91 Name All the Managers— in Order

Remember in school when you learned about the U.S. presidents? It included memorizing them in order, from George Washington to the present day.

Here's a challenge of similar significance: name all 19 of the Padres' managers—in order—since their inaugural season in 1969.

Preston Gomez got first crack at managing the team when it debuted. GM Buzzie Bavasi brought him south from the Dodgers, where Gomez had been coaching third base.

Don Zimmer was coaching third base for the Padres in 1972 when he replaced Gomez 11 games into the season.

Zim lasted two years before John McNamara took over in 1974. McNamara lasted until he was fired midway through the 1977 season.

This began a stretch of six managers in six years.

Coach Bob Skinner was interim manager for one game—a win—before Alvin Dark arrived from Chicago to take over the team. Dark finished out the season. He was fired during 1978 spring training in 1978 and pitching coach Roger Craig took over.

Craig, who led the Padres to the franchise's first winning season (84–78 in 1978) lasted through 1979.

Jerry Coleman came down from the broadcast booth in 1980, then went back upstairs when Frank Howard managed in 1981, skippering only 110 game because of a midseason strike.

Dick Williams followed in 1982, going 81–81 two straight seasons before leading the Padres to the 1984 NL pennant when they posted a franchise-record 92–70 mark. A disappointing 83–79

Padres Skippers

Managers (Years)	W–L (Win Pct.)
Preston Gomez (1969–72)	180–316 (.363)
Don Zimmer (1972–73)	114–190 (.375)
John McNamara (1974–77)	224–310 (.419)
Bob Skinner (1977)	1–0 (1.000)
Alvin Dark (1977)	48–65 (.425)
Roger Craig (1978–79)	152–171 (.471)
Jerry Coleman (1980)	73–89 (.451)
Frank Howard (1981)	41–69 (.373)
Dick Williams (1982–85)	337–311 (.520)
Steve Boros (1986)	74–88 (.457)
Larry Bowa (1987–88)	81–127 (.389)
Jack McKeon (1988–90)	193–164 (.541)
Greg Riddoch (1990–92)	200–194 (.508)
Jim Riggleman (1992–94)	112–179 (.385)
Bruce Bochy (1995–2005)	951–975 (.494)
Bud Black (2006–15)	649–713 (.477)
Dave Roberts (2015)	0–1 (.000)
Pat Murphy (2015)	42–54 (.438)
Andy Green (2016)	

outcome followed in 1985. Williams walked away on the eve of the 1986 season.

More instability followed, with Steve Boros managing in 1986 and Larry Bowa from 1987 to 1988. GM Jack McKeon fired the fiery Bowa 46 games into the 1988 season and made himself manager.

McKeon lasted until the 1990 All-Star break, when he turned the team over to coach Greg Riddoch. Riddoch posted a winning season in 1991—going 84–78—and was 78–72 in 1992 when he was fired by new GM Joe McIlvaine. Coach Jim Riggleman took over and managed the team through the 1994 season.

The franchise's greatest period of managerial stability followed, with former catcher Bruce Bochy taking over in 1995. Bochy guided the Padres to the 1998 World Series after a franchise-record 98–64 season. His 951 victories over 12 seasons are the most by any Padres manager.

Bud Black replaced Bochy in 2007—perhaps so they wouldn't have to change the initials on the towels—and lasted eight-plus seasons before being fired 65 games into the 2015 season.

Bench coach Dave Roberts was interim manager for one game—a loss—before Pat Murphy was summoned from Triple-A El Paso to take over the team.

Murphy was told he would not return an hour after the season ended.

GM A.J. Preller's search landed the franchise's 19th manager when Andy Green was hired.

Got all that?

92 Take a Tour of Petco Park

Fans have 81 opportunities a year to see the Padres at home, but they have virtually every day to see the Padres' home.

The team offers a behind-the-scenes guided tour of Petco Park that takes fans from down in the dugout to up in the press box, from the warning track to the bullpen, and everywhere in between.

The tours include a view of private luxury suites, the Western Metal Supply Co. building, the Beach, and the Park at the Park.

Guests get to know the history of the ballpark as well as little-known facts about the area during the 80-minute tour that covers more than a mile. They get to enjoy unique views of downtown San Diego, the Coronado Bridge, and San Diego Bay.

Tours are conducted year-round, except on certain days when special events are in town, such as the ComicCon convention each July.

Typical tour times are 10:30 AM and 12:30 PM during the week, with a 3:00 PM tour added on Saturdays. Tour times vary on game days during the season and sometimes require a game ticket to participate in the tour.

The Padres recommend the tours for class field trips, Little League teams, youth groups, company outings, tourists, and, of course, baseball fans.

Groups, families, and individuals are welcome as walk-ups. Groups of 25 or more must make reservations at least 10 business days before their tour date.

The tours involve climbing stairs and walking up ramps. The team emphasized the tours are wheelchair accessible, although wheelchairs are not provided for guests.

Ticket prices range from $8 to $12. Tickets are available at Padres.com or the Advance Ticket Windows at Petco Park. Information is available at the Tour Hotline at (619) 795-5011 or by emailing tours@padres.com.

Gazing out from home plate at Petco Park affords visitors a view of the Western Metal Supply Co. building incorporated into the ballpark's design, the giant video board that debuted during the 2015 season, the Park at the Park located beyond center field and the downtown San Diego skyline that has been enhanced in the decade since Petco opened. (Kirk Kenney)

93 Western Metal Supply Co. Building

In the late 1990s, owners John Moores and Larry Lucchino scouted several areas to build a new place for the Padres to play.

When the East Village location was pinpointed for Petco Park, there were several buildings scheduled for demolition to make way for the downtown ballpark.

At the same time, the owners wanted something special about the place that would help tie San Diego's past to its present and future.

They found it sitting right there on the corner of 7th Avenue and K Street—the Western Metal Supply Co. building.

Amazingly, it was originally among the buildings scheduled to be demolished. Of course, Petco wouldn't be the same without it.

Inspiration came from more than 2,500 miles away. Lucchino, who was with Baltimore in the early 1990s when the Orioles were building a new ballpark, was likely reminded of the existing B&O Warehouse located beyond right field at Camden Yards.

The Western Metal Supply Co. building was even better because it could be incorporated into the ballpark itself. In fact, one corner became a focal point—and a starting point—for the rest of the ballpark.

The corner of the Western Metal building has a strip of yellow angle iron from ground to roof that serves as the left-field foul pole.

"It seems to fit so well," longtime Padres broadcaster Ted Leitner said. "It looks like they put the Western Metal building in after they built the ballpark to give it that old flavor. There's nothing else like that."

The 51,400-square foot, four-story brick building was designed in 1909 by architect Henry Lord Gay. The Western Metal Supply Co. served much of Southern California.

It was filled with metal products for wagon makers, blacksmiths, and others. As times changed, so did the supplies it stocked. But the business went bankrupt in the 1970s. The building, though placed on the San Diego Historical Resources Board registry, sat there vacant for years.

The Padres gave it new life. Renovation of the building made way for a gift shop on the first floor, suites on the second and third floors, a restaurant on the fourth floor, and rooftop seating.

"It's not just the building and its age being there and fitting so well," Leitner said. "It's the idea of hitting in the first row, second row, third row, on to the roof. That's a pretty fair poke for a home run."

It's 336 feet to clear the left-field fence. Watching a home-run ball bounce off the brick building is pretty cool.

It beats a wrecking ball any day of the week.

Going 82–80

Division champions have been given a playoff berth ever since divisions were created in 1969.

The 2005 Padres launched a discussion to reconsider that when they won the National League West with an 82–80 record.

"It's going to take over .500 ball to win this division, I firmly believe that," Padres manager Bruce Bochy had predicted in mid-August.

Actually, the Padres could have won the division even if they had finished seven games under .500.

The Padres' 82–80 record translated to a .506 winning percentage. They replaced the 1973 Mets (82–79, .509), whose record had stood for 32 years as the worst to win a division.

There was some concern coming into the final week of the regular season that the Padres could become the first division winner with a losing record.

The Padres were 77–79 through 156 games. They saved the embarrassment of having a losing record by winning five of their last six games.

They would have finished at least eight games behind any other division winner in the major leagues and 18 games back of St. Louis (100–62) in the NL Central. There were eight other teams in the majors with better records than the Padres that didn't make the playoffs.

The Padres finished five games ahead of second-place Arizona (77–85), despite scoring fewer runs (684) than they allowed (726).

Part of the Padres' struggles—as well as their NL West counterparts—dealt with injuries. Only two starters from San Diego's Opening Day lineup—right fielder Brian Giles and left fielder Ryan Klesko—did not spend time on the disabled list.

In the best-of-five divisional playoffs, the Padres were swept in three straight games by the Cardinals—losing on scores of 8–5, 6–2, and 7–4—to finish the season with an 82–83 overall record. They became the only playoff team in history to lose more games than they won.

Still, Padres CEO Sandy Alderson downplayed all the talk over the team's poor winning record.

"This is something that happens once every 30 years," Alderson said. "It's an unusual situation. Would it be better if we were one of the other four teams in the division at the end of the year? I don't think so. I'd rather be a footnote to history than not in history at all."

95 Going Ape on the Padres' Plane

Among the upgrades the Padres enjoyed after the team was purchased in the mid-1970s by Ray Kroc was the purchase of a private jet so the team could travel in style.

There would be no more sitting around airports enduring travel delays. No longer would players be shoehorned into seats on planes lacking leg and elbow room.

Kroc's generosity extended beyond the team. Before the 1979 season, the plane was used for a mission of mercy.

It was flown to Colorado to pick up Abe the gorilla, who was brought to the San Diego Zoo to cheer up (and hopefully mate with) Bouba.

According to a UPI story, the female "has suffered from loneliness and depression since her lifelong friend Albert died last October from old age."

So Kroc and his wife Joan donated the team's 727 to give Abe a lift.

"The Krocs felt this would be something good for San Diego and would help out the zoo," said Ballard Smith, Padres executive vice president. "It so happened we had the plane scheduled to go up Friday, so we extended the trip a bit to make the gorilla pickup."

The seats and floor covering in the first-class section were removed to make room for Abe's cage.

Journalists were invited to document the occasion. They sat in coach with other members of the traveling party.

Downwind, as it turned out.

Hopefully, Abe got in a shower and a shave before being introduced to Bouba. Bringing Abe to San Diego otherwise went off without a hitch.

For all the good intentions, however, it was not a match made in heaven.

Zoo spokesman Jeff Jouett remembered Bouba and Abe getting into "a very dramatic slapping match." Abe had romantic inclinations, but Bouba wasn't interested.

They ended up going their separate ways—Bouba to a zoo in Pennsylvania and Abe to a zoo in Houston.

96 Cammy's Snickers Bar

The Padres made a big push in 1996 to improve their fan following south of the border, traveling for a three-game series against the New York Mets in Monterrey, Mexico.

Planning took the better part of a year. Pulling it off in a foreign country was a serious undertaking.

Don't laugh, but it is best remembered with Snickers.

Padres third baseman Ken Caminiti came down with something before the last game of the series.

"When I got sick the night before, I didn't know what I had," said Caminiti, who had severe cramping in his calves, hamstrings, and forearms as well as diarrhea.

He could barely move when he woke up in the morning but somehow made it to the ballpark.

Caminiti immediately received two IVs, although manager Bruce Bochy still wasn't counting on having his third baseman for the game.

"Once the first bag went in me, I started focusing a little bit better," Caminiti said. "Bruce was looking at me—and I said, 'I'm starting to feel better. Give me a chance.'"

A few minutes before first pitch, Caminiti said, "Let's go."

"They wanted to take my vitals again," Caminiti said, "but I said I didn't have time for that. I felt I was good enough to go. I ran one sprint, threw two baseball warm-ups, then played third base."

Still woozy and wobbly, Caminiti called for a Snickers bar before his first at-bat.

"Snickers?" trainer Todd Hutcheson repeated.

"Snickers," Cammy confirmed.

Then he homered leading off the second inning. Caminiti followed with a three-run homer in the third. He was replaced in the fifth after striking out with the Padres ahead by four runs on the way to an 8–0 win over the Mets.

"What it comes down to, I just don't ever know what I can do, so I give myself a chance to see," Caminiti said. "Unless I've got something broke, I'm always going to try to help the team."

After that, Caminiti incorporated the candy into his daily diet.

"I'm making sure I eat one a day before the game," he said. "I don't know if they have anything to do with it, but they're good and I'm having fun with it."

Padres fans did their part, bringing Snickers to the ballpark to make sure the slugger had a steady supply.

"They've been throwing them and dropping them off and leaving them in the bullpen, saying 'Give those to Cammy.' We've got a ton of them in there," he said.

Teammate Tony Gwynn marveled at it all.

"The first day home (from Monterrey), he hit a grand slam," Gwynn said. "The next time up he gets a two-run single. In five at-bats he had four hits, three home runs, 10 RBIs, three IVs, and two Snickers. The guy is amazing."

Caminiti finished the season with a .326 batting average, 40 home runs, and 130 RBIs and was a unanimous selection as National League MVP.

Snickers took out full-page ads following Caminiti's heroics, tapping into his feats when fueled with the product. The candy company also said opponents should be thankful he hadn't eaten the king-size version.

Just imagine.

Enzo Hernandez

Padres shortstop Enzo Hernandez became a crowd favorite in the early 1970s and it had nothing to do with his hitting or fielding.

When Hernandez came to the plate, public address announcer John DeMott had an unusually catchy way of introducing the 5'8" Venezuelan's number and name: "NumberElevenEnzooooooHernandezzzzzzzzzzzz."

Fans loved it.

There's no way to explain it.

Hernandez, who debuted with the Padres in 1971, was the primary beneficiary of the franchise's inability to acquire a legitimate everyday shortstop.

"Hernandez could solve our shortstop problem for years to come," Padres manager Preston Gomez said when introducing his new shortstop.

If only.

Hernandez appeared in 143 games in 1971. He distinguished himself that season by driving in the fewest runs of any regular player in major league history. He had 12 RBIs, tying the total of Pittsburgh's Goat Anderson in 1907. Hernandez, however, accomplished it in 549 at-bats while Anderson had only 413 at-bats.

He averaged two RBIs a month. Imagine.

Bob Fontaine, Padres director of player personnel, once said of Hernandez: "Enzo doesn't get on base as much as he should, or score as often as he should, because he doesn't walk enough and because he hits too many balls in the air and not on the ground. And he doesn't bunt enough."

Not exactly a glowing scouting report.

Hernandez somehow lasted six seasons on the Padres roster before being released early in the 1977 season after former first-round draft pick Bill Almon replaced him at shortstop.

Hernandez had a career-high 34 RBIs in 1975. He also had a National League best 24 sacrifice bunts that season.

A career .224 hitter, Hernandez did contribute on the base paths, averaging 21.5 stolen bases a season.

Popularity isn't always explained by statistics. Hernandez is proof of that.

98 Buy a Painting from Gene Locklear

When Gene Locklear was barely old enough to hold a brush or a bat, he already knew what he wanted to be when he grew up.

"I really wanted to be a professional artist and a professional baseball player," Locklear said. "I loved to paint, and I loved to play ball. If you had asked me when I was six or seven what I was going to do, that's what I would have told you. I'd do both."

Locklear, a full-blooded member of the Lumbee Indian Nation, grew up in Pembroke, North Carolina, a place where in the 1950s dreams rarely became reality.

"As a kid from a small country town," Locklear said, "I figured my chances of becoming a ballplayer were probably something like one in a million. I had the common sense to realize I'd better have something to fall back on. So I painted."

Locklear did develop the talent to play baseball and was one of about two dozen Native Americans to reach the major leagues. He debuted in 1973 with Cincinnati. There wasn't much room on the roster of the Big Red Machine for the young outfielder, and Locklear was traded to the Padres in midseason that year.

Locklear played parts of four seasons in San Diego before finishing his five-year career with the Yankees. His .274 career batting average—which included a .321 average, five homers, and 27 RBIs for the 1975 Padres—would earn Locklear a multimillion-dollar contract these days. In the 1970s, he needed to make money in the offseason to make ends meet.

And so he painted.

"While I was in high school, my mom and dad sacrificed for me to go to art school," Locklear said. "I finished high school with a commercial art degree.

"The first painting I ever sold was for $5. I now sell one painting for more than my parents used to make in a whole year, so the sacrifice was worth it."

Locklear, who still makes his home in a San Diego suburb, had his first one-man show in 1985.

In the three decades since, Locklear has had his work displayed in both the White House and the Pentagon. According to his website, genelocklear.com, Locklear has had paintings commissioned by the NFL, the NBA's Atlanta Hawks, and the Padres as well as professional golfers Phil Mickelson and Tiger Woods.

Locklear favors sports-themed and Native American subjects for his art and he also does some abstract work. He has done everything from small paintings to 30-foot murals, working with oils, acrylics, and pencils.

The person who purchased that $5 Locklear painting got quite a bargain. Some of his paintings sell now for $20,000.

"You know you have the ambition and you hope you have the talent," Locklear said.

Few people have held a brush or a bat with more authority.

99 Garth Brooks Makes a Hit

It wasn't among Garth Brooks' greatest hits, but the country superstar was pretty proud of it all the same.

Brooks, pinch-hitting in a spring training game for the Padres in 1999, bounced a pitch from Chicago White Sox left-hander Mike Sirotka under the glove of second baseman Ray Durham for a single. It was the first—and only—hit for Brooks.

"It's hard to get a hit at this level," White Sox first baseman Frank Thomas said. "The way he's hustling and working hard, it's something I can't fathom. He's changed a lot of people's minds about what he's doing. I think everyone thinks it's great."

There isn't usually much demand for 37-year-old outfielders who never rated a second look the first time around. But Brooks, who played high school baseball growing up in Oklahoma, was different.

Brooks signed as many autographs as Tony Gwynn during the spring, fans flocking to get a glimpse of the singer.

Brooks signed a minor league contract with the Padres before the spring. In addition to realizing a childhood dream, Brooks also was trying to gather support for his Touch 'Em All Foundation, a charity for children. He signed up dozens of major leaguers, who pledged to make contributions based on their number of home runs, strikeouts, and other statistics during the season.

Brooks would have been only too happy to contribute, but he was 0-for-spring before getting his only hit in 22 at-bats.

"I think (the Lord) got the message," said Brooks, who had the ball retrieved by Thomas after his hit. "You keep doing things right and hope it falls."

Brooks took his lead off first following the hit. Thomas played behind the bag.

"Yes," Brooks said, "the thought to steal came into my mind."

There could only be so much drama in the day, however.

Brooks went 1-for-22 during the spring, collecting his only RBI on an infield out in his final plate appearance.

"It's been good—no, great—for baseball," Padres manager Bruce Bochy said.

Padres GM Kevin Towers joked that the club tried to retain Brooks by offering him a "Trevor Hoffman deal, $32 million for four years." Towers said Brooks "turned us down. He said he could make that much in a weekend."

 **In Closing...**

The save became an official Major League Baseball statistic in 1969, the same year the Padres became a major league team.

And while they have not been among the most successful franchises over the past five decades, the Padres have enjoyed a rather rich history in regard to those who save games.

The Padres have had two Hall of Fame closers through the years in Rollie Fingers (Class of 1992) and Goose Gossage (Class of 2008).

Padres Top 10 Career Saves Leaders

552—Trevor Hoffman
134—Heath Bell
108—Rollie Fingers
83—Goose Gossage
80—Huston Street
78—Mark Davis
64—Craig Lefferts
49—Gary Lucas
39—Craig Kimbrel
38—Randy Myers

There was great anticipation that Trevor Hoffman would join them in 2016. The Padres' career saves leader fell short in his first year of eligibility, receiving 67.3 percent of the vote from members of the Baseball Writers Association of America.

In fact, Ken Griffey Jr., who received a record 99.3 percent, and Mike Piazza, who was on 83 percent of ballots, were the only players who received the minimum 75 percent required for election.

"First and foremost I want to congratulate Ken Griffey Jr. and Mike Piazza," Hoffman said in a statement after voting results were announced. "This is a class of tremendous players and people, both deserving of the title Hall of Famer. While the news today wasn't the news I was hoping for I am humbled and honored to have been on the ballot and in the conversation with players of this caliber.

"If and when the day comes that I receive the ultimate honor in our game, I look forward to sharing with my family, friends, teammates, the Padres organization, and most importantly, the fans."

Gaining entry to the Hall of Fame has not been easy for closers.

Fingers and Gossage are among five relievers—Bruce Sutter (2006), Dennis Eckersley (2004), and Hoyt Wilhelm (1985) are the others—enshrined in Cooperstown. John Smoltz (Class of 2015) was primarily a starter, but his three-plus years as Atlanta's closer likely put his HOF candidacy over the top.

Sutter is the only one in the group who never started a game in his career. Hoffman would be the second.

"I kind of prepared myself for something where I might come up a little short," Hoffman told MLB.com.

Added Hoffman: "To be honest with you, I'm ecstatic with the number. You know…you're left and right, this and that, but you never really know where you stand. Until there's a number, you really don't know how (voters) felt about your career….To have that number (67.3) is extremely encouraging."

Jack Morris and Gil Hodges are the only two players to receive 60 percent of the vote and not eventually get into the Hall of Fame. Of course, it took them years to rise to that figure. Morris received just 22.2 percent in his first year of eligibility in 2000. Hodges received 24.1 percent in his first year on the ballot in 1969.

If recent trends are any indication, Hoffman can expect to get elected within the next two years.

Craig Biggio (2015), Barry Larkin (2012), Roberto Alomar (2011), and Carlton Fisk (2000) all were elected in their second or third year of eligibility after receiving at least 50 percent in their first year on the ballot.

In a statement following the voting results, the Padres said: "Regarding Trevor Hoffman falling short in his first year of eligibility, we share our fans' disappointment in today's results. Few others have represented a franchise in Major League Baseball the way Trevor and his family have represented the Padres over the last three decades.

"While it may be impossible for us to be objective, Trevor is a true Hall of Famer in our eyes and the eyes of all San Diegans. We hope that well-deserved recognition comes his way in the near future."

Sources

Newspapers
Associated Press
Atlanta Journal-Constitution
Baltimore Sun
Cincinnati Enquirer
Chicago Tribune
Denver Post
Los Angeles Times
Milwaukee Journal-Sentinel
New York Post
New York Times
Philadelphia Inquirer
San Diego Evening Tribune
San Diego Union
San Diego Union-Tribune
San Francisco Chronicle
St. Louis Post-Dispatch
USA TODAY
Washington Post

Magazines
Baseball America
Boys Life
Coach and Athletic Director Magazine
San Diego Magazine
Sporting News
Sports Illustrated
Time

Websites

Baseball-reference.com
Baseballhall.org
ESPN.com
Famouschicken.com
Fantography.com
Genelocklear.com
MLB.com
NBCsandiego.com
NPR.org
Padres.com
SABR.org
Signonsandiego.com
YouTube.com (Dock Ellis & the LSD No-No by James Blagden)

Books

Bavasi, Buzzie, and John Strege. *Off the Record* (Chicago: Contemporary Books, 1987).

Center, Bill. *Padres Essential: Everything You Need to Know to Be a Real Fan!* (Chicago: Triumph Books, 2007).

Chandler, Bob, and Bill Swank. *Bob Chandler's Tales from the San Diego Padres Dugout* (New York: Sports Publishing LLC, 2006).

Coleman, Jerry, and Richard Goldstein. *An American Journey: My Life On the Field, In the Air, and On the Air* (Chicago: Triumph Books, 2008).

Garvey, Steve, and Skip Rozin. *Garvey* (New York: Times Books, 1986).

Kroc, Ray, and Robert Anderson. *Grinding It Out, The Making of McDonald's* (Chicago: Contemporary Books, 1977).

McKeon, Jack, and Tom Friend. *Jack of All Trades* (Chicago: Contemporary Books, 1988).

Porter, David, and Joe Naiman. *The San Diego Padres Encyclopedia* (New York: Sports Publishing LLC, 2002).

Slusser, Susan. *100 Things A's Fans Should Know & Do Before They Die* (Chicago: Triumph Books, 2015).

Strasberg, Andy. *Fantography: San Diego Baseball* (Charleston: Arcadia Publishing, 2014).

Swank, Bill. *Baseball in San Diego: From the Padres to Petco* (Charleston: Arcadia Publishing, 2004).

Williams, Dick, and Bill Plaschke. *No More Mr. Nice Guy: A Life of Hardball* (San Diego: Harcourt, Brace, Jovanovich, 1990).

Winfield, Dave, and Tom Parker. *Winfield: A Player's Life* (New York: Norton, 1988).